The Poetry of Céline Arnauld
From Dada to Ultra-Modern

LEGENDA

LEGENDA is the Modern Humanities Research Association's book imprint for new research in the Humanities. Founded in 1995 by Malcolm Bowie and others within the University of Oxford, Legenda has always been a collaborative publishing enterprise, directly governed by scholars. The Modern Humanities Research Association (MHRA) joined this collaboration in 1998, became half-owner in 2004, in partnership with Maney Publishing and then Routledge, and has since 2016 been sole owner. Titles range from medieval texts to contemporary cinema and form a widely comparative view of the modern humanities, including works on Arabic, Catalan, English, French, German, Greek, Italian, Portuguese, Russian, Spanish, and Yiddish literature. Editorial boards and committees of more than 60 leading academic specialists work in collaboration with bodies such as the Society for French Studies, the British Comparative Literature Association and the Association of Hispanists of Great Britain & Ireland.

The MHRA encourages and promotes advanced study and research in the field of the modern humanities, especially modern European languages and literature, including English, and also cinema. It aims to break down the barriers between scholars working in different disciplines and to maintain the unity of humanistic scholarship. The Association fulfils this purpose through the publication of journals, bibliographies, monographs, critical editions, and the MHRA Style Guide, and by making grants in support of research. Membership is open to all who work in the Humanities, whether independent or in a University post, and the participation of younger colleagues entering the field is especially welcomed.

ALSO PUBLISHED BY THE ASSOCIATION

Critical Texts
Tudor and Stuart Translations • *New Translations* • *European Translations*
MHRA Library of Medieval Welsh Literature

MHRA Bibliographies
Publications of the Modern Humanities Research Association

The Annual Bibliography of English Language & Literature
Austrian Studies
Modern Language Review
Portuguese Studies
The Slavonic and East European Review
Working Papers in the Humanities
The Yearbook of English Studies

www.mhra.org.uk
www.legendabooks.com

RESEARCH MONOGRAPHS IN FRENCH STUDIES

The *Research Monographs in French Studies* (RMFS) form a separate series within the Legenda programme and are published in association with the Society for French Studies. Individual members of the Society are entitled to purchase all RMFS titles at a discount.

The series seeks to publish the best new work in all areas of the literature, thought, theory, culture, film and language of the French-speaking world. Its distinctiveness lies in the relative brevity of its publications (50,000–60,000 words). As innovation is a priority of the series, volumes should predominantly consist of new material, although, subject to appropriate modification, previously published research may form up to one third of the whole. Proposals may include critical editions as well as critical studies. They should be sent with one or two sample chapters for consideration to Professor Diana Knight, Department of French and Francophone Studies, University of Nottingham, University Park, Nottingham NG7 2RD.

Editorial Committee
Diana Knight, University of Nottingham (General Editor)
Robert Blackwood, University of Liverpool
Jane Gilbert, University College London
Shirley Jordan, Newcastle University
Neil Kenny, All Souls College, Oxford
Max Silverman, University of Leeds

Advisory Committee
Wendy Ayres-Bennett, Murray Edwards College, Cambridge
Celia Britton, University College London
Ann Jefferson, New College, Oxford
Sarah Kay, New York University
Michael Moriarty, University of Cambridge
Keith Reader, University of Glasgow

PUBLISHED IN THIS SERIES

20. *Selfless Cinema? Ethics and French Documentary* by Sarah Cooper
21. *Poisoned Words: Slander and Satire in Early Modern France* by Emily Butterworth
22. *France/China: Intercultural Imaginings* by Alex Hughes
23. *Biography in Early Modern France 1540–1630* by Katherine MacDonald
24. *Balzac and the Model of Painting* by Diana Knight
25. *Exotic Subversions in Nineteenth-Century French Literature* by Jennifer Yee
26. *The Syllables of Time: Proust and the History of Reading* by Teresa Whitington
27. *Personal Effects: Reading the 'Journal' of Marie Bashkirtseff* by Sonia Wilson
28. *The Choreography of Modernism in France* by Julie Townsend
29. *Voices and Veils* by Anna Kemp
30. *Syntactic Borrowing in Contemporary French*, by Mairi McLaughlin
31. *Dreams of Lovers and Lies of Poets: Poetry, Knowledge, and Desire in the 'Roman de la Rose'* by Sylvia Huot
32. *Maryse Condé and the Space of Literature* by Eva Sansavior
33. *The Livres-Souvenirs of Colette: Genre and the Telling of Time* by Anne Freadman
34. *Furetière's* Roman bourgeois *and the Problem of Exchange* by Craig Moyes
35. *The Subversive Poetics of Alfred Jarry*, by Marieke Dubbelboer
36. *Echo's Voice: The Theatres of Sarraute, Duras, Cixous and Renaude*, by Mary Noonan
37. *Stendhal's Less-Loved Heroines: Fiction, Freedom, and the Female*, by Maria C. Scott
38. *Marie NDiaye: Inhospitable Fictions*, by Shirley Jordan
39. *Dada as Text, Thought and Theory*, by Stephen Forcer
40. *Variation and Change in French Morphosyntax*, by Anna Tristram
41. *Postcolonial Criticism and Representations of African Dictatorship*, by Cécile Bishop
42. *Regarding Manneken Pis: Culture, Celebration and Conflict in Brussels*, by Catherine Emerson
43. *The French Art Novel 1900-1930*, by Katherine Shingler
44. *Accent, Rhythm and Meaning in French Verse*, by Roger Pensom
45. *Baudelaire and Photography: Finding the Painter of Modern Life*, by Timothy Raser
46. *Broken Glass, Broken World: Glass in French Culture in the Aftermath of 1870*, by Hannah Scott
47. *Southern Regional French*, by Damien Mooney
48. *Pascal Quignard: Towards the Vanishing Point*, by Léa Vuong
49. *France, Algeria and the Moving Image*, by Maria Flood
50. *Genet's Genres of Politics*, by Mairéad Hanrahan
51. *Jean-François Vilar: Theatres Of Crime*, by Margaret Atack
52. *Balzac's Love Letters: Correspondence and the Literary Imagination*, by Ewa Szypula
53. *Saints and Monsters in Medieval French and Occitan Literature*, by Huw Grange
54. *Laforgue, Philosophy, and Ideas of Otherness*, by Sam Bootle
55. *Theorizing Medieval Race: Saracen Representations in Old French Literature*, by Victoria Turner

www.rmfs.mhra.org.uk

The Poetry of Céline Arnauld

From Dada to Ultra-Modern

RUTH HEMUS

LEGENDA

Research Monographs in French Studies 58
Modern Humanities Research Association
2020

*Published by Legenda
an imprint of the Modern Humanities Research Association
Salisbury House, Station Road, Cambridge* CB1 2LA

ISBN 978-1-78188-831-5 *(HB)*
ISBN 978-1-78188-832-2 *(PB)*

First published 2020

All rights reserved. No part of this publication may be reproduced or disseminated or transmitted in any form or by any means, electronic, mechanical, photocopying, recording or otherwise, or stored in any retrieval system, or otherwise used in any manner whatsoever without written permission of the copyright owner, except in accordance with the provisions of the Copyright, Designs and Patents Act 1988, or under the terms of a licence permitting restricted copying issued in the UK by the Copyright Licensing Agency Ltd, Saffron House, 6–10 Kirby Street, London EC1N 8TS, *England, or in the USA by the Copyright Clearance Center, 222 Rosewood Drive, Danvers MA 01923. Application for the written permission of the copyright owner to reproduce any part of this publication must be made by email to legenda@mhra.org.uk.*

Disclaimer: Statements of fact and opinion contained in this book are those of the author and not of the editors or the Modern Humanities Research Association. The publisher makes no representation, express or implied, in respect of the accuracy of the material in this book and cannot accept any legal responsibility or liability for any errors or omissions that may be made.

Trademark notice: Product or corporate names may be trademarks or registered trademarks, and are used only for identification and explanation without intent to infringe.

© *Modern Humanities Research Association 2020*

Copy-Editor: Charlotte Brown

CONTENTS

	Acknowledgements	ix
	Introduction: The Mysterious Case of Céline Arnauld	1
	PART I. EARLY EXPERIMENTS IN WRITING	
1	From Romania to Paris: *La Lanterne magique* (1914)	11
2	Contesting the Novel: *Tournevire* (1919)	22
3	Collision and Collage in *Poèmes à claires-voies* (1920)	35
4	Liminal Spaces and Refrains in *Point de mire* (1921)	47
	PART II. AVANT-GARDE COLLABORATOR	
5	Dada Actions: Magazines and Manifestos (1920–21)	61
6	Founding a Journal: Ambition and Vision in *Projecteur* (1920)	74
7	Battles with Breton: 'Les Faux Managers' (1924) and Projectivism	85
	PART III. WRITING BEYOND DADA	
8	The Lyric Traveller: Longing and Belonging in *Guêpier de diamants* (1923) and 'Diorama' (1925)	101
9	Music and Madness in *La Nuit rêve tout haut et Le Clavier secret* (1934)	115
10	Cycles of Time and Nature in *Heures intactes* (1936) and *Les Réseaux du réveil* (1937)	127
11	War, Exile, and Precarious Peace: *La Nuit pleure tout haut* (1939) and *Rien qu'une étoile, suivi de Plains-chants sauvages* (1948)	139
	Conclusion: A Triple Margin: Gender, Nationality, and Ultra-Modernity	151
	Bibliography	159
	Index	169

ACKNOWLEDGEMENTS

This book has been a long labour of love. Gratitude goes to The Leverhulme Trust who first put faith in my project with the award of an Early Career Fellowship based at Royal Holloway back in 2007. This permitted me not only to continue research for the book but to establish an academic career. A network of scholars of the avant-garde have been colleagues or correspondents over the years including Elza Adamowicz, Patricia Allmer, Peter Dayan, Stephen Forcer, Sarah Hayden, Giuliana Pieri, Eric Robertson, and the Mélusine community. Working with curators Ina Boesch and Nadine Schneider in Switzerland, and Ana María Bresciani and Karen Reini in Norway, to showcase Arnauld in Dada exhibitions has been inspiring. Artist Audrey O'Brien, and above all my co-conspirators composer-musician Sonia Allori and visual artist Vaia Paziana, have revitalized Arnauld's work in collaborative creative practice. They are honorary Dada women. In the early stages I spent significant time in solitary research tracking textual traces of Arnauld. Victor Martin-Schmets was similarly on her trail and was a generous interlocuteur. He is to thank for getting Arnauld's work out there again in print. Students on my final-year course 'Wanton Women: Artists and Writers of the French Avant-Garde' have kept dialogue going, as have PhD students Lauren Faro and Abigail Richards. Last-minute translation queries have taxed Soizick Solman, and Karine and Héloïse Gaspais, testing their ingenuity. It is a privilege, now, to have my book published in Legenda's RMFS series. Diana Knight showed belief in my book proposal, gave extensive and valuable feedback, and pointed out blunders with immense diplomacy. Charlotte Brown painstakingly copy-read my text. Graham Nelson has guided me efficiently and patiently through each stage of production.

Over thirteen years ago Pierre and Josette Janssen showed me warm hospitality when I visited their home. At this point Céline Arnauld became a real person, 'Tante Carola'. In the late writing stages of this book I came across a card written to me by Mme Janssen. I had recently married. She urged 'soyez heureux surtout'. Coming across forgotten written words is salutary. This book is dedicated to my husband Gary, and our children Ben, Lucy and Sam. You have shown me unstinting support and always matter the most.

R.H., August 2020

INTRODUCTION

The Mysterious Case of Céline Arnauld

Céline Arnauld, c'est la Poésie même.[1]

[Céline Arnauld is Poetry itself.]

The name Céline Arnauld (1885–1952) recurs in literary journals and reviews of the early twentieth-century avant-garde but only occasionally in accounts and histories of it. Primary sources thus yield tantalising traces of an enigmatic figure whose narrative resists full disclosure. Arnauld is a seeming paradox. She was a writer of French. She was not French. She was Dada. She was beyond Dada. She was a marginal female voice. She was a prolific poet. She was an agitator. She was a wordsmith. But after a long journey of research, discovery, and reflection the conclusion that Céline Arnauld was poetry, that she was her poetry, is one with which I concur. It is apt in placing emphasis firmly on the rich set of texts she produced, and which speak for themselves. And it is apt in its recognition of her revelry in language and form in a period of heady experiment in interwar Paris.

Arnauld was one of five women whose interventions I underscored in *Dada's Women*.[2] My research was driven by curiosity about names that appeared frequently in primary literature but whose presence was largely unaccounted for in histories, whose stories remained wholly or partially written, and whose work was too frequently skipped over. That project acknowledged the interventions made by five women — Emmy Hennings (1885–1948), Sophie Taeuber (1889–1943), Hannah Höch (1889–1978), Suzanne Duchamp (1889–1963), and Céline Arnauld — in three geographical hubs (Zurich, Berlin, and Paris) across the visual arts and literature. In challenging the notion of Dada as an artistic venture only realised by men I focused above all on these women's credentials as Dadaists. The research I began there on Arnauld informs the current study but with a crucial difference: instead of concerning itself only with her activities connected to the relatively short manifestation of Dada in Paris, it will situate that important work in a more comprehensive timeframe that takes in the poet's life before and after Dada. It will also take a more elastic approach to the question of affiliations and categorisations. In addition to underscoring characteristics that her work has in common with Dada, it will highlight the ways in which her work diverges from it too.

This turn is in accordance with an emerging trajectory in feminist scholarly treatments of avant-garde women. The identification of lacunae in women's participation in movements, including Dada, Surrealism, Constructivism, and Futurism, cried out for interrogation and research into whether, how, and under what circumstances women not only took part in but took forward innovations in the arts in the early twentieth century. Women in Dada, for example, arose as an important object of study in the early 2000s. Nadia Sawelson-Gorse's *Women in Dada: Essays on Sex, Gender and Identity* (2001) engaged with representations of gender identity in Dada works by women and men, and in the playing out of group dynamics, above all in New York.[3] A 1999 set of German-language essays, edited by Britta Jürgs, dealt more extensively with women in Europe, as well as those based in New York, and declared its opposition to a purely masculinist conception of the movement, 'Dada was not just a man's thing!'; 'Dada is feminine'.[4] More recently, Paula K. Kamenish's *Mamas of Dada: Women of the European Avant-Garde* (2015) followed a similar model to *Dada's Women* in showcasing a selected set of individuals, among them Arnauld.[5]

A wealth of under-researched case studies has subsequently led to a more profound analysis of these women as individuals who resist easy classification and insertion into a canon. Both Amelia Jones and Irene Gammel have highlighted writing, visual artworks, and performances by the German-born, New York-based Baroness Elsa von Freytag-Loringhoven (1874–1927), for example. They have succeeded in positioning her not just as an eccentric adjunct to the triumvirate of Marcel Duchamp, Francis Picabia, and Man Ray in New York but as an artist whose creative turns anticipated performance art, whose writing is thematically and formally radical, and whose art object *God* (1915) can be posited as a forerunner to Duchamp's 1917 *Fountain*.[6]

Curatorial work, too, has been instrumental in a sea-change in the recognition of women Dadaists. While a small exhibition at the Francis Naumann Gallery in New York in 2006 put the spotlight on 'Dada's Daughters', that is women working in the USA, a more extensive show dedicated to Dada's women that would take in European women was long overdue. The centenary year of Dada's beginnings in Zurich was the stimulus for such game-changing interventions. Two exhibitions took up the challenge. 'Dada Anders / Dada Differently' took three artists as its focus, Sophie Taeuber, Hannah Höch, and Baroness Elsa von Freytag-Loringhoven.[7] The curators chose three German-speaking artists working in different geographical centres: Zurich, Berlin, and New York. In communications for the exhibition they emphasised the need to bring women who participated in Dada 'out of the shadows', not least by underscoring multimedia and performance work. Welcoming the increasing renown of both Höch and Taeuber, they also pointed to the baroness as the least well-known of the three artists.

'Die Dada La Dada She Dada', meantime, which opened in 2014 at the Forum Schlossplatz in Aarau, just outside Zurich, both stole a march on the centenary and comprehensively tackled the question of women's participation and their legacies.[8] It subsequently travelled to two more locations in Zurich, the Museum Appenzell, and the Manoir de la Ville de Martigny, in 2015 up until the beginning of 2016. Conceived by the journalist Ina Boesch, it was co-curated with the director of the Forum Schlossplatz, Nadine Schneider. Five individuals were selected as case studies: Taeuber, Höch, and the Baroness, as well as the Cologne-based artist Angelika

Hoerle (1899–1923) and, gratifyingly, Arnauld. The geographical and national range was more ambitious, and in this instance a multimedia and multidisciplinary approach placed due emphasis on literature too. Significantly, the curators of 'Die Dada La Dada She Dada' also commissioned five contemporary Swiss women video artists to each produce new work 'in dialogue' with one of the five Dada women.[9]

This spotlight on women in Dada followed on from the vital 'rediscovery' of women in Surrealism, to whom critical appreciation and academic attention were turned in the 1990s.[10] Scholarly research by Mary Ann Caws, Whitney Chadwick, and, more recently, Patricia Allmer, has been vital in bringing to academic and popular attention individuals including Claude Cahun, Leonora Carrington, Frida Kahlo, Lee Miller, Meret Oppenheim, Dorothea Tanning, and Remedios Varo. Again, this has enabled more profound research into individual cases. The rich material produced on Leonora Carrington in the centenary of her birth in 2017, for example, included a book-length biography, a collection of short stories, a theatrical performance of her novel *The Hearing Trumpet*, a television documentary, and a plethora of press articles that have reached wide-ranging international audiences.[11] Her re-emergence goes far beyond her fascinating biography and relationship with Max Ernst and supersedes the simplistic categorisation of her as a 'surrealist woman' that she herself resisted.

Here we can again turn to Arnauld, who, prophetic about the possibility of being written out of memoirs, understood how protagonists, critics, and scholars shape knowledge in ways that might be contradictory to lived experience. In 1925 Arnauld published a book composed of several parts. *L'Apaisement de l'éclipse* [The Appeasement of the Eclipse] is preceded by a prose text 'Diorama', itself prefaced by an 'Avertissement aux lecteurs' [Note to Readers]. Its composite nature alone suggests stages, a process, a thinking and writing-out-loud.[12] The first short text, a mix of the prosaic and the poetic, gives us a rare insight into the author's views of her writing. Notably, she addresses the question of how to describe her writing, asserting that she does not wish to be confined by association with any one trend:

> Si on se voyait tenté de rapprocher maintenant mon inspiration et mon esthétique de celles de certaines écoles modernes qui font quelque bruit aujourd'hui, je prie que l'on considère combien ma poésie est restée elle-même. [...] Je ne voudrais pas que ceux qui ignorent mon œuvre me rattachent arbitrairement à l'un ou à l'autre de ces mouvements. (OC, p. 176)
>
> [If anyone should be tempted now to align my inspiration and my aesthetic to those of certain modern schools that are making the headlines today, I would ask them to consider how far my poetry has remained the same. [...] I would not like those who don't know my work to attach me arbitrarily to one or other of these movements.]

This seeming paradox points to the shifting and insecure experiences of this poet and, subsequently, the difficulty for the scholar in trying to locate her. It is a challenge that she experienced and that this research aims to confront. In this book I want to address and respect Arnauld's plea that she should not be annexed to or absorbed within the narrative of a single movement by considering the full range of her written output.

Gender is at play here but not exclusively. Stephen Forcer's book *Modernist Song: The Poetry of Tristan Tzara*, for example, offers a pertinent example of a case in which association with a movement can be limiting. Forcer points to the long writing career of Tristan Tzara (1896–1963) whose set of works beyond Dada had been sidelined. In this case, myth was in danger of obscuring material.[13] Although this instance was one of fame rather than neglect, these two examples have in common that the broader career of an avant-garde participant can result in the glossing over of a more substantial and varied *œuvre*. Add to that the relative neglect of Dada in relation to Surrealism, of writing in relation to the visual arts, and of women writers in comparison with men, and the pressing nature of the issue is apparent.

Arnauld published twelve single-authored books, comprising poetry, prose, dialogues, and an experimental novel. Finding and compiling this work entailed a lengthy and obstinate search. She was scarcely acknowledged in scholarly accounts of the avant-garde, she was frequently omitted from indexes (for books and archives), and there was neither biography nor bibliography. Only by going painstakingly through copies of avant-garde reviews, sometimes following up generous leads from a call out to the 'Mélusine' academic community of scholars of Surrealism, sometimes simply 'cold-calling', could I establish the extent of her contributions.[14] As for her single-authored books, some are held by the Bibliothèque nationale de France (BnF) and some by the British Library, but others I had to track down in second-hand bookshops until I had acquired the full set (excepting *La Lanterne magique*, about which more in Chapter 1). During this process I also gathered reviews of her work in literary magazines and anthologies. In parallel, another researcher, Victor Martin-Schmets, based in Belgium, was engaged in the same quest. His careful editorship and subsequent publication of Arnauld's complete works in 2013 stole a march on my own bibliographic findings and plans for publication. More positively, it facilitated my project to write about her; her work, now back in print, could finally be more widely accessed, read, and discussed.[15]

Recognising Arnauld's presence in Dada has been, and remains, a valid endeavour, one that was a crucial first step not only in establishing her place within avant-garde circles, but in reconfiguring perceptions of Dada. But her existence cannot be confined to the high point of Dada activity in Paris that coalesced relatively briefly, albeit loudly, around 1920–1921. Her body of work reveals a longer span of work and life that took her from Romania to Paris, where she enrolled at the Sorbonne and met her husband the Belgian poet Paul Dermée (1886–1951), through participation in literary circles in the 1920s and 1930s, to hiding in the south of France in the Second World War, and to a final decade of poetic output in the 1940s. There are huge gaps in her biography and many details of her life remain to be uncovered. This was exemplified early on by the fact that the BnF listed her as having been born in Nice and having French nationality until I alerted them to her dual identity. In fact she was a Romanian Jewish émigré, born Carolina Goldstein, who adopted the pseudonym 'Céline Arnauld' on arrival in Paris in 1914, and for whom French was a second language.[16]

I have already cited Arnauld herself, as a means to get to her voice and to explore the tensions in her creative life. 'Diorama', a creative semi-autobiographical text published as part of *L'Apaisement de l'éclipse*, is an evocation of Arnauld's writing trajectory in which she sets out her publications as signposts. The text speaks explicitly of a journey, and implicitly of exile and longing. I will use that project as a framework for my own chapters, taking each of her book-length works from this period to structure the first part of my study, granting analytical space and time to each. My first chapter is unusual in that the book itself has disappeared. *La Lanterne magique* [The Magic Lantern], 1914, nevertheless offers a springboard from which to introduce an interest in visual technologies that would run through Arnauld's writing career. This first chapter will also sketch out some brief biographical details, not least setting up her status as an émigré. A second chapter focuses on a 1919 experimental novel *Tournevire* [Sea-Shanty] that shares ground with fairy tales and the fantastic in style and theme, and which will be situated in the avant-garde project of revolutionising the novel. The emphasis of my third chapter will be formal experiment. Selected texts from the 1920 collection *Poèmes à claires-voies* [Openwork Poems] will be analysed for their collisions of language and use of verbal collage. Guillaume Apollinaire, greatly admired by Arnauld, will be adopted as an important point of reference here. Thematically some strands will begin to emerge that are closely connected with form, namely juxtapositions between apparently oppositional concepts, not least nature and technology. In a fourth and final chapter in this section on early experimental writing, I will discuss a second volume, *Point de mire* [Focal Point], published in 1921, to draw out what I see as Arnauld's interest in liminal spaces: between the urban and the rural; night and day; life and death. Formally I will consider recurrences of words and ideas, combinations and repetitions, that offer a strategy of layering within and across individual poems.

In the second part of the book I will underscore and discuss a question to which Arnauld points somewhat ambivalently, that is her involvement in avant-garde movements. This builds on work in *Dada's Women* that sought to acknowledge her place in the Dada group and briefly looked ahead to emergent Surrealism. This element will critically approach her 'voice' and her 'fit', or otherwise, in that context, and bring out tensions in those relationships. Her contributions to journals, especially Dada magazines, will be the focus of a first chapter. Her editorship of a one-off magazine *Projecteur* (1920) will be the object of a second chapter that considers her ambitions beyond the group, not least in her conception of a new term *projectivisme* [projectivism]. A third and final chapter takes up the tensions in her relationship with André Breton and Surrealism. In its entirety, this element of the book interrogates the question of Arnauld as an avid collaborator, on the one hand, and, on the other, as an individual whose creative ambitions were sometimes at odds with group play and politics.

In the third part of the book I will continue the project that Arnauld began in 'Diorama'. I will add her later volumes as signposts in a voyage that extended beyond Dada, through the 1920s, 1930s, and into the 1940s. *Guêpier de diamants* [Diamond Trap], from 1923, will be examined together with the aforementioned 'Diorama'. These texts are marked by journeys, actual and metaphorical, that will be analysed for their reflections on movement and motivation. 'Diorama', especially, will be posited as a turning-point in her relationships and career ambitions, with questions of nationality, exile, and marginality paramount. Sound and music will come to the fore in *La Nuit rêve tout haut et Le Clavier secret* (1934) [The Night Dreams Aloud and The Secret Keyboard], as well as notions of madness and creativity as possible salvation. Two volumes in quick succession, *Heures intactes* [Unbroken Hours] and *Les Réseaux du réveil* [Awakening Networks], published 1936 and 1937 respectively, offer meditations on time, with plentiful reference to the cycles of night and day, the weather, seasons, and the natural world. Connections to Arthur Rimbaud's *Une saison en enfer* [A Season in Hell] will be made in an analysis of the first extended tripartite poem. In the second, natural landscapes — earthly, marine, and celestial — are heralded as the dramatic location of human life and creativity. Where the first work is full of conflict, the second is marked by optimism, joy, and abundance. Arnauld's own nods to pre-avant-garde poetry will be taken up in this chapter as a discursive point that deters a too-easy assimilation of her work to the groups of the avant-garde and which challenges a neat linear categorisation of poetic style, function, and influence. In the fourth chapter a lengthy span of time and change is deliberately tackled. From *La Nuit pleure tout haut* [The Night Weeps Aloud], published in 1939, to a last volume *Rien qu'une étoile, suivi de Plains-chants sauvages* [Nothing but a Star, followed by Free Plainsongs], appearing in 1948, these works are set against a backdrop of personal and political upheaval, from premonitions of conflict, to concealment during the war, to a precarious peace.

The question of what the engaged writer might do after the apparent end or so-called death of the avant-garde is one that is frequently discussed.[17] In the 1930s and 1940s Arnauld, a relatively marginal, isolated figure, had to find her place in a rapidly-changing socio-political, cultural, and economic landscape that both inspired her and finally abandoned her. She survived the 1939–1945 war but did not live long past the death of her husband. Her death by suicide in 1952 marked an unhappy end to a resilient life. In my Conclusion I will reflect on this individual's fate in her context and in the current moment. In doing so I hope to underscore her interest as a case study for interwar experimental writing, between form and narrative, past and present, the personal and political.

Arnauld played with the flexibility of language and perceived the elasticity of history. Anniversaries offer opportunities to rehearse what we know of events and people but also to review our perceptions. The centenary of Dada's beginnings in Zurich gave rise to prolific and multiple revisionings of Dada that took an open and often radical approach to manifestations and participants. Arnauld is a case in point. When I first started tracking her work in 2002 I could not have begun to imagine that she would be showcased in the first European exhibition ever to be devoted to women in Dada, nor that she would become the inspiration for a performance staged at the Schauspielhaus in Zurich.[18] The significant work undertaken to pay heed to women's participation in Dada and Surrealism can be said to have opened up the possibility of viewing these individuals as not only attached to movements into which they might be reinserted, but as artists and writers with complicated relationships to those groups, and with creative lives and legacies that exceed them.

In her 'Avertissement aux lecteurs' (cited above), in which she articulated a rejection of any schools or movements, Arnauld wrote of her books as being pertinent to those with an interest in 'la poésie ultra-moderne' [ultra-modern poetry] (*OC*, p. 177). The title of this book pays homage to her, in this respect. It also reflects my own journey of research as a feminist scholar as I seek to allow myself and readers a more expansive acknowledgement that takes in not only her interventions in Dada but her insistence on her own individuality. My hope is to undertake a journey that tackles ambition, vision, and persistence in a case that is at once enigmatic and salutary.

Notes to the Introduction

1. Gérard de Lacaze-Duthiers, review, 'Céline Arnauld', *Interventions*, 1 (December 1923), 2; repr. in Céline Arnauld and Paul Dermée, *Œuvres complètes. Tome 1 — Céline Arnauld*, ed. by Victor Martin-Schmets (Paris: Classiques Garnier, 2013), pp. 571–77 (p. 571). Further references to this collection are given after quotations in the text, using the abbreviation *OC*. Although I have worked in most cases from the original publications (books and journals), I will cite this volume for its comprehensiveness and reasons of accessibility. All English translations are my own unless stated otherwise. Where published translations exist I have done my best to use them.
2. Ruth Hemus, *Dada's Women* (London & New Haven, CT: Yale University Press, 2009).
3. Nadia Sawelson-Gorse, *Women in Dada: Essays on Sex, Gender and Identity* (Cambridge, MA: MIT Press, 2001).
4. Britta Jürgs, 'Dada war keine reine Männersache!' and 'Dada is weiblich', in *Etwas Wasser in der Seife: Portraits dadaistischer Künstlerinnen und Schriftstellerinnen* (Berlin: Aviva, 1999), pp. 7, 10.
5. Paula K. Kamenish, *Mamas of Dada: Women of the European Avant-Garde* (Columbia: University of South Carolina Press, 2015). The other women are Hennings, Höch, Gabrielle Buffet (1881–1985), Germaine Everling (1887–1975), and Juliette Roche (1884–1980).
6. Irene Gammel, *Baroness Elsa: Gender, Dada and Modernity — A Cultural Biography* (Cambridge, MA: MIT Press, 2002); Amelia Jones, *Irrational Modernism: A Neurasthenic History of New York Dada* (Cambridge, MA, & London: MIT Press, 2004); Elsa von Freytag-Loringhoven, *Body Sweats: The Uncensored Writings of Elsa von Freytag-Loringhoven*, ed. by Irene Gammel and Suzanne Zelazo (Cambridge, MA: MIT Press, 2011).
7. Sabine Schaschl, Margit Weinberg Staber and Evelyne Bucher, 'Dada anders / Dada Differently', exhibition, Museum Haus Konstruktiv, Zurich, 25 February–8 May 2016.
8. 'Die Dada La Dada She Dada', exhibition, Forum Schlossplatz Aarau, 25 October 2014–18 January 2015; Museum Appenzell, 22 March–28 June 2015; Le Manoir de la Ville de Martigny, 3 October 2015–10 January 2016.
9. Anne-Julie Raccoursier (1974–) was paired with Arnauld, producing the video work *Projecteur* (2014).
10. Key studies include Whitney Chadwick, *Women Artists and the Surrealist Movement* [1985] (London: Thames & Hudson, 1991) and *Mirror Images: Women, Surrealism and Self-representation* (Cambridge, MA: MIT Press, 1998); *Surrealism and Women*, ed. by Mary Ann Caws, Rudolf E. Kuenzli and Gwen Raaberg (Cambridge, MA, & London: MIT Press, 1991); Penelope Rosemont, *Surrealist Women: An International Anthology* (London: Athlone Press, 1998), a welcome intervention on writing; and Patricia Allmer, *Angels of Anarchy: Women Artists and Surrealism* (Munich: Prestel, 2009), a catalogue to accompany an exhibition at Manchester Art Gallery (26 September 2009–10 January 2010). Two more recent additions are: Whitney Chadwick, *The Militant Muse: Love, War and the Women of Surrealism* (London: Thames & Hudson, 2017), and *Intersections: Women Artists / Surrealism / Modernism*, ed. by Patricia Allmer (Manchester: Manchester University Press, 2016). See also Patricia Allmer, 'Feminist Interventions: Revising the Canon', in *A Companion to Dada and Surrealism*, ed. by David Hopkins (Chichester: Wiley-Blackwell, 2016), pp. 366–81, for a useful summary of academic work in this area.

11. Joanna Moorhead, *The Surreal Life of Leonora Carrington* (London: Virago, 2017); Leonora Carrington, *The Debutante and Other Stories* (London: Silver Press, 2017); *The Hearing Trumpet*, presented by Dirty Market, Theatre Delicatessen, London, 4–29 April 2017; *Leonora Carrington: The Lost Surrealist*, directed by Teresa Griffiths, produced by Rachel Hooper (BBC4, 2017).
12. Céline Arnauld, *L'Apaisement de l'éclipse, passion en deux actes; précédé de Diorama, confession lyrique* (Paris: Écrivains réunis, 1925); *OC*, pp. 175–219. I will come back to this tripartite text in Chapter 8.
13. Stephen Forcer, *Modernist Song: The Poetry of Tristan Tzara* (Oxford: Legenda, 2006).
14. The 'Liste Mélusine' is run by the 'Association pour l'étude du surréalisme', convened by Henri Béhar. See: <http://melusine-surrealisme.fr> [accessed 10 April 2020]. I am grateful to all those who responded to my request for information.
15. Martin-Schmets is also the author of the only piece of academic writing published on her prior to my own work, see 'Céline Arnauld, épouse Paul Dermée, poète dadaïste', in *Les Oubliés des Avant-Garde*, ed. by Barbara Meazzi and Jean-Paul Madou (Chambéry: Université de Savoie, 2006), pp. 171–82. His subsequent editorship of the collected works has been invaluable. The volume also includes an introduction, biography, and contemporary reviews of Arnauld's work and is the first of seven volumes devoted to Arnauld and Dermée.
16. For a chronology of both lives researched by Martin-Schmets see 'Chronologie de Céline Arnauld et de Paul Dermée', in *OC*, pp. 21–26.
17. See, for example, Paul Mann, *The Theory Death of the Avant-Garde* (Bloomington & Indianapolis: Indiana University Press, 1991).
18. 'Die Dada La Dada She Dada', exhibition (noted above); *Vergessenes Gelächter* [Forgotten Laughter], a two-person theatrical production of music and words that was performed at the Theater Tuchlaube in Aarau (15, 19 November 2015, 18 January 2016) and the Schauspielhaus in Zurich (11 June 2016), by Isabelle Menke and Bo Wiget. The tendency towards interpretations of avant-garde women's work by artists working today has been crucial in opening up possibilities beyond rigid historicisation. It evinces the pressure to refer and defer to a canon of male contemporaries and underscores the work's relevance now.

PART I

Early Experiments in Writing

Fig. 1.1. Portrait of Céline Arnauld by Alice Halicka, in *Point de mire, poèmes* (Paris: Jacques Povolozky & Cie, Collections Z, 1921).
© ADAGP, Paris and DACS, London 2020

CHAPTER 1

From Romania to Paris: *La Lanterne magique* (1914)

Je consultai la *Lanterne magique* de mon enfance, et à la clarté de la réalité cruelle, je vis que ma vie était ailleurs.[1]

[I consulted the *Magic Lantern* of my childhood, and in the clarity of cruel reality, I saw that my life was elsewhere.]

The question of displacement is at the heart of the avant-garde. Its international nature has long been feted. Statements issued by the protagonists, including those of Dada, have been readily repeated in later narratives that celebrate it as eclectic, diverse, mixed, multicultural, multinational, and multilingual. If only by dint of repetition, however, these claims can become stale. As Paul Éluard wrote in the first issue of his journal *Proverbe* (February 1920), 'Les mots s'usent à force de servir, et quand ils ont une fois réussi ne donnent plus beaucoup d'eux-mêmes' [Words wear out through being used, and once they have succeeded they have nothing more to give]. The label 'international', applied to Dada, arguably fades with usage, turns to trope, and is scarcely interrogated. Zurich, Berlin, Paris, and New York each has its own special version of Dada, one that is claimed, nurtured, and propagated by many literary- and art-historical accounts as a national phenomenon, even though a rejection of nationalism was at its core. Meanwhile, both Dada's geographical reach within Europe, let alone beyond, and the richness of cultural backgrounds within each city-based group, have at times been underestimated. The international label may indicate that Dada appeared in multiple geographical 'centres', but it does not necessarily acknowledge the fact that within each now celebrated hub Dada's members came from numerous national cultures.

The 2016 Zurich centenary sparked a variety of interventions that more closely interrogated the nature and extent of cultural diversity in Dada. Exhibitions, performances, walking tours, and symposia drew attention to lesser-known participants from different national backgrounds and called up transnational networks. The Cabaret Voltaire, for example, staged 165 early-morning tributes to individuals associated with Dada as part of its 'Obsession Dada' programme. Scheduled at 6.30 am, these short homages were intended to distract citizens from Zurich and beyond from their everyday routine and monotony. Notably, they took an expansive approach to Dada participants that bore witness to plural nationalities and geographies, as well as so-called major or marginal men and women respectively.

Another venue that brought to the fore Dada's eclectic scope was the Kunsthaus, Zurich. Like the 165 days of 'Obsession Dada', its exhibition 'Dadaglobe Reconstructed' was the result of an extraordinary venture of time and commitment, in this case by Adrian Sudhalter, who took up Tzara's unfinished quest to create a transnational anthology of the movement.[2] Sudhalter delved into Tzara's mass of correspondence, in which he wrote to more than fifty peers from ten countries requesting photographic portraits, photographs of artworks, literary and design contributions.[3] Over one hundred of these artefacts, now dispersed, were meticulously researched and gathered. The set-up and supporting contextual material reminded us of the geographical spread of participants, Tzara's extensive pre-internet networking, the web of connections and collaboration that constituted Dada, and the will to evade both nationalist and individualist interests.

The exhibition 'Dada Afrika', meanwhile, took on the tricky topic not of global participants but of influences.[4] The interest in dissolving boundaries and borders underlying 'Dadaglobe' is also apparent here but where 'Dadaglobe Reconstructed' took up Tzara's curation of Dada, the perspective of 'Dada Afrika' was firmly postmodern. Where 'Dadaglobe Reconstructed' was fascinating and valuable for its revelations into Tzara's perception of the movement, his network of participants, and his plans for writing its history, 'Dada Afrika' looked back from today's vantage-point at some emerging if not always explicit trends among Dada artists. Thus the curators highlighted the ways in which many individuals drew on and were inspired by cultures outside Europe in their search for renewed means of expression. In displaying Dada artworks and world artefacts side-by-side it drew attention to the global stimuli at play in early twentieth-century European artistic circles. 'Dada Afrika' widened the net from a too-narrow European focus. Building on a move away from national claims to Dada, it underlined the globalisation already underway in the early twentieth century and the will to avoid parochialism, raising questions, too, about the problematics of intercultural appropriation.

Each of the three centenary events discussed, 'Obsession Dada', 'Dadaglobe Reconstructed', and 'Dada Afrika', are underpinned by their emphasis on Dada's heterogeneity and eclecticism, presenting a plethora of artists in a non-hierarchical and anti-individual way. It is worth noting, additionally, that there were no single retrospectives of so-called major figures in Zurich in the centenary. These events, in sum, have played an important role in a more thorough appraisal of Dada's diversity that goes beyond glossing and that complements the greater scholarly attention paid to Dada women.

As for national and cultural backgrounds, Tom Sandqvist's book *Dada East: The Romanians of the Cabaret Voltaire* is pertinent to this study of Arnauld. Here, Sandqvist draws attention to the important number of Romanian participants at the beginnings of Dada in Zurich, namely Tristan Tzara, Arthur Segal, and the brothers Marcel, Jules, and Georges Janco, who together made up as much as half of the founding group. In examining the pre-Dada Romanian context and acculturated backgrounds of these participants, he challenges a tendency to easy assimilation, and instead emphasises the inevitable, albeit not measurable, workings of Romanian and Jewish culture and context on the origins and early ventures of Dada, including influences of folklore and eastern European Yiddish culture alongside western European trends such as Futurism and Symbolism. Rather than simply buy into a levelling internationalism, he makes convincing claims for his own Dada-style proclamation, 'Ex oriente Dada — Dada comes from the East'.[5] His research does not take for granted Dada's multinational flavour, but instead considers in more detail its ingredient notes.

Central and Eastern European countries were experiencing enormous turmoil and change in the early decades of the twentieth century. The devastating effects of the First World War had reverberated across Europe, west to east, but with the breakdown of the old empires (Austro-Hungarian, Hohenzollern, Russian, and Ottoman), new independent states in central and eastern Europe had still to establish themselves. Artists and writers in these states doubtless shared similar feelings of disgust as their western counterparts with war, the failure of progress and the huge blow to the ideals and values of civilisation, but many were also enthusiastic about the potential for change and independence. Avant-garde movements flourished in states from the Baltic to the Balkans, but the call to a universal modernist language was balanced in many cases with a keenness to draw on and develop visual and linguistic vocabularies suited to the traditions, sources, and self-image of a particular nation.[6] In tandem, utopianism and a belief in the possibilities of social change are apparent in many modernist manifestations in contrast, for example, to some of the more nihilist proclamations of Dada in Zurich and Berlin.

Having fought with the 'Entente' during the First World War, Romania was awarded Transylvania in the Paris Peace Treaty, thus massively expanding its territory, taking in what was Hungarian land as well as many of its citizens. Postwar Romania was largely conservative but rebellious writers and artists, including Victor Brauner and Ilarie Voronca, set up a prolific avant-garde network in Bucharest, producing journals, pamphlets, artworks, and 'Picto-Poetry' in the 1920s and 1930s.[7] Earlier still, Tzara, Segal, and the Jancos were making their contributions to Dada in Zurich, and Dada was an important reference point and stimulus to the avant-garde scene back in Bucharest, as would be Surrealism after it.[8]

Sandqvist's study is focused on Zurich Dada but his list of Romanians in that conurbation can be complemented by further delving into those in Paris Dada. The multinational argument is less compelling in the case of the Paris group than in the Zurich group when it comes to the balance of background cultures there. Zurich, after all, had attracted exiles fleeing the war. In addition to the many artists and writers who coalesced around Dada, its historians can boast the presence of James Joyce and the short stay of Lenin.[9] Artistic activity in Paris was inevitably affected by the outbreak of war in 1914, but in the 1920s, once war was over, a new wave of activity could flourish and Paris exercised its draw once again. During the nineteenth century linguistic, cultural, and political links between Romania and France had been encouraged and strengthened. As Anne Quinney writes,

'France was viewed as a cultural beacon' and even 'symbolized the "soul sister"' of Romania as it sought to establish a collective identity somewhere between its eastern European neighbours and the West.[10]

Paris Dada, however, appears to have been resolutely non-diverse. In *Dada's Women*, I drew attention to a 1920 photograph of the Dada group, principally to highlight gender imbalance: in a group of thirteen Arnauld is the only woman.[11] It is pertinent to revisit that same image now (reproduced at the start of Part II) to note its make-up of nationalities. Of the thirteen individuals, eleven were born either in France or Belgium. The other two are Romanian, both Jewish. The first, Tzara, is well-known to us as a Dada luminary and contender for the moniker 'father of Dada'. Born Samuel Rosenstock in Moinesti, his work and life have rightly been the object of considerable popular and scholarly attention.[12] The other, much less discussed but all the more intriguing for that, is Céline Arnauld.

As we will see, Arnauld was not what her name suggests. Born in Calarasi, Romania, on 27 December 1885, her real name was Carolina Goldstein. That brief sentence with its referential function belies the fact that this basic biographical information more-or-less lay dormant for decades. In those sources that did provide information on her, her year of birth was most often given as 1893 or 1895, and only sometimes as early as 1885.[13] Her place of birth, meantime, drew not a blank but a plethora of places. It was listed only in some sources as Romania, and otherwise as Nice, France, including by the International Dada Archive at the University of Iowa Libraries, and in the database of the BnF, until I requested a correction. Beyond the obvious, that is, a lack of knowledge about this individual, perpetuated by a lack of interest, this confusion could point to an assimilation by Arnauld into Frenchness.[14]

Calarasi sits on the Borcea branch of the Danube, at the border with Bulgaria, just sixty miles from Romania's capital Bucharest. Arnauld was from a Jewish family, possibly one of the many that had sought refuge from oppression by the tsar in Russia a generation before. Her mother died when she was young. Though provincial by birth, it appears that she travelled abroad extensively with her father, a diplomat, including to India, Greece, Turkey, and Italy. Following his death, she completed her schooling in Romania, living with her maternal family.[15] In 1914 she moved to Paris to study at the Sorbonne. A year later she met the Belgian-born Camille Gérard Zéphirin Janssen, known as Paul Dermée, across the street at a lecture in the Collège de France. Records show that the couple married at the town hall in the fifth arrondissement of Paris on 19 November 1914, the month before Arnauld's twenty-ninth birthday. They were to spend the rest of his lifetime and nearly all of hers together, both using alternative names, as the literary couple Céline Arnauld and Paul Dermée.

It was not uncommon for writers in avant-garde circles to adopt pseudonyms, and for a variety of reasons. Some made deliberate attempts to sever linguistic and symbolic connections with their national backgrounds. The Berlin Dada artist John Heartfield, known for his political photomontages, was born Herzfelde, but anglicised his name in a deliberate rejection of German nationalism. The Swiss artist Arp, meanwhile, favoured the first name 'Jean' over 'Hans'. Others played with gender, and on a less permanent basis, slipping in and out of names like a suit of clothes, which allowed experimentation with shifting identities. So it was that Marcel Duchamp took on an alter-ego under the name 'Rrose Sélavy'. In journals language play extended to anagrams of names, such as 'Paul Draule' for Paul Éluard.

Without doubt the assumption by Goldstein of the name 'Céline Arnauld' is of enormous significance to her self-identity and reception and may not so readily be consigned to ludics. Her swapping of two Romanian-Jewish names for two French-Christian names permitted, facilitated, or at least proposed an assimilation into French social and cultural life. Meanwhile her roots were in large part obscured. The choice Goldstein made in changing her name mirrors that of Samuel Rosenstock, who remodelled himself as 'Tristan Tzara'. Both individuals achieved their stroke of identity-changing so effectively that their original names have been little used, and only recently acknowledged and discussed in any depth. In Arnauld's case, Goldstein remained as good as buried for over half a century. We have discussed neglect. An example of her resurrection is just as telling. In 1977 the American poet Clayton Eshleman was asked to translate some of her poetry. He was unimpressed by her 'run-of-the mill' writing and instead wrote his own story, *The Gospel of Celine [sic] Arnauld*. 'I found myself discovering the "gospel" of the gradual release of Celine Arnauld from the bourgeois Catholic mind of her era', he writes. As well as disparaging her writing and recasting a narrative for her, this latter, usurping male poet makes erroneous assumptions about her national and religious background.[16]

Switching names publicly and professionally does not summarily erase the personal and private of course. Pierre Janssen, the son of Dermée's brother, recalled to me in an interview his recollections of his uncle and aunt. Asked about their names he specified of Arnauld, 'elle était connue sous le nom de Céline Arnauld' [she was known under the name Céline Arnauld]. Privately, though, they retained their names, 'quand j'étais petit je les ai connus sous les noms d'Oncle Camille and Tante Carola' [when I was little I knew them as Uncle Camille and Aunt Carola]. More complicated, he suggested, was the matter of civil or state names, where he assumed she was 'Carolina Dermée'.[17] This myriad naming points to a negotiation of identities and calls to mind Gayatri Chakravorty Spivak's notion of the voice of the subaltern.[18] Goldstein-Arnauld-Dermée occupies a place that does not correspond to binary oppositions, between self and other, central and marginal, and east and west. Indeed, the voice will come up as a recurring motif in her work, above all discussed in Chapter 9.

We will never know much about this émigré's personal and life experiences. How did she integrate or assimilate? Did she bury her cultural past, her religion, and her traditions along with her name, or did she walk a line between the peripheral figure and naturalised Francophile? The slippery, nebulous borders between this writer's two identities surely exceed a rigid dichotomy and can scarcely be resolved through biographical research, where gaps persist and facts are evasive. But the little that we do know of her life story offers an intriguing backdrop for consideration of her interactions with other currents in writing, and above all for readings of her writing.

While Sandqvist has highlighted the semi-forgotten fact of Romanian input into Zurich Dada, more recent scholarship has begun to extend that question to the French avant-garde. In a 2019 article, for example, Sami Sjöberg specifically discusses writers. His approach is distinguished by a more explicit consideration of the question of Jewishness and his application of the concept transnationalism to the Franco-Romanian avant-garde. He deploys it to evince a straightforward 'intra-dichotomy', or overblown duality between centre and periphery, insider and outsider. Instead he argues for parallelism and multiplicity in the avant-garde's project of 'flows of ideas, cultural products, and people across national borders'.[19] Suffice it to say, the question of whether traces of Arnauld's cultural and linguistic background are to be found in her work in Paris is compelling and complex. It reminds us not to blindly focus on connections with Frenchness, Dada and/ or Surrealism, but to permit the myriad influences and trends proliferating in avant-garde and modernist circles in the interwar years. Sjöberg identifies this new turn in scholarship thus, 'the current understanding of the European avant-gardes highlights transnational networks, paradigmatic parallelism, and linguistic multiplicity, rather than rigid unilateral relations between centres and peripheries'.[20]

At the start of this chapter the note from 'Diorama' on *La Lanterne magique* evokes an intuitive escape, a journey, a search for life that was to be found 'ailleurs'. On the one hand its author may well have found her home in the French capital. Certainly, she remained there until her death, and it is in Paris that she found her husband and established her writing career. We know from correspondence and calling-cards that they lived at various addresses around the capital.[21] Although she had travelled with her father, there is no evidence that she travelled abroad from Paris, and her nephew confirms that she never returned to Romania, 'même en voyage' [even for a visit].[22] The other side of this biographically-centred speculation is that she was forever slightly adrift, always a foreigner by birth, nationality, religion, culture, education, accent, and language. As Janssen put it, when pushed about how she sounded (something that of course evades us and about which I wanted to know), 'elle parlait français avec un petit accent mais couramment quand même' [she spoke French with a slight accent but fluently nonetheless]. Whether Arnauld felt 'at home' is an irresolvable question. It is doubtful whether she herself would have been capable of answering such a complex question simply or fully.

For matters of language and expression we must turn to her texts. What is remarkable about Arnauld is that she constantly innovated with a language that was not her first, but a learned, second language. Its shared roots as a Romance language meant some grammatical and lexical similarities, and from the nineteenth century French was perceived in Romania as a language of culture and education. Arnauld deployed and interrogated her adopted language with extreme vigour and originality. Her vocabulary, her play with words, and her inventiveness are extraordinary. Indeed, it may be precisely her acquaintance with French as an acquired language, divorced from her nationality, that gave her the liberty to observe, re-invent, love, and critique it. That experience may be liberating. Nevertheless, her position as a foreign speaker among so many French native speakers may not have been straightforward. This adopted language permitted her intellectual currency and international exchange but the robustness of her affinities, of community and commonality, remains unknown.

This knowledge, then, adds another layer of intrigue to our investigation. Susan Rubin Suleiman has written convincingly about the double intolerability of the woman avant-garde writer, 'The avant-garde woman writer is doubly intolerable, seen from the center, because her writing escapes not one but two sets of expectations / categorizations; it corresponds neither to the "usual revolutionary point of view" nor to the "woman's point of view"'.[23] Already marginal in terms of her willingness to challenge convention, the writer's status as a woman intensifies or redoubles the threat that she poses. She, and her writing, escape expectations and categories. The examples Suleiman employs in the French context offer fruitful connections to Arnauld's case. As she shows in relation to Surrealism, the question is far more than a biographical one; it is about the inventiveness and slipperiness of language itself, as deployed by women on the margins of patriarchal structures.

Arnauld's relative isolation as a woman writer in Dada remains of vital interest to this study, as it takes up her writing life in relation to the avant-garde and beyond; that is its relation to what came before and what was to come. Likewise, the rich, elusive nature of her writing continues to inspire my readings of her work in relation to gender. But there is a third element to this shifting matrix of location, that is nationality. As a foreign woman avant-garde writer, Arnauld is arguably not only doubly intolerable, but triply intolerable. Her case offers a remarkable, untapped case study of a Jewish, Romanian-born émigré who infiltrated the Parisian literary scene at an explosive point in individual and collective experiment. As Quinney proposes, those writers of Romanian origin in France constitute a form of *francophonie*, 'one of exchange, borrowings, and crossovers', that has been largely neglected.[24]

From sketchy yet tempting biographical details, we need to turn firmly to texts, to the poems, manifestos, sentences, phrases, and words that are left to bear witness not only to Arnauld, difficult enough to trace, but to Goldstein, whose identity has been even more deeply concealed. But first, another mystery. According to her own declarations, Arnauld's first single-authored publication was *La Lanterne magique* [The Magic Lantern]. While this title appears in lists of publications by the author at the front of some of her early volumes, it has so far proved impossible to locate a copy.[25] Its publication date listed as 1914, it seemingly coincides with Arnauld's (or rather Goldstein's arrival) in Paris. I have begun to wonder whether it ever actually existed in the first place. One theory is that the poet invented for herself a published title as a means of establishing the credentials of her newly-christened alternative ego, the writer Céline Arnauld, and to ease access to getting her work in print. On the other hand, it is likely that, quite simply, no copies were preserved. It would, after all, most probably have been a thin, cheaply-produced pamphlet with a small print-run.[26] Indeed, while it is listed in her first four subsequent volumes published in Paris (*Tournevire, Poèmes à claires-voies, Point de mire, Guêpier de diamants*), by the time of *L'Apaisement de l'éclipse* in 1925 it was being designated 'épuisé' [out of print]. In later volumes it is not listed at all.

Its disappearance notwithstanding, the mere fact of Arnauld's choice of title is of interest. The magic lantern, an early type of image projector, was first developed in the seventeenth century. Using a concave mirror, it gathers light, projecting it through one or multiple slides, featuring a painted image. The light is magnified by a lens to produce an enlarged image. As technology improved so did the light source, from oil lamp to electric light, allowing ever-more sophisticated models of this entertainment machine. Magic lanterns continued to be used through the nineteenth century both for storytelling within the home and as a form of popular, mass entertainment. Movement was introduced by mechanical operation, with a slide, turned on a disc, moving over a stationary slide. Additionally, in the nineteenth century in particular, illusionists made use of the magic lantern to stage 'phantasmagoria', producing ghosts and supernatural phenomena for impressed, or impressionable, audiences. In the twentieth and twenty-first centuries, the basic projection principle persists in children's bedside lamps.

This resonance of childhood is evoked by Arnauld in 'Diorama', cited at the beginning of the chapter, in which she alludes to her first publication as *'La Lanterne magique* de mon enfance' [*The Magic Lantern* of my childhood] (*OC*, p. 183). Here is one of the signposts to which I referred in the Introduction. The note draws an autobiographical association between her first book of poetry and childhood and permits a connection between the apparatus and childhood. Though the publication is lost this reference in the later text, linking the magic lantern and childhood, invites a discussion of Arnauld's choice of title, not least in relation to the work of Marcel Proust. *Du côté de chez Swann* [The Way by Swann's], the first volume of his series *A la recherche du temps perdu* [In Search of Lost Time], was published in 1913, the year prior to Arnauld's publication. In the opening pages, the narrator describes his experience of being given a magic lantern as a child. Intended as a distraction to cheer him up, it is installed over the lamp in his bedroom. The narrator describes the story relayed by the slides, and evokes the impact this apparatus has on transforming his environment:

> Certes je leur trouvais du charme à ces brillantes projections. [...] Mais je ne peux dire quel malaise me causait pourtant cette intrusion du mystère et de la beauté dans une chambre que j'avais fini par remplir de mon moi au point de ne pas faire plus attention à elle qu'à lui-même. L'influence anesthésiante de l'habitude ayant cessé, je me mettais à penser, à sentir, choses si tristes.
>
> [Certainly I found some charm in these brilliant projections. [...] But I cannot express the uneasiness caused in me by this intrusion of mystery and beauty into a room I had at last filled with my self to the point of paying no more attention to the room than to that self. The anaesthetizing influence of habit having ceased, I would begin to have thoughts, and feelings, and they are such sad things.][27]

For Proust, the lantern offered neither passive entertainment nor superficial distraction. The narrative, and above all the transforming effect of light and images, triggered changes in the boy's perception of himself, his values, and the world around him.

Although it is not possible to establish whether Arnauld's choice of title for her first publication was inspired by reading Proust, it is the case that not only this title, but other metaphors and ideas in her work resonate with those in this passage. The notion of the transformative power of the visual, of renewal of perception, and notably the term 'projection' prove to be crucial aspects of her work. Proustian connections aside, Arnauld's choice of a visual term to signal the content of her volume is already noteworthy in and of itself. It suggests a link between the visual and the verbal for both writer and reader. The set of texts (its subtitle is 'poèmes') might be imagined, then, as a series or sequence. Just as the slides in the lantern reveal another image, the turning of the page in the book might be said to reveal another 'picture'. Also relevant here is the notion of accumulation, and a materiality or process at work in the revelation of ideas, by words printed in a book, as by images painted on slides. In referencing a piece of apparatus used to project images and to powerfully convey stories to an audience, a precursor to film, Arnauld's first choice of book title begins an association between linguistic and optical, and poet and projectionist, that will be reprised and developed in later written texts. That interest will turn out to be perennial in Arnauld's work, as will be seen in discussions of both her poetry and prose throughout this book.[28] Meantime *La Lanterne magique* remains, like Proust's time, irrecoverable, enigmatic, lost.

Before we leave this untraceable book behind, it is worth noting one more reference that might further illuminate our quest to reconstitute it and which points ahead to some of Arnauld's key concerns. *La Lanterne magique* is the title of a 1903 short film by the magician-turned-filmmaker Georges Meliès. In it two clownish characters build a structure that mimics a magic lantern on a giant scale. The box appears to project the actions of interacting couples on a moon-like disc of light, before being opened, time after time, to release surprising collections of characters, from dancing girls, to ballet dancers, to policemen. A strange, outsized, Punch-like figure appears towards the end, looming over the clowns, who have been fighting over one of the women, and the policemen, who have arrived to break it up.

The film begins intimately, as if in a child's bedroom, turns into a performance that resembles a variety show, and culminates in a dramatic fight. It is physical, entertaining, exaggerated, and out-of-scale. It mixes genres and media, from magic lantern to stage show to puppet show. Human actors play fictitious characters (caricatures even), whose images might have been projected by the apparatus of the lantern, but who instead burst out of it and revert to bodies, and which are subsequently filmed by a camera and screened, becoming mediated images again. The viewer's attention, surely, is on the medium.

In the next chapter I will introduce and consider Arnauld's earliest surviving single-authored text, *Tournevire* (1919). Viewing Meliès's film brings to the fore ideas about dramatisation, magic, illusion, and characterisation that are key to getting to grips with a text that Arnauld categorises as a novel, but which calls up visual and aural elements of folklore and theatre. Where Meliès uses filmed images, the poet uses words. He has the visual at his disposal and can depict movement, but the form is silent; she relies on words to evoke the visual and includes written songs to point to sound. Like Meliès she draws on familiar, conventional characters but seeks too to try out new form. She looks for a new direction for the novel in a time of emerging technologies, not least film, even as she draws on ritual and tradition. This first analysis will set her up as an experimental writer of modernity, indeed ultra-modernity, whose intertextual references prove to be rich and varied.

Notes to Chapter 1

1. Arnauld, 'Diorama', in *L'Apaisement de l'éclipse, passion en deux actes; précédé de Diorama, confession lyrique*, [n.p.] (*OC*, p. 183).
2. Adrian Sudhalter, 'Dadaglobe Reconstructed', exhibition, Kunsthaus, Zurich, 5 February-1 May 2016; MOMA, New York, 12 June-18 September 2016.
3. *Dadaglobe Reconstructed*, ed. by Kunsthaus, Zurich (Zurich: Scheidegger & Spiess, 2016).
4. 'Dada Afrika', exhibition, Museum Rietberg, Zurich, 18 March-17 July 2016; 5 August-7 November 2016, Berlinische Galerie; 18 October 2017-19 February 2018, Musée de l'Orangerie, Paris. *Dada Africa: Dialogue with the Other*, ed. by Ralf Burmeister, Michaela Oberhofer and Esther Tisa Francini (Zurich: Scheidegger & Spiess, 2016).
5. Tom Sandqvist, *Dada East: The Romanians of the Cabaret Voltaire* (Cambridge, MA: MIT Press, 2006), p. 13.
6. The exhibition catalogue *Graphic Modernism: From the Baltic to the Balkans, 1910–1935*, ed. by S. A. Mansbach (New York: New York Public Library, 2007), was useful in informing this background.
7. Research into the avant-garde in Romania has also been important in acknowledging its reach beyond the centrifugal pull of scholarship on Zurich, Paris, and Berlin. For an account of Romanian women writers, for example, see Olga Gancevici, 'Littérature féminine des avant-gardes roumaines', in *Les Oubliés des Avant-Garde*, ed. by Meazzi and Madou, pp. 183–96.
8. A notable resource that takes in both movements is a special issue of the journal *Dada/Surrealism*, devoted to Romanian participants in the avant-garde at home and abroad. See *From Dada to Infra/Noir: Dada, Surrealism and Romania*, ed. by Monique Yaari and Timothy Shipe, special issue of *Dada/Surrealism*, 20.1 (2015). *La Réhabilitation d'un rêve: une anthologie de l'avant-garde roumaine*, ed. by Ion Pop (Paris: Maurice Nadeau, 2006), also spans different movements.
9. In his play *Travesties* (1974), Tom Stoppard imagines a meeting between Tzara, Joyce, and Lenin.
10. Anne Quinney, 'Introduction', in *Paris-Bucharest, Bucharest-Paris: Francophone Writers from Romania*, ed. by Anne Quinney (Amsterdam & New York: Rodopi, 2012), p. 13. This collection of essays, dealing with writers of Romanian heritage writing in French, is another useful intervention. Introduced by Quinney, it includes essays on Tzara, E. M. Cioran (1911–1995), Benjamin Fondane (1898–1944), Eugène Ionesco (1909–1994), Isidore Isou (1925–2007), Panaït Istrati (1884–1935), and one woman, Ana de Noailles (1876–1933). Also worth noting is *France-Romania: Twentieth-Century Cultural Exchanges*, ed by Gavin Bowd, special issue of *Forum for Modern Language Studies*, 36.2 (2000), that includes, but is not devoted to, aspects of the avant-garde.
11. Hemus, *Dada's Women*, p. 166. The individuals are Louis Aragon, Théodore Fraenkel, Éluard, Clément Pansaers, Emmanuel Faÿ (back row); Benjamin Péret, Dermée, Philippe Soupault, Georges Ribemont-Dessaignes (middle row); Tzara, Arnauld, Picabia, Breton (front row).
12. For relevant studies see Marius Hentea, *TaTa Dada: The Real Life and Celestial Adventures of Tristan Tzara* (Cambridge, MA, & London: MIT Press, 2014); Forcer, *Modernist Song*.
13. I too got her date of birth wrong in *Dada's Women*, p. 194. My embarrassment has given way to a sort of delight in this resistance to fixity.
14. One exception to the general rule of neglect is provided by Giovanni Lista. A brief but pithy biography includes the correct place and year of birth, albeit the precise date is awry, see *Dada libertin & libertaire* (Paris: l'Insolite, 2005).
15. Notes on her parents' deaths, her studies, and her travels are taken from Victor Martin-Schmets,

'Bibliographie analytique des revues littéraires belges: *La Revue mosane*', in *Le Livre et l'estampe: revue semestrielle de la Société Royale des Bibliophiles et Iconophiles de Belgique* (Brussels, 1994), p. 104.
16. Clayton Eshleman, 'A Note on the Text', in *The Gospel of Celine Arnauld* (Berkeley, CA: Tuumba Press, 1977), [n.p.].
17. Pierre Janssen, interview conducted by Ruth Hemus with Pierre and Josette Janssen in their home in Vallangoujard, 12 November 2007. I am grateful to both for their hospitality and generosity, and to Madame Janssen for her warm correspondence.
18. Gayatri Chakravorty Spivak, *A Critique of Postcolonial Reason: Toward a History of the Vanishing Present* (Cambridge, MA: Harvard University Press, 1999).
19. Sami Sjöberg, 'Any Other Transnationalism: Romanian Jewish Emigrants in Francophone Avant-Garde Literature', *French Studies*, 73.1 (2019), 33–49 (p. 33). Sjöberg's analysis of the impact of Jewishness is detailed and robust, for example his analysis of the Kabbalah as a 'now-forgotten border-crossing literary feature' (p. 38). Anther useful resource is an essay collection *Jewish Aspects in Avant-Garde: Between Rebellion and Revelation*, ed. by Mark H. Gelber and Sami Sjöberg (Berlin: De Gruyter, 2017).
20. Sjöberg, 'Any Other Transnationalism', p. 35.
21. 17 rue Berthollet, 5th arrondissement; 29 rue du Mont-Cenis, 18th arrondissement; 23 rue des Morillons, 15th arrondissement; 16 rue Cassini, 14th arrondissement.
22. Janssen, interview with Hemus, 12 November 2007.
23. Susan Rubin Suleiman, *Subversive Intent: Gender, Politics and the Avant-Garde* (Cambridge, MA, & London: Harvard University Press, 1990), p. 15.
24. Anne Quinney, 'Introduction', in *Paris-Bucharest, Bucharest-Paris*, ed. by Quinney, p. 13. Her proposal recognises differences between this project and studies of Francophone writers from former French colonies that have been the focus of postcolonial studies.
25. I became so determined at one point to find this book that I began to trawl through a list of publications drawn from the catalogue of the BnF, just in case something might have been misattributed. At that time (2008) there were eighty-four entries for 'La Lanterne magique'.
26. Martin-Schmets notes that twenty-five copies were produced ('Notices et variantes', *OC*, pp. 461–569 (p. 463)). This information may have come from a 1923 review by Lacaze-Duthiers, 'Céline Arnauld'.
27. Marcel Proust, *A la recherche du temps perdu*, ed. by Jean-Yves Tadié, 4 vols (Paris: Gallimard, 1987–1989), I, 17–18; *In Search of Lost Time*. Vol. 1, *The Way by Swann's*, trans. by Lydia Davis (London: Penguin, 2002), p. 14.
28. For an article on this topic see Ruth Hemus, 'Dada's Film Poet: Céline Arnauld, in *Modernism's Intermedialities: From Futurism to Fluxus,* ed. by Rhys Davies and Chris Townsend (Newcastle upon Tyne: Cambridge Scholars Publishing, 2014), pp. 66–80.

CHAPTER 2

Contesting the Novel: *Tournevire* (1919)

> J'ai lu et relu avec un profond plaisir intellectuel ce roman plein d'une ardente fantaisie suggestive et d'une couleur virile. J'ai lu ce livre en prison, c'est dire que j'en sais de parties par cœur. — F. T.[1]
>
> [I have read and re-read this novel with profound intellectual pleasure. It is filled with ardent, suggestive fantasy and virile colour. I read this book in prison, such that I know parts of it by heart.]

Writers associated with the historical avant-garde are known for the variety of their textual productions, from short prose and poetry, manifestos and aphorisms, to dialogues and dramatic texts, either published in pamphlets, performed, or both. These endeavours were informed by rapidity, spontaneity, direct action, and collaboration. They constituted a refusal of conventional literary channels and their supporting institutional structures and a rejection of established forms and genres. Avant-garde movements, including Dada and Surrealism, reacted against the individual act of writing and of reading fiction, turning, in theory at least, from lengthy, crafted, solitary pursuit to improvised, accelerated, transmission: from writer to printer to reader, or writer to stage to viewer. That contact was based on chance, change, and collaboration. Audience intervention was privileged in performances. And in publishing the emphasis was on ephemeral journals and pamphlets, fast-produced and fast-moving, to be printed, sold, and read before the next new arrival. The elevated status bestowed on these journals by scholars, collectors, and curators today, their 'aura' as art objects, to use a term by Walter Benjamin, could scarcely have been envisaged at the time.[2]

The first known text published by Arnauld is *Tournevire* [Sea-Shanty]. Like so many journals and books of the time, which were often published in limited print-runs, any surviving copies offer valuable material indices.[3] In this instance two hundred copies were printed, as well as twenty-five special editions, by the publisher 'Éditions de l'Esprit nouveau'.[4] The book comprises only sixty-eight pages of narrative and is unpaginated. The plain cover of *Tournevire* belies a visual treat within: a portrait of the author by Henri Laurens (see the front cover). Drawn in black ink with a splash of blue gouache, it is Cubist in style. The single, circular eye, prominent against its blue background, takes on greater resonance after reading the book, in which, as we will see, the eye recurs as motif. The compelling image of the author, meanwhile, resists straightforward identification and figuration and bears witness to her location in a vibrant verbal-visual cultural scene.

The timing of this text is notable. Published in May 1919 it pre-dates Dada's debut in Paris (Picabia arrived there that year, publishing the first Paris edition of his journal *391* in November; Tzara arrived only in early 1920). This makes *Tournevire* an early experiment both in Arnauld's writing career and that of the avant-garde. Most interestingly, in relation to both her case and broader trends, the book is heralded on the front cover as a 'roman' [novel]. This is a bold and unusual choice. It is with Surrealism, sometime later, that the novel comes to be interrogated and reworked both in theoretical statements and in experiments with automatic writing. How to locate this text, then, in the trajectory of the avant-garde novel — the most well-known being the (later) surrealist novel — or trends in Modernism? To what extent does it either adhere to our expectations of the novel or forge new ground? It soon becomes clear that this book defies conventions in its peculiarities of length, content, and style. It is indisputably a difficult read. These factors — the scarcity of the book, its independence from any group or trend, and its confounding nature — have contributed to the fact that *Tournevire* remains undiscussed in analyses of avant-garde literature. Its contemporary endorsement by the futurist leader F. T. Marinetti, cited as an epigraph to this chapter, gives weight to an insistence on granting it some attention.

In *Aspects of the Novel* (1927), E. M. Forster sets out the elements that define the form, such as storyline, characters, and plot, before drawing our attention to the resistance and innovations heralded by Modernism. Some of the formal characteristics that Forster elucidates, as well as his observations, will be used in the following analysis of *Tournevire*. Forster proposed, 'And now we must ask ourselves whether the framework thus produced is the best possible for a novel. After all, why has a novel to be planned? Cannot it grow?'[5] We will see how in many ways *Tournevire* defies novelistic conventions, from characterisation to causality. The questions that emerge, then, are: which traditions, if any, does it draw on, or how might we understand it as a form? *Tournevire* proves itself to be a defiant and insubordinate piece of writing that seemingly resists its own categorisation throughout. But how far does it succeed in cultivating an alternative framework?

The title of the text is strikingly unusual and unfamiliar. The word *tournevire* is a marine term, dating to the seventeenth century. It refers to an old navigation tool, to ropes or rigging used to lift an anchor. It comes from the two verbs *tourner et virer*, an amalgamation of the conjugation *tourne et vire*, which translate into English as 'turn and heave' or 'turn and turn around'. The notion of cyclical movement evoked by this initially mystifying word was picked up in a review of the novel by Fernand Divoire: 'Cela tourne et vire, vient parfois de quelque part et ne va nulle part, et laisse l'impression d'un coffret où de jolies pierres sont éparsés' [It turns and turns around, at times comes from somewhere and goes nowhere, leaving the impression of a treasure chest in which pretty stones are scattered].[6] This observation of a non-teleological narrative structure is entirely apt. It proposes a dizzying reading based on moments of discovery rather than a plot that follows a linear logic. That same impression emerges from a more modern use of the term in the south of France. A *tournevire*, here, can denote a procession of sailing vessels, circling for display to spectators.

I have also come across *tournevire* as the title of an old marine song, a game played at fairs ('jeu de tournevire', or wheel of fortune), and — today — the name of a folk group for children. My proposed translation as 'Sea-Shanty' seeks to encompass seafaring, singing and the cyclical. It is based on a reading of the text that identifies journeying and song as crucial elements in the narrative. These multiple possibilities emerge, too, from Arnauld's signposting of *Tournevire* in 'Diorama': 'Je quittai donc cette compagnie vagabonde, mais j'emportai avec moi le sujet tragique de cette histoire qui chanta, par-dessus les têtes des lions fantasques, le lever de l'ancre de mon roman *Tournevire*' [So I left that vagabond company, but I took away with me the tragic subject of this story that sang, above the heads of the fantastical lions, of the lifting of the anchor in my novel *Tournevire*] (OC, p. 183). From this single sentence, we get a sense of elements that emerge and collide in the text, from its troupe of human and non-human characters, to its loose plot of displacement and uprooting with an unclear destination, to its mix of forms (theatrical, musical) and genres (the fantastic, the tragic).

The text is structured into six sections, each given a title and numbered by roman numerals. The opening section 'Au théâtre des nouveaux-nés' [At the Theatre of the Newborns] plunges the reader immediately into something more akin to a theatrical scene than an opening chapter of a novel. This effect, already proposed by the heading, is achieved on the first page by a mix of dialogue and relatively brief descriptive lines. The opening speaker issues commands and edicts from the very first line, 'Vite — Vite, dépêchez-vous' [Quickly — Quickly, hurry up]. It heralds a moral human drama or epic tale in which there will be both tragedy and comedy, 'n'oubliez pas qu'il faut pleurer et rire à la fois aujourd'hui — surtout rire' [don't forget that today you'll have to cry and laugh at the same time — especially laugh] (OC, p. 33). That phrase is repeated twice, presumably aimed as much at the reader as between the protagonists.

The sense that what we are reading is the verbalisation of a theatrical experience is reinforced by explicit references to staging, from a red curtain parting in two (twice in the first section), to a balustrade, decor, sound coming from the wings, boards, scenery, and greasepaint. In other examples of meta-theatrical language one character is described as stepping forward to the middle of the stage, another waiting at the edge of it. At one point there is 'no-one on stage'. Less explicitly, there are lines which, were it not for their conjugation in the past tense, read like stage directions, 'Mirador se tourna vers celui qui parlait' [Mirador turned to the character who was talking], 'Mirador s'avança furieux en serrant les poings' [Mirador stepped forward furiously, clenching his fists] (OC, p. 33). These prosaic pointers to action are interspersed with poetic images. What is absent is any description that might be designated as realist.

In this first chapter, or scene, of six, we are caught between tragedy, fairy tale, and dreamscape. Mirador [Watchtower], who responds to the first voice, is our first protagonist. He announces the death, from the cold, of Luciole [Firefly], seemingly his beloved and our story's heroine. His dialogue gives way to a description of

Luciole in her death pangs. Surrounded by candelabras, she wears a white veil with black pearls and lace, as a cast of characters steps up to say their goodbyes. It is as if the enactment of a play is being described to the reader, but the scene becomes increasingly fantastical. A star appears, for example, with an eye in its centre, and goes to settle on Luciole. Meanwhile, fairy-tale symbols and tropes, including a well and a mirror, enter the narrative, and the couple is carried away to the forest in a carriage drawn by a white bear and an ogre. The reader, already, travels between play, fairy tale, and dream.

Many of the characters are typical of myth and legend. Alongside the protagonists Mirador and Luciole, there is a clown (Matassin), a juggler (Gadifer), a fairy (Morgane), an angel (Azaril), a bogey-man, an ogre, and a white bear.[7] Other minor characters include a mayor, a village idiot, an athlete and a former artist, generic types that point to the potential for fairy tale as social satire. The mayor, for example, resides over the fictional 'Bar-le-Fol'. The meaning of 'le fol' as crazy together with the designation of the place as a bar undermines this municipal official's realm.[8] The cast of characters, for a short text, is immense. The reader scarcely gets to know or understand characters and is denied any psychological connection. Whilst there are indications of romance between Mirador and Luciole, as well as infatuation for the latter on the part of Gadifer and the village idiot, the relationships and alliances between them are never clear. If characterisation is a feature of the conventional novel, as discussed by Forster, 'The novelist [...] makes up a number of word-masses [...], gives them names and sex, assigns them plausible gestures, and causes them to speak by the use of inverted commas, and perhaps to behave consistently. These word-masses are his characters', it is here rejected.[9] *Tournevire*'s characters certainly speak but they are indeterminate. Their make-up is implausible and their actions inconsistent, seemingly motivated by chance rather than objectives, fortuitous as opposed to imperative. They are never fully described, introduced, or explained. Like half-remembered acquaintances, or characters in dreams, they are remnants.

In the second chapter the action moves to a new location, 'Chez les rapins' [At the Art Apprentices]. In this section a nightmarish meal is described. It begins prosaically, everyone gathering at the table at seven o'clock precisely. The expectations of a social occasion are at first upheld, 'D'après les conventions mondaines on devrait arriver à l'heure [According to social conventions one should always arrive on time] (*OC*, p. 38). But such niceties soon prove superficial as a planned discussion about the vermin in the artist's lodgings gives way to macabre interventions. The piece of meat on the table turns out to be a new-born baby that moves and bleeds when cut and the wine from the tap turns to blood. These are unsettling and uncanny visions.

A knock on the door heralds the first in a series of arrivals. It is Mirador (they call him 'the damned' before we learn that it is him) desperately communicating Luciole's disappearance in a whirlwind. His story is a confusion of the pragmatic (he says he has informed the police) and the fantastical:

> Une grenouille accoucha de deux perles
> tandis qu'un ver luisant montait
> vers mon cou (*OC*, p. 39)

[A frog gave birth to two pearls | whilst a glow-worm was climbing | up my neck]

Gadifer aligns himself with Mirador and Luciole, claiming enchantment of all three by the fairy Morgane, who soon appears to upset any notion of a society event. If the invasive wind and collapsing chandelier are plausible, subsequent apparitions of a descending star and a floating Luciole are entirely fantastical. Chaos and panic give way, and the silver mirror proves to be both symbolic and divisive. As each character pitches their stake for it, they abandon any civilities and coherence. The mirror assumes the importance of a possible solution to the enigmas faced by characters and readers alike.

The third section's setting, 'Chez le croque-mitaine' [At the Bogeyman's], makes a transition from the interior to the exterior. From a dark and semi-ruined building, the troupe emerges in response to the arrival of an important guest, the mayor. A *fête* is being organised, it transpires, and the group is worried that it cannot deliver Luciole and Mirador to act their parts. Luciole is missing, presumed dead. Arrangements again are interrupted by sinister happenings. Mirador pleads for Luciole, recounting another tale, in which the natural and modern worlds cross and blur. References to electric and rail accidents collide with darkening skies, the moon, stars and winds, as well as a nightingale. Spider webs and a falling mirror-ball both portray fragility. Finally, Mirador sets out with the troupe. The scene ends with a bad omen:

> Au bout de la route
> un œil noir
> s'ouvrait (*OC*, p. 46)

[At the end of road | a black eye | was opening]

In the original copy, the lines are staggered across the page, the typography intensifying their dramatic effect. This black eye might be read, here, as a symbol of watching, perhaps as a camera eye.

Suspicion surrounding Mirador emerges strongly in this section. 'Qu'est-ce donc — un fou — un malade — un poète peut-être?' [What is this then — a madman — a sick person — a poet perhaps?], the mayor asks (*OC*, p. 45). The answer is given as all three, the first by Matassin, the second by the bogey-man, and the third, violently and definitively, by Gadifer. The notion of Mirador and Luciole as outsiders or visionaries is more explicit here, as is the ease with which they are judged, dismissed, or banished by society and supposed allies alike. The fragility of existence might well be read as the difficulty of the poet's life. The main characters could even be read as Arnauld and Dermée.[10] When sections of *Tournevire* are reprinted in Arnauld's 1936 anthology, she will add an epigraph, 'Qu'est-ce qu'un poète? S'il s'agit de l'honorer, rien; s'il s'agit de le persécuter, tout' [What is a poet? For honour, nothing; for persecution, everything]. This citation, attributed to

Victor Hugo writing about William Shakespeare, underlines her perception of the poet as misunderstood and marginal.[11]

Where the first three chapters were named according to setting, the fourth appears to relate more directly to plot. Titled 'Condemnation', thus explicitly linking to the events, tone, and language of the previous section, it sees the start of the *fête* at last. A circus tent is the location, filled with action, from athletic performances to juggling, to dancing. Again, there are references to literature. The festival is being held in honour of a poet who had died the previous week 'dans l'indifférence générale' [to general indifference], presided over by a mayor described as 'lettré précieux' [precious and well-read] (*OC*, p. 47). The longest section of prose in the entire text ensues, unbroken by dialogue. But far from offering straightforward description it contains a series of vignettes about each of the characters' actions, complicated by further visualisations, together building a kaleidoscope of activity. Our troupe is joined by a squirrel, a giraffe, beetles, frogs, and a tortoise. There is singing, shouting, swinging, juggling, swaying, and climbing. A fairy-tale world is brought to life with seemingly unbridled imagination and juxtaposition of creatures and objects. These fragments come together as a cavalcade begins, a great success.

But the sense of menace is never far away. This brittleness is encapsulated in our protagonists, 'Ivres de bonheur, Luciole et Mirador se regardèrent effrayés' [Drunk with happiness, Luciole and Mirador looked fearfully at one another] (*OC*, p. 48). There are whispers of an accident, never explained. The dark eye, the star, a pair of magic scissors appear, and the crowd and mayor begin to turn against the couple. The rest of the group retreats to make its decision behind closed doors before pronouncing that Mirador be condemned to death and Luciole to banishment. The festivities have turned sour; a festival of condemnation is instead declared; Mirador expresses his fears in a final song. The marvellous has become dystopian.

In the fifth scene, 'Exécution', Luciole wakes up and the reader, with her, wonders where reality lies. But it was not all a dream. She realises that Mirador has been condemned and must be saved, that her friends have abandoned him, and that no-one had succeeded in saving her since her accident. Led to the forest by a village idiot, she finds the troupe holed up together in a house. In her desperation she begs Gadifer for help. The well is turned into a scaffold for Mirador's execution. Abandoned by all, including Morgane the fairy, he disappears. Over five scenes, the theatre of the newborns has turned into a theatre of death.

The book culminates in a sixth section 'Le Miroir des songes' [The Mirror of Dreams] in which the style changes altogether. Here, selected characters sing, one by one, in a contest to win the mirror that will deliver up the secret of one's dreams and knowledge of the future. There are self-conscious references to staging, again, in this culminating section, not least 'les cabotins se regardaient entre eux méchamment, car cette fois-ci il y avait un prix pour le gagnant: non pas l'honneur — le butin!' [the luvvies looked at one another wickedly, since this time there was a prize for the winner: not honour — the booty!] (*OC*, p. 57). Matassin, the ogre, the bear, the former artist, the idiot, Cantanette, and Gadifer deliver songs, each subsequently looking into the mirror, these performances interspersed with dialogue and grappling on stage and in the wings. The scene concludes with Gadifer. As Luciole takes her leave of him, Mirador's voice rises from behind the curtain. His five-line address derides the attacks made against him, and defiantly states that from the insults (stones) he has built his own house. The mirror takes flight with Morgane and the curtain falls. The last lines take us offstage:

> À la sortie du théâtre
> le maire plia le genou
> et aida Luciole à monter dans sa calèche. (OC, p. 72)

> [At the exit of the theatre | the mayor went down on one knee | and helped Luciole into her carriage.]

Luciole, it seems, has triumphed over all. She has survived the troupe, escaped the performance, and won over society.

The reader's expectation of a narrative or novelistic structure is confounded by the serial scenes, which shift from location to location, and which are not clearly linked. They are not treated to an easy text, but must wander, along with the cast of itinerant characters, through a sometimes magical, sometimes baffling and absurd experience. The landscape is knowingly theatrical. What is striking, from the first lines, is the preponderance of dialogue, which intersperses with relatively short descriptive passages, and which, equally, makes of this text more a script for a performance, or even a screenplay, than a novel. These narrative passages sometimes move forward the action but are often flights of fancy. The culmination of the books in songs mixes written fiction with the devices of popular or musical theatre.[12] At other times, the theatrical setting is overridden by lines that conjure up a dreamscape, especially at those moments when the sun, star, or moon takes on the guise of a character. As in Chapter 1, Méliès comes to mind, in this case his 1907 film *L'Éclipse du soleil en pleine lune* [The Eclipse: Courtship of the Sun and Moon], in which celestial bodies are anthropomorphised. With its spectacle of an erotic eclipse, figures riding shooting stars, and a meteor shower, it transcends the rational and eclipses logic with humour and theatricality.

Another inspiration may have been the circus, a hugely popular form of entertainment in the early decades of the twentieth century. A description by Jed Rasula calls to mind *Tournevire*, 'Replete with acrobats, orchestras, and exotic animals, circuses offered fantasies and marvels to adults well before they gradually became "family entertainment"'.[13] As well as travelling circuses, he refers to the prolific success of fixed venues such as the Luna Park theme parks. The thrill of being disoriented and surprised by apparitions and attractions, from animals to song to lights, is arguably echoed by Arnauld's fantastical novel. Tellingly, she goes on to refer to Luna Park in a poem (see Chapter 5) and to the circus in a review (see Chapter 7). As noted by Forcer, in Dada writing 'the tropes of magic, magicians, circuses and fairs are common'.[14] High culture is not revered; literature is infiltrated by modern and popular forms.

The first quotation I cited by Forster (above) refers to drama in its continuation:

> Why need [the novel] close, as a play closes? Cannot it open out? Instead of standing above his work and controlling it, cannot the novelist throw himself

into it and be carried along to some goal that he does not foresee? The plot is exciting and may be beautiful, yet is it not a fetish, borrowed from the drama, from the spatial limitations of the stage? Cannot fiction devise a framework that is not so logical yet more suitable to its genius?[15]

Arnauld draws on the theatrical or cinematic to evoke a visual and aural spectacle that reaches beyond the novel. She rejects too its conventions, from a neat ending to planning, from causal plot to boundaries on the imagination of landscape and space. The reader's attention is drawn throughout to the unruly nature of the text. Is this literary fiction that requires a private reading, a script for a play to be performed, or a screenplay for a film? It is more apt to refer to a 'viewer-reader', perhaps, than a reader. We are outside, looking in, trying to decipher this hybrid text that seems to grope towards or occupy a sub-genre of its own.

Tournevire is neither a novel nor a script in any conventional sense. Its storyline, characters, and plot are inconstant, baffling, and even unsatisfying. Its resistance to convention arguably pre-empts the experiment of the surrealist novel that would emerge in the next few years. Breton would set out his distaste for the novel in his 1924 'Manifeste du surréalisme', 'l'attitude réaliste, inspirée du positivisme, [...] m'a bien l'air hostile à tout essor intellectuel et moral. Je l'ai en horreur, car elle est faite de médiocrité, de haine et de plate suffisance' [The realistic attitude, inspired by positivism, [...] clearly seems to me to be hostile to any intellectual or moral advancement. I loathe it, for it is made up of mediocrity, hate, and dull conceit].[16] Narrative coherence, description, and observation of the external world take a back seat in the surrealist project, with naturalism and realism vehemently rejected. In this respect common ground can be found with *Tournevire*, which neither assumes omniscience nor feigns credibility.

Surrealism would test the potential of the novel to espouse values including chance, spontaneity, and automatic writing. Breton's *Nadja*, for example, written in 1928, tracks the author's journey through Paris, charting chance moments and unexpected encounters, above all with a young woman Nadja.[17] Its mix of verbal and visual — it includes numerous photographs, more or less evidently connected with the narrative — also represented a powerful reworking of the novel as form. These fact-fiction mixes still sought to represent snapshots of moments in time, the inner workings of the mind, and to escape logic. Nonetheless, it is not radically divorced from the format of the novel and a narrative persists. In an analysis of the avant-garde novel Tania Colliani writes of the avant-garde's rejection of the novel as being grounded in the primacy of the 'poétique' over 'prosaïsme'. She writes, 'Le jeu entre les frontières de la prose et de la poésie, du réel et de l'irréel, de l'impossible et pourtant vraisemblable, confère cette atmosphère exotérique et merveilleuse à certains romans avant-gardistes' [Playing with the frontiers between prose and poetry, the real and unreal, the impossible and yet feasible, confers on some avant-garde novels this atmosphere of the exoteric and the marvellous].[18] That description applies to Arnauld's project, but it is one of a kind.

Arnauld's attention to folkore and fairy tale reminds us of her cultural roots, even as she seeks to revolutionise form and genre. She forges her own version of the marvellous. Steven Mansbach, for example, asserts that the eastern European avant-garde moved more readily than the western between idioms, from the narratives of mythology and folklore, to non-figuration and abstraction. In this way it brought in the local and universal, the popular and progressive.[19] With its mix of the fairy tale and the theatrical *Tournevire* calls up traditions of oral and dramatic storytelling, but its sense of the absurd and resistance to narrative clarity renders it modern. Images, sound, gesture, and action are everything. Drawing on storytelling and performance it is an ultra-modern fairy tale in a modernist framework. It precedes the surrealist rejection of the novel's description and employs free association to a greater extent than the work of Breton. It is the advanced guard of absurdist drama, at least in experiment if not success. Finally baffling as a standalone text, it reveals hints of elements to come in Arnauld's writing, including liberated imagination, resistance to realism, rejection of narrative coherence, free mixing of symbols and pure indulgence in the possibilities of language as a pursuit in itself. When an anthology of Arnauld's work is produced in 1936, one chapter of *Tournevire*, 'Condemnation', is included, together with six of the songs.[20] In this latter publication they are not attributed to characters. Interestingly they lose little without context. Free of the determination to make narrative sense, the reader might even gain more from these free-standing texts.

It appears that Arnauld planned, and may have drafted, more 'novels' following *Tournevire*. A title, *Serpentine*, was signalled in *Poèmes à claires-voies* the following year as a 'roman'. *La Lune dans le puits* [The Moon in the Well] was noted as forthcoming in that volume and in her journal *Projecteur*. The fact that in the former it was 'féerie' and the latter 'comédie' underscores the author's free play with genre. Five years down the line *L'Apaisement de l'éclipse* (1925) signalled *Le Musicien des marées* [The Musician of the Tides] as a 'roman poétique'. This title she had already given to a poem in the 1923 volume *Guêpier de diamants*.[21] However, none of those was published, leaving *Tournevire* to stand alone in its rebuttal of an imposing tradition. Its early experiment as an alternative working of the novel as performance sets it apart.

There is, however, one further published text that can be usefully discussed in relation to *Tournevire*. 'Jeu d'échecs' [Game of Chess] was printed at the front of *Point de mire* in 1921, dedicated to Dermée (*OC*, pp. 103–08). A resistance to the conventions of genre is apparent once again. Supposedly a volume of poetry, *Point de mire* opens with this text, labelled 'a lyrical dialogue'. 'Jeu d'échecs', we know from the programme, was performed at the 'Festival Dada', the second major Dada performance event staged in Paris, at the Salle Gaveau on 26 May 1920, and which featured sketches by Aragon, Breton, Ribemont-Dessaignes, Soupault, and Tzara, among others. Dada performances in Paris frequently featured short dramas and dialogues, some of which were reproduced in journals or in later single-authored anthologies.[22] The group's interest in performance may be seen as disaffection for esoteric and paper-bound written language, in favour of more immediate communication with audiences, instigated by Zurich Dada.

'Jeu d'échecs' was later published in Arnauld's 1936 *Anthologie*.[23] In the first published version, in *Point de mire*, the two characters are named 'Dolome' and

'Cantalèbre'. In the later version, these have been changed to 'Le Roi' [The King] and 'Le Fou' [The Bishop] respectively.[24] Those latter monikers underscore the conceit of a verbal chess game. The characters appear trapped in an absurd and fateful situation, an inescapable social set-up, a stylised form of combat, signified by the chess board. Like the two characters in the later *En attendant Godot* (*Waiting for Godot*), by Samuel Beckett, their steps are prescribed and free will limited.[25] Yet the spoken responses each character makes to the other do not follow a rational pattern: each appears to pursue, and unload, subconscious thoughts, to produce language and ideas that have somehow been triggered by the other's words or actions. The extent to which their actions and words are determined by society and fate, as opposed to the degree to which they can draw on reserves of imagination and the subconscious, are thus thrown into relief.

The King is the most confined by his position and expectations. His predicament is to be in a rigid, confined system, in which status, function, tradition, place, materiality, and ritual are far more important than the life of the individual. Nevertheless, Arnauld suggests that he has access to something beneath the surface, 'moi le seul gardien des hallucinations' [I the sole guardian of hallucinations] (*OC*, p. 103). In his last speech he declares, 'Enfin que me voulez-vous? Je suis le roi, la route épineuse des assassins est la mienne — je vous nargue tous — vos paroles sonnent faux — faux — faux — on ne prend pas mon cœur aux échecs' [What exactly is it you want of me? I am the king, mine is the thorny route of assassins — I scoff at you all — your words sound false — false — false — they will not take my heart at chess] (p. 107). Lonely and in demand, he cannot make meaningful contact in the social game, cannot trust language, and exits.

In contrast to the failing King, the other character, 'Le Fou', is insightful and prophetic. He is given the last word, in fact a song, which he delivers alone. A jester (rather than bishop) in the French game, he could be compared with the Dada project. Unfettered by social convention and expectations, he follows his thoughts and expression, 'je suis l'unique affront' [I am the unique affront], he repeats twice in a final three-stanza poetic refrain (pp. 107, 108). The characters also refer to a third figure, who never actually speaks or features, that is the 'curé' [parish priest]. Representative of religion, he is not even granted a voice, and is the object of ridicule. The text's irreverence towards religion is most apparent in the shortest turn of dialogue in the whole drama, when the King pronounces — and Arnauld gives the direction 'prophétique' [prophetically] — 'Le Christ n'a jamais aimé personne' [Christ never loved anyone] (p. 106).

Language is paramount and, although its arbitrariness and failings as a stable tool for communication are exposed, it is also shown to offer potential. This is made most explicit by 'Le Fou' who, just before his song, ends with a declaration of the 'fécund buisson universel des mots' [universal fecund bush of words] (p. 107). The notion of spontaneous expression is vividly evoked here, and can be related to the Dada project. Tzara is an important reference point. Willard Bohn notes:

> Jacques Baron has argued that the subject of Tzara's plays is really the birth of language via the destruction and reconstruction of the word. Thus, the Dada

poets wished to stimulate thought and to achieve new states of consciousness by manipulating their (verbal) medium.[26]

The rules of verbal interaction are thwarted and thematised.

Finally, it is important to draw attention to the preponderance and recurrence of chess in Dada visual and verbal texts. From as early as 1912, for example, Marcel Duchamp used images related to chess in visual and written work to explore human relationships, especially sexual relations, exploring the metaphor for themes including the notion of predetermined moves.[27] In a chapter on women Dada poets, Forcer neatly encapsulates its importance as 'a regular part of the iconography and homosocial mythology constructed by and between male Dadaists'. He goes on to discuss a text by Gabrielle Buffet-Picabia, 'Gambit de la Reine' [Queen's Gambit], that also draws on chess. He writes of 'a woman making a first move into the ludic environment of male-orchestrated Dada'.[28] Such scholarship permits us to vary our points of comparison from recourse only to the men of Dada. Increasing attention paid to the women of the avant-garde demonstrates that they were playing with this game too.[29]

Arnauld is drawn to the codes of fairy tales, fables, and games, perhaps because of their power to shape thought and uphold moral and social systems. The King's first phrase in 'Jeu d'échecs' reflects explicitly on this issue, 'La clé des histoires enfantines est une cravate étroite qui serre les paroles' [The key to children's stories is a tight tie that constricts speech] (*OC*, p. 103). By reformulating familiar genres, she ponders the ways in which language imposes itself through narratives, beginning with childhood. Her work envisages a prelogical existence, when language is less fettered, narrative more fantastical, and when the imagination might be less constricted. And, like fairy tales, the worlds that are conjured are not only joyful and utopian but frequently dark and dystopian. It is these elements, language, fable, dialogue, narrative sequences, and song, that connect 'Jeu d'échecs' with *Tournevire*. Each exposes social relations as fraught. The allusions to performance — to staging and drama and circus — draw attention to the arbitrary nature of words and gestures. Agency is threatened, identity as performativity is pre-empted. Both texts cross the boundaries of written and spoken texts, fiction, and performance. Not entirely successful as written texts, they occupy a space between the avant-garde theatre of the early decades of the twentieth century in Paris and post-war absurdist theatre. As Annabel Melzer states, 'The iconographic fantasy level of the Dada plays and performances [...] were not equalled in the contemporary theatre until the 1960s'.[30] Arnauld's self-referential fusions of form, her appeal to the psychological and physical in verbal and visual sparring, take their place in this trajectory.

Notes to Chapter 2

1. F. T. Marinetti, untitled review, in *La Critique et Céline Arnauld* [pamphlet of collected reviews] (Paris: [c. 1925?]), p. 3 (*OC*, p. 469).
2. Walter Benjamin, 'The Work of Art in the Age of Mechanical Reproduction', in *Illuminations*, trans. by Harry Zorn (London: Pimlico, 1999), pp. 211–44.
3. Some copies of the first edition (my own) were displayed for the first time at the 'Die Dada La

Dada She Dada' exhibitions in Switzerland 2015–2016. The prominent showcasing of a Dada woman writer was especially welcome.
4. See *OC*, p. 465, for full details of three types of edition, as well as written dedications listed from found copies. This bibliographical information is provided for each of the works to be discussed in this study in a section ('Notices et variantes', *OC*, pp. 461–569).
5. E. M. Forster, *Aspects of the Novel* (Harmondsworth: Penguin, 1966), p. 95.
6. Fernand Divoire, untitled review, in *La Critique et Céline Arnauld*, p. 3 (*OC*, p. 469).
7. Morgane le Fay, for example, is an enchantress in Arthurian narratives, appearing in medieval works by Chrétien de Troyes and Marie de France, and variously reprised by writers, artists, and film-makers over the centuries.
8. *Le Fol* recalls *Le Fou* or the 'bishop' in chess, a potential link to the dialogue 'Jeu d'échecs' discussed below.
9. Forster, *Aspects of the Novel*, p. 55.
10. If we take up a note by Étienne-Alain Hubert, we could also read Gadifer as Pierre Reverdy. The editor of the journal *Nord-Sud*, Reverdy had worked closely with Dermée before the two fell out acrimoniously. Hubert writes, 'Céline Arnauld était entrée en guerre avec *Tournevire* [...]; ce roman poétique [...] était chargé d'attaques allusives contre Reverdy [Céline Arnauld went to war with *Tournevire* [...]; this poetic novel [...] was loaded with allusive attacks on Reverdy]' (Pierre Reverdy, *Œuvres complètes. Nord-Sud, Self-Defence et autres écrits sur l'art et la poésie (1917–1926)* (Paris: Flammarion, 1975), p. 340); cited by Schmets, *OC*, p. 465.
11. Céline Arnauld, *Anthologie Céline Arnauld: morceaux choisis de 1919 à 1935* (Brussels: Cahiers du Journal des poètes, 1936), p. 7 (not repr. in *OC*).
12. For English translations of 'Farandole' and 'Cinéma' see Kamenish, *Mamas of Dada*, pp. 70–72.
13. Jed Rasula and Tim Conley, 'Introduction', in *Burning City: Poems of Metropolitan Modernity*, ed. by Jed Rasula and Tim Conley (Notre Dame, IN: Action Books, 2012), p. xviii. A section of this massive anthology of 541 texts by modernist and avant-garde writers gathers poems about the circus, cabaret, and zoos. See 'Whipcracks and Megaphone Chants', pp. 222–49.
14. Stephen Forcer, *Dada as Text, Thought and Theory* (Oxford: Legenda, 2015), p. 22.
15. Forster, *Aspects of the Novel*, p. 95.
16. André Breton, *Manifestes du surréalisme* (Paris: Gallimard, 1979), p. 16; *Manifestoes of Surrealism*, trans. by Richard Seaver and Helen R. Lane (Ann Arbor: University of Michigan Press, 1972), pp. 6–7.
17. André Breton, *Nadja* (Paris: Gallimard, 2000).
18. Tania Colliani, 'Les Avant-gardes et la narration: pour une poétique anti-prosaïque', *Cahiers de Narratologie*, 24 (2013), 1–13 (p. 4).
19. S. A., Mansbach, 'Methodology and Meaning in the Modern Art of Eastern Europe', in *Between Worlds: A Sourcebook of Central European Avant-Gardes, 1910–1930*, ed. by Timothy O. Benson and Éva Forgács for the Los Angeles County Museum of Art (Cambridge, MA, & London: MIT Press, 2002), pp. 290–303.
20. They are 'Arlequin' [Harlequin], 'Remorqueur' [Tugboat], 'Cinéma', 'Pacotille' [Junk], 'Farandole', and 'Magie [Magic]'.
21. Céline Arnauld, *Guêpier de diamants, poèmes* (Antwerp: Éditions Ça ira, 1923), p. 170. The title also reminded me of Apollinaire's poem 'Le Musicien de Saint-Merry' [The Musician of Saint-Merry]. See Guillaume Apollinaire, *Calligrammes: Poems of Peace and War (1913–1916)*, trans. by Iain Lockerbie (Berkeley & Los Angeles: University of California Press, 1980), pp. 70–77 (in French and English).
22. See programmes for the 'Manifestation Dada' and 'Festival Dada', for example, in *Documents Dada*, ed. by Yves Poupard-Lieussou and Michel Sanouillet (Paris: Weber, 1974), pp. 36–37 & 45. In March, she had played a 'femme enceinte' [pregnant woman] in the inaugural performance of Tzara's *La Première Aventure céleste de Monsieur Antipyrine* at the 'Manifestation Dada de la Maison de l'Œuvre'. This time her own text is performed.
23. Arnauld, *Anthologie Céline Arnauld*, pp. 41–46.
24. The chess piece 'Le Fou' is equivalent to the bishop in the English version of the game. Its literal translation as 'jester', however, points to an entirely different set-up, frame of reference, and

understanding. In the French game, and in Arnauld's text, a king and jester are pitted against one another.

25. Samuel Beckett, *En attendant Godot* (Paris: Bertrand-Lacoste, 1993), first performed in 1953; *Waiting for Godot* (London: Faber & Faber, 2015), first performed in English in 1955.
26. Willard Bohn, *The Dada Market: An Anthology of Poetry* (Carbondale & Edwardsville: Southern Illinois University Press, 1993), p. xvii; from Jacques Baron, *L'An du surréalisme, suivi de L'An dernier* (Paris: Denoël, 1969).
27. See, for example, David Hopkins, *Marcel Duchamp and Max Ernst: The Bride Shared* (Oxford: Clarendon Press, 1998), pp. 13 & 119–20.
28. Forcer, 'Decoding Dada: Women Dada Poets and Homosocial Dada', in which he deals with Arnauld, Buffet-Picabia, and Marguerite Buffet (in *Dada as Text, Thought and Theory*, pp. 10–46 (pp. 12 & 15)). Gabrielle Buffet-Picabia, 'Gambit de la Reine', *Dada*, 4–5 (February 1919), 19.
29. Yet another example, this time a visual artist, is Dorothea Tanning. See *Dorothea Tanning*, ed. by Alyce Mahon (London: Tate Modern, 2019). Exhibitions at the Museo Nacional Centro de Arte Reina Sofia (3 October 2018–7 January 2019) and Tate Modern, London (27 February–9 June 2019) have been instrumental in extending recognition of her multimedia work.
30. Annabel Melzer, *Dada and Surrealist Performance* (Baltimore, MD, & London: John Hopkins University Press, 1994), p. xiv.

CHAPTER 3

Collision and Collage in *Poèmes à claires-voies* (1920)

Arnauld's novel remained a one-off experiment. What followed, however, was a prolific period of invention in poetry, signalled by a text that in its very title suggests openness. *Poèmes à claires-voies* [Openwork Poems], published in 1920, is Arnauld's first surviving volume of poetry, and appeared during the height of Dada's manifestation in Paris. It was swiftly built upon by *Point de mire* in 1921. In this chapter and the next I seek to tease out some of the formal and thematic characteristics of these two volumes.[1] As a starting-point my readings of form will draw out connections with Apollinaire and the notion of verbal collage. That technique's production of juxtapositions gives rise to thematic collisions of ideas and images that will begin to emerge in this chapter, and that will be further unpacked in Chapter 4.

A review, published in the magazine *Action*, both exposes some tensions and offers a way into this first volume:

> La directrice de *m'Amenez'y* est une des muses du *Dadaïsme*. Ce volume serait plutôt dans la 'tradition' du cubisme de Jean Cocteau. Il y a là d'exquises choses, de petites merveilles de sensibilité ténue, dansante, cachée et magnétique, dont la lecture est le plus savoureux des divertissements.[2]
>
> [The director of *m'Amenez'y* is one of the muses of *Dadasim*. This volume is rather in the 'tradition' of Jean Cocteau's cubism. There are exquisite things in it, little marvels of a delicate, dancing, hidden and magnetic sensibility, the reading of which is the most delicious of diversions.]

This short review, authored by Renée Dunan, relates to a research question that underpins this study; how to locate Arnauld's poetry within a literary landscape. If the term 'muse', used to relate Arnauld to Dada, strikes us now as problematic, connoting passivity over agency, so too does a reference point that conflates Cocteau and Cubism. The reviewer faces a thorny task in seeking comparisons that make sense to the reader. More affirmatively, Dunan's conundrum reminds us of the intertextual context of the literary avant-garde, the innovative nature of Arnauld's writing, and the instability of any kind of 'tradition' as backdrop.

The challenge of categorisation is familiar to feminist scholars seeking to describe, justify, or benchmark women's writing in relation to some sort of canon.

Dunan's reference to Arnauld as one of the muses of Dadaism was an effort to mark out her importance to the nascent Dada *groupe du jour*. It is apposite, too, to acknowledge what came before. Arnauld greatly admired Apollinaire, in particular. On 31 December 1916 Dermée had co-organised a banquet in his honour, following his return from war service. In a much later text 'Le Banquet', published after Apollinaire's death, Arnauld relates this event, including her impressions of his voice, 'lyrique et tendre', his encouragement and discovery of young poets, and her poignant wish that she had known him better so that she might have enjoyed his support. But even here she is careful to head off facile comparisons, asserting that poetry was evolving in new directions to that of Apollinaire. It was appropriate to think of new poets as admirers, enthusiasts, and friends, she asserts, rather than as the disciples of a master. 'Enthousiasme et admiration ne sont pas allégeance' [Enthusiasm and admiration are not allegiance], she concludes.[3] The pamphlet was published at some point between 1919 and 1924. As we will see in Part II, Arnauld's insistence on independence was becoming acute at this point, and Dermée shared it. Although he went on to co-launch the magazine *L'Esprit nouveau* in 1920, its title a nod to Apollinaire, he too would take a distance from a too-close alliance.[4] Without a doubt, though, this influential figure on the Parisian scene was an important reference point for both poets.

Arnauld's *Poèmes à claires-voies* was published on 5 March 1920 in a print run of two hundred, plus ten deluxe copies, by 'Éditions de L'Esprit nouveau'. It contains seventeen relatively lengthy poems. Some of these were also published in journals. In that same month 'Sous-marin' [Submarine] appeared in print in Picabia's *391*, 12, and 'Avertisseur' [Alarm] in Dermée's *Z*. Additionally, a shorter version of the poem 'Entre voleurs' [Among Thieves] was included in Éluard's *Proverbe*, 4 (April-May 1920). Much later, eight poems would be selected for Arnauld's 1936 anthology, prefaced by a well-known quotation in French translation from *The Tempest* by Shakespeare, 'Nous sommes faits de la même étoffe que les rêves' ('We are such stuff | As dreams are made on') (IV.1.156–57). What we can take from this retrospective gesture, as we analyse the early collection, is an emphasis by its author on the illusory, fleeting nature of human existence.

I have translated the title of the collection into English as 'Openwork Poems'. The term 'à claires-voies' suggests a structure that lets in light. It can refer to functional or ornamental objects, frequently in wood, stone, or metal that contain numerous openings. A common use of 'à claire-voie' for example is for architectural elements such as fencing, slatting, partitions, or balustrades. In churches it designates an upper level, pierced with windows, rising above the roofline, designed to allow in light and can be translated as 'clerestory'. It is also a marine term, applied to articulated glazing that lets in daylight to a loading area or hold below deck. We might think, too, of railway bridges, or the fretwork of glass and iron in railway station roofs. For the reader of French the two-word construction 'light' and 'way' points immediately and literally to the characteristic of allowing in light through an otherwise solid object. The visual metaphor suggests chinks and gaps rather than solidity and opacity. Formally it can be connected to collage, to the bringing together of disparate fragments in a composition that nevertheless leaves spaces and blanks. That idea, of verbal collage, is a notion that will be pursued in this chapter as a characteristic of Arnauld's work, and which ties in with Dunan's use of the term 'Cubism'.

Figuratively we can read Arnauld's title as an entirely suitable choice for her collection of poems. Its suggestion of a fashioned but relatively loose network aptly evokes both the collection of standalone poems, brought together within the pages of the book, and the poet's free association of words that makes up the individual poems. It signals creatively constructed work that nevertheless remains open to associations and meanings, and of grammatical and semantic openings that are left for the reader to complete. My English translation, 'Openwork', also brings to mind and pays homage to *The Open Work* by Umberto Eco.[5] Admittedly the association is tempting for the reader of English, since the original Italian title of Eco's 1962 work (*Opera aperta*) and the French of Arnauld's (*claires-voies*) are mediated by the translator's choice. But it is not so far-fetched to consider shared ground in the will to permit and privilege reader responses in the reception of a work of literature.

The first poem in the collection shares its name with the volume. 'Claires-voies' is a forty-eight-line poem set over two pages (*OC*, pp. 75–76). Its first stanza plunges the reader into that no-man's land between night and day, sleep and waking:

> Le cauchemar des clairs-obscurs
> hante le promeneur
> au bord du matin

[The nightmare of chiaroscuros | haunts the walker | at the morning's edge]

The reader identifies with the figure of the walker, a psychic sleepwalker almost, whose imaginative journey between night and the dawning of light is evoked as the poem continues. Contrasts between light and dark signalled in the first line characterise the entire poem. The term 'clair-obscur' explicitly sets a visual mood, referring to a technique of painting in which the range and contrasts of light and dark are exploited. Like the Italian term *chiaroscuro*, usually employed in English, the French contains a tension between the terms *clair* [light] and *obscur* [dark], with the *clair* echoing too the first half of the poem's title. The poem goes on to describe a gradual coming to light. In the second stanza the light creeps its way slowly in ('A tâtons la lumière se glisse') to succeed the night. In the latter stages of the poem the (assumed) human figure, advancing through time, merges with the light, rendered by a hybrid of Arnauld's invention, a 'promeneur-lumière' [walker-light], another collision of terms. The light is personified so that one wonders whether the walker is not, after all, the light stealing in, the rays of the rising sun.

Pain and joy are also set up as oppositions. In the earlier half of the poem there is an undeniable sense of suffering: the haunting nightmares in the first stanza; 'la douleur du soir' [the evening's pain], remembered as a sort of hangover from the evening before in the second; 'trois douleurs' [three pains] that 'possess' the walker in the third. These are all but extinguished as the morning light advances, with just one reference back to 'les douleurs bleues' [the blue pains] in the latter part, still present at the edges of memory. The 'bleu' in French also calls up its meaning as a noun, that is a bruise.

The indices of anguish present in the first three stanzas, which build in length from three to four to six lines, are overtaken by the sounds and sights of awakening activity. The gradually advancing light in the second stanza is accompanied by 'l'eau de jet-prière' [the jet of prayer-water] issuing from a fountain in a park, a first suggestion of location. The water, a combination of the physical rush of water and spiritual hope of prayer, extinguishes the pain. The restorative power of water recurs in the next (fourth) stanza, prayer having evolved into play. Arnauld builds a collage, line by line, the sense coming together only as fragments build. From 'l'aurore en maillot' [dawn in a swimsuit] in the first line, to 'le caprice du jet d'eau' [the caprice of the fountain] in the second, to the appearance of children (from the chateau) introduced in the third, a picture of children playing in water is constructed. Baskets of snowballs and nests are added to this idyllic scene of outdoor play that verges on being a child's-eye view. 'Aux claires-voies' recurs as a qualifier, evoking the latticework of the basket and arguably implying too the tangle of the nests. An idea of location is revealed little by little, a word introduced here and there to build a context: a park, fountain, chateau, nests, ground ivy, pond, pebbles, a bell, a forest (the last word of the poem). These are signifiers of the natural and man-made elements of a formal French park, coming to life in a morning. Here is an urban microcosm, a communal site of modern metropolitan life.

After this fourth stanza the structure of the poem becomes looser. Reading rhythms are changed by experimentation with typographical layout, with lines indented and staggered across the page. Far from suggesting a negative disintegration, the fragments that emerge are bursts of imagery, advancing and receding, acted out on the page. Thus, for example:

> De chaque caillou
> s'élève une prière
> vers les douleurs bleues

[From every pebble | a prayer rises | towards the blue pains]

The prayers appear to issue forth hopefully from the pebbles, before being pulled back towards sorrow, reminiscent, perhaps, of the lapping of water. In all, the image reminds us of Apollinaire's poem 'La Colombe poignardée et le jet d'eau' [The Bleeding-Heart Dove and the Fountain].[6] In this celebrated pictorial calligram the jets of water from a fountain offer a prayer to comrades from the 1914–1918 war, topped by a dove of peace.

As Arnauld's poem continues, positive images and emotions encroach. The sights and sounds are exultant: laughter, cries, and joy are listed as breaking out, a bell rings, 'six coups d'allégresse' are heard, suggesting a clock striking six o'clock, the sound jubilant. Children play together, the water jet rises in prayer and an umbrella is described as being in ecstasy. Dancing Pierrots regain their nests. This term seemingly conflates the marionettes used in puppet shows for children in some French parks with birds. Openness and fullness are emphasised and appear to prevail. What was glimpsed from the edge (the edge of the morning, of the sky, of the pond, of the sun), is now experienced fully, with verbs such as *inonder* [flood] and *envelopper* [envelop]. The uncertain cusp of morning has turned to day.

The openwork (likely fencing here) has 'opened its eyes' (in the fourth stanza) to mysteries, and then its soul (in the ninth stanza), this uncertain image suggesting the latticework of iron fencing and gates that conceal and gradually reveal the park, the community space, within.

In its evocation of a morning awakening or journey in time, 'Claires-voies' shares common ground with 'Avertisseur' ('Alarm'), another poem from this volume (OC, pp. 80–81). Its form recalls the *Reihungsstil* (or serial style) of Expressionist poetry. In a series of staccato phrases, it evokes a commute, from the moment of getting up, and out of bed, through to travelling on a train. With its fragments of rapid, multisensory experiences, related in a succession of short lines, it echoes speed and motion. The short first lines build momentum. The fourth line, the word 'Matin' ('Morning'), for example, dispenses with pronoun and verb in favour of a single noun that conveys all that is required. The rhythm of the reading experience is underscored by the appearance of the text on the page, which recalls the railway it evokes. These short lines might be said to echo sleepers. This harmony of form and content can be most readily appreciated by seeing and reading it in Dermée's one-off magazine *Z*, where it was published in 1920. That magazine's unusually long, thin format (23 x 31 cm, but folded to make a pamphlet half the width) offers the optimum material support.

The poem's fleeting images are saturated with lyrical beauty:

> est-ce l'étalage du soleil
> sur les fenêtres du wagon
> ou l'inspiration anti-alcool
> du matin en papillotes
>
> is it the display of sunlight
> on the carriage windows
> or the anti-alcohol inspiration
> of the morning in paper curls[7]

A description of the station master is beautifully concise, yet evocative and sensuous:

> le chef de gare sans raison
> [...]
> divague en jonglant avec les colis
> sévèrement remplis du café réveil-matin
>
> the station master for no apparent reason
> [...]
> rambles on while juggling the packages
> full to the brim with alarm-clock coffee

Sights, sounds, smell, and movement are concisely conveyed. In the ways they crash and tumble together, truncated phrases reflect the speed, confusion, and exhilaration of early morning urban activity both inside and outside the train.

Scattered through the staccato impressions are phrases that might be received as snippets of overheard dialogue. 'Arrêt première station' has been translated by Willard Bohn as 'Stop first station', but 'First stop' would be a more effective rendering of an announcement by the guard. Greetings also punctuate the text. 'Mes amis mes amis' and 'Ohé mes très chers amis' ('My friends my friends', 'Hello my very dear friends') might again be assumed to emit from the guard, speaking to the train's passengers, or could be the interjections of a passenger to their fellow travellers. These fragments of spoken language, together with sensory evocations, remind us of Apollinaire's integration of colloquial language and expressions in poems including 'Lundi rue Christine' ('Monday in Christine Street').[8] Here, too, the speakers are not specified, the words instead becoming part of a verbal-visual tapestry of everyday sensations and experiences.

The apparent friendliness and innocuousness of the lines discussed above are problematised, however, by another category of address, that is the imperative. The first address is followed immediately by the warning:

> ne vous fiez pas à l'étincelle
> le feu prend partout
> même dans vos cervelles
>
> don't trust in sparks
> fire erupts everywhere
> even in your brains

Three lines after the second direct address, an accusation and another command follow in quick succession:

> Vos paroles sont des schrapnells
> sur les roues tournesol
> Les cimetières s'allongent jusqu'à l'herbe morte...
> PRENEZ GARDE
> AUX TOMBES OUVERTES
>
> Your words are shrapnel
> on the sunflower wheels
> The cemeteries extend to the dead grass...
> WATCH OUT
> FOR THE OPEN GRAVES

These direct addresses are jarring for the reader, who wonders whether the warning is more widespread. The ambiguity of the title — as an alarm clock (the start to the commuter's day) or as a warning — is apparent. The last stanza brings us to the sense of caution contained in the title.

Indeed, the poem is shot through with ominous moments. From 'Les rails en pleurs ('The rails in tears'), to 'la pluie tombe méfiante et mesquine' ('the rain falls suspicious and petty'), personification brings the mechanical, natural, and human into a shared sphere of fearfulness. Written only two years after the end of the First World War, the poem undoubtedly contains an undercurrent of fear about new technology, and of caution over the horrifying misuse of machinery, transport, and mass movement alongside its positive potential.[9]

This is not, though, a didactic poem. Rather, it mimics the digressions and loopings of the mind. The commuters are half-asleep, caught between the previous night's dreams and the sounds, sights, and smells that assail them. The changing nature of their experience as they move forward is captured. The windows of the carriages offer a succession of sights that are in constant motion, from sunlight to rain, sunflowers to wheels, an aeroplane above, a cemetery and open graves below. This is travel, but it is neither linear nor straightforwardly progressive. Elements from the start recur at the end. 'Les sentiments | descentes de lit' ('Sentiments | getting out of bed') becomes 'les sentiments en descente de lit' ('feelings of getting out of bed'). The wings of an aeroplane, glimpsed in l. 5, recur in l. 24. In both cases they are associated with a balance of emotions. Latterly they are described as 'trop fragiles' ('too fragile'). These impressions convey a simultaneous excitement and anxiety about aeroplanes in modernist literature. Their appearance in the sky was still relatively novel, pointing to the potential for ingenuity, on the one hand, and deployment in conflict on the other. These elements co-exist thanks to a collage technique that eschews a single-point perspective. The point of view is constantly changing.

'Avertisseur' takes its place in a trajectory of avant-garde literature that celebrates everyday urban interactions, encounters, and displacements, from Charles Baudelaire's influential concept of the city *flâneur*, proposed in his 1863 essay 'Le Peintre de la vie moderne' [The Painter of Modern Life], to Breton's wandering narrator in the 1928 novel *Nadja* (noted in Chapter 2).[10] It also recalls the fragmentation and multi-faceted nature of experiments in painting at the time, from images of the Eiffel Tower by Sonia Delaunay and Robert Delaunay, to the Futurists' evocation of individuals, machines, and cities in motion, to the Berlin Dadaists' city photomontages, such as George Grosz and Heartfield's *Leben und trieben in Universal-City, 12 Uhr 5 Mittags* [Life and Work in Universal City. 12:05 Noon] (1919) and *Metropolis* (1932) by Paul Citroen. 'Avertisseur' has a rapid, pacey, almost filmic quality, appealing both to the ear and the eye.

The apparent celebration of modernity and urbanity in 'Avertisseur', its indication of the new potential of mass transit to move the individual around the city in a short space of time, reminds us, too, of Marinetti's evocation of the city, 'An ordinary man in a day's time can travel by train from a little dead town of empty squares, where the sun, the dust, and the wind amuse themselves in silence, to a great capital city bursting with lights, gestures and street cries'.[11] Arnauld's poem is, however, tempered by a level of caution not found in the Futurists' elevation of machine technology. The semi-glimpsed sights of 'Avertisseur', like 'Claires-voies', bear traces of a dark underbelly. Tears, suspicious and petty rain, and words like shrapnel, combine to produce a sense of menace, shaking the reader out of any commuter-complacency.

The motif of transport, present in many of Arnauld's poems and typical of avant-garde and modernist literature, is central also to 'Sous-marin' (*OC*, p. 91). Appearing in *391* only eleven days after 'Avertisseur' had been published in Dermée's journal *Z* (12 March and 1 March respectively), it has in common with that poem the inclusion of trains and the proposal of danger, even tragedy. In the case of 'Sous-marin', however, an underwater world is additionally evoked. The first lines of this twenty-one-line poem place the reader in a liminal space between the sky above and a stretch of water below, using familiar imagery to bring to mind a night-time landscape:

> Sous l'avalanche d'étoiles
> une nappe de velours
> s'étend
> sur le bonheur sommeil
> de deux voleurs scaphandriers

[Beneath the avalanche of stars | a velvet cloth | extends | over the happiness sleep | of two deep-sea diver thieves]

The image is apparently harmonious until the notion of a thieving incursion pierces the surface of the water and with it the reader's sense of a harmless peace. The word 'thief' suggests an intrusion, but 'le bonheur sommeil' counters any sense of drama with a more peaceful notion of crossing into an underwater world.

The second stanza reads:

> Seul avec Dieu
> l'œil sous-marin grand ouvert
> enchante la merveille dévastée'

[Alone with God | the wide-open underwater eye | enchants the devastated marvel]

The mysterious eye sees what we, the readers, cannot, and may even have brought about 'the devastated marvel'. 'La merveille dévastée' is given a definite article rather than indefinite, referring to a context, a tragedy that has come before but to which the reader is not privy. The eye is frequently present in Arnauld's poetry, an indication of her fascination with visual perception and ways of relating the imagination to the external world. Here it is an entity in its own right, assuming the ability not only to see but to enchant. In combination with God (the first line of this second stanza), it suggests a fatalistic power which might not only be witness to but possibly cause of some sort of accident, and at the very least a powerful mediator of experience.

The third stanza, a single line, transports the reader back above the surface of the water to the sleeping-cars of a train passing or crossing the 'rive escalier' [stairway shore], reminding them of the modern human world above. As well as actual travels across, through, and below this physical landscape, there are suggestions of emotional journeys. 'L'amertume enfantine d'un amour' [the childish bitterness of a love] is described in the distance, beyond the twinned concepts or obstacles of 'une colline' [a hill] and 'un soupir' [a sigh]. The eight of spades signals bad luck but uncertainty reigns. 'La bonne aventure de cette night tragique' [The great fortune of this tragic night], for example, is highly paradoxical.

In the fifth stanza the natural world of birds and insects that we encountered in *Tournevire* and that we will see so frequently invoked in Arnauld's poetry intervenes, and in a typically magical way, 'Hannetons-marionnettes | yeux d'hiboux qui faites la quête' [May-bug-marionettes | owl eyes passing round the collection hat]. 'Hanneton' is most commonly translated as a 'May bug' (or cockchafer), the name for a large brown beetle found in late spring and early summer.[12] The marionettes of the poem 'Claires-voies' appear again, their fusion with insects creating some uncanny semi-animate creature. The rapid juxtaposition with 'owls' eyes' in the next line and the anthropomorphic action of passing round a collection hat combines to conjure a nocturnal being that exists somewhere between bird, animal, doll, and human, watching big-eyed over what is now specified as a tragedy. The semantic insecurity of the stanza is compounded by the conjugation 'faites'. The second person of *faire* [to do] is chosen instead of the grammatically correct *font* (third person plural), presumably to make and enjoy the rhyme between 'faites' and 'quête', which at the same time seems to address the reader and maintain ambiguity as to the subject (are the owls' eyes a feature of the May-bug-marionnettes or a separate entity?).

In the final stanza 'la nappe de velours' [the velvet cloth] is repeated from the second line of the first stanza, this time strewn with flowers and sorrows, and calling up the scene of a tragedy marked by mourners. These 'fleurs' and 'douleurs' have assonance with 'velours' and are rhymed too with 'la rive des pleurs' [the shore of tears] in the final line of the poem. This choice to use rhyme as a conventional structure, relatively unusual in Arnauld's poetry, produces a lulling, almost soporific effect, echoing the sleepy feel of the poem, and leaving the imprint of a sorrowful elegy as the final impression of the poem.

The other recurrence in the final stanza is the sleeping-cars that pass or cross the shore. 'La rive escalier' in the fourth stanza is echoed here by 'la rive des pleurs', the latter qualifier, positioned at the very end of the poem, offering a defining resonant image. Like many of Arnauld's poems, 'Sous-marin' grants no easy narrative and maintains ambiguity, not least in its scarcity of verbs and favouring of nouns and adjectives, themselves sometimes neologisms or odd juxtapositions. One interpretation of the poem is that it refers to the aftermath of an accident. The notion of underwater interlocutors, the night-time setting, and the indices of sorrow and devastation all convey the idea of recent tragedy. The 'diver thieves', with their 'happy sleep', might be the victims of drowning, their good fortune gone bad. The 'sous-marin' of the title can be either adjective or noun. In the latter, a submarine vessel might have sunk, the object of marvellous devastation observed by the eye, or even itself the eye alone now with God. Since 'rive' 'can mean the bank or shore of a river, lake, or sea, the context remains ambiguous. Above ground, the refrain 'les sleeping-cars ont passé la rive' [the sleeping cars have crossed the shore], repeated twice, suggests life continuing nonetheless. Arnauld's interest in travel at this time is typical of the historical period during which she lived. While offering exciting possibilities to cross space and 'compress' time, it was also hazardous, the losses at sea and scrapping of submarine vessels still recent in 1920, and civilian train travel punctuated by regular accidents. Less literally, the poem might be an evocation of the porous zone between wakefulness and sleeping, the conscious and unconscious, with the shoreline as a border and immersion as surrender, a trope frequently deployed in surrealist artistic production.

This analysis of three of the poems in *Poèmes à claires-voies* offers only a taster of the seventeen poems published there. Though necessarily limited in scope, it gives some sense of the formal characteristics and themes of Arnauld's poetry, including preoccupations with the edges of time, the collision between rural and urban, and the conflicting emotions of hope and sorrow. Metaphors of flight and light take in both the natural world (birds and insects) and the possibilities of new technologies such as modern modes of transport. Frequent turns to the marvellous, fantastical, and dreamlike are tested to express the apparently inexpressible. These case studies also point to the ways in which Arnauld brings words together to make fusions, her use of certain words and phrases as recurring motifs, and her approach to building visual images as collages.

The latter approach underscores one of the key strategies of the Parisian avant-garde, common to writers and artists. Pioneered by the Cubists and celebrated by Apollinaire, it offers complexity over coherence, defies linearity and logic, and encompasses multiple moments and perspectives. As Ivan Goll will state four years later in his 'Manifeste du surréalisme', which looks back to Apollinaire as well as forward, 'L'image est aujourd'hui le critère de la bonne poésie. La rapidité d'association entre la première impression et la dernière expression fait la qualité de l'image' [The image today is the criterion of good poetry. The rapidity of association between the first impression and of the last expression makes for the quality of the image].[13] Dunan's reference to Cubism as well as Dada, in the short review with which we began, acknowledges this current and its intertextual impact in the early decades of the twentieth century. The latter part, 'Il y a là d'exquises choses, de petites merveilles de sensibilité ténue, dansante, cachée et magnétique', offers an appropriately lyrical response that draws attention to the liveliness of the work, its alluring and elusive component imagery, and the necessity of an active response on the part of the reader.

Reading Arnauld's poems serially gives rise to new appreciations. This is especially true given the intertextual nature of her writings. To give just a few examples: the title of the seventh poem in the volume, 'A tâtons' [Gropingly], is familiar to the reader from the inclusion of this phrase in the first 'Claires-voies'. There, 'A tâtons la lumière se glisse' [the light creeps its way] conveys a sense of proceeding little by little. In this same poem 'tourne et vire' [turn and turn around] recalls her 1919 poetic novel *Tournevire*, the marine term linking to her repeated references to boats and to water. The term 'claires-voies' appears twice more in poems in her next volume of poetry *Point de mire*. In 'Surtout ne regarde pas' [Above All Don't Look] we read, 'Ces morts l'œil collé aux claires-voies' [These dead ones, eyes glued to the openwork] (*OC*, p. 117). In 'Symphonie' [Symphony] the term appears again, like a trace, a return to poems already read, 'la tanière aux claires-voies de harpe' [the lair with its harp's openwork] (*OC*, p. 120). We will see further repetitions of the term as late as seventeen years later, in *Les Réseaux du réveil* (see Chapter 10). The words impress on the mind, layer after layer, even as the meaning remains flexible, elusive, slippery, ungraspable. It is as if Arnauld wants to wring every meaning and possibility out of the linguistic sign, deploying it again and again at different moments, yet the reader is still given considerable room for manoeuvre. The 'openwork' of the title is entirely apt, conjuring up a network of visual and verbal connections characterised by gaps and openings that resist closure. The next chapter will delve in more detail into this tendency to iterate and reiterate, to build frameworks or fretworks of terms that get close to objects and concepts, but that remain porous and incomplete. With these terms the texts both relay and delay meaning in seemingly endlessly chains of linguistic play.

Notes to Chapter 3

1. For an earlier article on this volume see Ruth Hemus, 'Céline Arnauld's *Poèmes à Claires-voies* (Openwork Poems)', in *Lost in Transmission: Preservation, Radicalism, and the Institutionalisation of the Avant-Garde(s)*, ed. by Rebecca Ferreboeuf, Fiona Noble, and Tara Plunkett (Basingstoke: Palgrave Macmillan, 2016), pp. 71–85.
2. Renée Dunan, 'Encycliques: *Poèmes à claires-voies*', *Action*, 3 (April 1920), 62. Many press reviews were gathered and reprinted by Martin-Schmets in *OC*, but not all. This one I discovered in the BnF; repr. in *Action: cahiers de philosophie et d'art, collection complète, mars 1920 à avril 1922*, ed. by Florent Fels and Marcel Sauvage (Paris: J-M Place, 1999), III, 62. The reference to *m'Amenez'y* will be discussed in Chapter 6, as will Dunan, who contributed a text to Arnauld's 1920 journal *Projecteur*.
3. She specifically refers to the publication of *Tournevire*, 'où éclataient tant de haines et de luttes inutiles' [when so many instances of hatred and unnecessary battles broke out]. See Céline Arnauld, 'Le Banquet', in Guillaume Apollinaire and others, *Apollinaire* (Paris: Editions de l'Esprit nouveau, [1919–1924]), [n.p.] (consulted in BnF). *Apollinaire* includes contributions by Pierre-Albert Birot, Dermée, Picabia, Roch Grey (Hélène Oettingen) and André Salmon.
4. The title refers, of course, to Apollinaire's essay 'L'Esprit nouveau et les poètes' [The New Spirit and the Poets], first published in *Mercure de France*, 1 December 1918 (Apollinaire, *Œuvres en prose complètes*, Bibliothèque de la Pléiade (Paris: Gallimard, 1991), pp. 948–53). Dermée also published a long article dedicated to Apollinaire, 'Guillaume Apollinaire', *L'Esprit nouveau*, 26 (June-July 1924), [n.p.]. For more on Dermée's motivations and ambitions, not always complimentary, see Victor Martin-Schmets, 'Céline Arnauld, épouse Paul Dermée, poète dadaïste', in *Les Oubliés des Avant-Garde*, ed. by Meazzi and Madou, pp. 176–77.
5. Umberto Eco, *The Open Work*, trans. by Anna Cancogni (Cambridge, MA: Harvard University Press, 1989).
6. Apollinaire, 'La Colombe poignardée et le jet d'eau', in *Calligrammes*, pp. 122–23 (in French and English).
7. For an English translation, which I am citing here, alongside the original French version, see *The Dada Market*, ed. by Bohn, pp. 18–19. That anthology also includes the short version of 'Entre voleurs' [Among Thieves] that was published in Paul Éluard's *Proverbe*, 4 (April 1920), a longer version of which appears in *Poèmes à claires-voies*. A third poem, 'Les Ronge-Bois' [The Wood-Gnawers], from *Projecteur* (May 1920), is also included, pp. 16–17. Bohn was rare and prescient in including Arnauld in his anthology. See also Kamenish, *Mamas of Dada*, pp. 74–76, for an alternative translation and analysis.
8. Apollinaire, 'Lundi rue Christine', in *Calligrammes*, pp. 52–57 (in French and English).
9. Forcer makes an interesting reading of this text as a prescient warning to the Dada group about the destructive nature of distrust, friction, and hostile rhetoric that would destabilise Dada (*Dada as Text, Thought and Theory*, pp. 23–27).
10. Charles Baudelaire, 'Le Peintre de la vie moderne', in *Œuvres complètes*, 7 vols (Paris: Calmann Lévy, 1885–1903), III, 68–73; 'The Painter of Modern Life', in *The Painter of Modern Life and Other Essays*, trans. and ed. by Jonathan Mayne (London: Phaidon, 1964), pp. 1–40.
11. F. T. Marinetti, 'Destruction of Syntax — Imagination without Strings — Words-in-Freedom 1913', in *Futurist Manifestos*, ed. by Umbro Apollonio (New York: The Viking Press, 1973), p. 96.
12. 'Pas piqué d'hannetons' is also a colloquial expression meaning 'great', 'brilliant, or 'wild' (eccentric).

13. Ivan Goll, 'Manifeste du surréalisme', in *Surréalisme*, 1 (October 1924), [n.p.]. This text appeared a month before Breton's surrealist manifesto.

CHAPTER 4

Liminal Spaces and Refrains in *Point de mire* (1921)

Avant tout, Céline Arnauld ne fait pas de littérature. Nous ne sommes pas pour les règles.[1]

[Above all, Céline Arnauld does not do literature. We are not in favour of rules.]

This extract, from a review of Arnauld's 1921 volume of poetry *Point de mire* [Focal Point] succinctly underscores the experimental approach taken towards literature by Arnauld that the previous chapter began to unpack. Authored by the playwright Antonin Artaud, it also bears witness to her place within avant-garde circles in Paris and offers a contemporaneous acknowledgement of her work by a respected figure. Artaud's statement that Arnauld 'does not do literature' aligns with a notion of literature as establishment, convention, or code. As she formulates it mockingly in a text 'Ombrelle Dada' [Dada Parasol], to be discussed in the next chapter, 'C'est ça la Poéesie, croyez-moi' [That's what Pooetry is, believe me] (*OC*, p. 448).

Artaud's review of *Point de mire* continues:

On espère peut-être de nous une explication logiquement raisonnable, une coordination raisonnée de ces poèmes! Il n'y en a pas. Céline Arnauld pense par associations d'idées. Une image appelle une autre image d'après des lois qui sont les lois mêmes de la pensée. Chaque poème est un corps complet et parfaitement organisé auquel des nécessités intérieures et lointaines imposent sa forme et sa dimension.

[Perhaps we are expecting a logically rational explanation, a careful coordination of these poems! There is none. Céline Arnauld thinks by association of ideas. One image calls up another image according to laws that are the very laws of thought. Each poem is a complete and perfectly organised body, its form and scope imposed by interior and distant necessities.]

Artaud's words anticipate frustration for the reader in the face of a body of work that is not thematically coherent. His characterisation of Arnauld's creative process as an 'association of ideas' stands in opposition to linearity, logic, and a planned rationale. It shares ground with the futurist concept of imagination without strings and the surrealist emphasis on free association, unhindered by conscious thought. Crucially this openness, and the possibility for making connections, applies to both writer and reader, the latter having ample room for interpretation. Indeed, they are required to participate in an active reading and generation of meaning. Narrative coherence is relegated in favour of words as shapes and sounds, as material entities to be savoured in themselves.

In what follows I will take heed of Artaud's warning. An overview of *Point de mire* cannot hope to find a unifying thread and it would be false to try to impose coherence on what is an eclectic collection. Paradoxically, however, the free reign of language results in reiterations of words. The more one reads, the more these emerge. Recurring words punctuate poems and sets of poems; images and ideas reappear with surprising regularity; linguistic repetitions and mutations become characteristics. While each poem is indeed complete in itself, as Artaud concludes, I propose that a reading that situates it in Arnauld's wider body of work yields a richness.[2] The associations of ideas that Artaud identifies occur within individual texts but they also recur across them. Favoured words, objects of contemplation, or indeed 'focal points', emerge in a single poem, through a set of poems, and then across volumes. They are deployed and redeployed, coming in and out of focus, acquiring meaning, changing emphasis, being made anew. They are both heavy with significance and elusive, always one step ahead.

Artaud writes of necessities that fuel Arnauld's writing. Formally, I argue, what drives this work is the emphasis on getting to the meaning of a word, of using and reusing it so that it is continually signifying anew. Bound up with that approach to language is a self-reflection in the texts on the poet as a seeker, a traveller, and an outsider, stretching the limits of language and ideas. Thematically we see Arnauld's interest in the edges of things, the liminal spaces between the natural and the urban, land and water, day and night, light and dark, waking and sleeping, life and death, human and non-human. These points of collision between elements from different spheres began to emerge in the last chapter and will be given further space here. Notions of formal and thematic juxtapositions will be built upon in an analysis that emphasises contrasts and oppositions, combinations and, importantly, repetitions. The result is a kind of vocabulary of visual motifs that might be said to characterise Arnauld's writing as she searches for the inexpressible between opposites. Some of these areas will be picked up and explored in more depth in subsequent chapters, including in relation to vision (Chapter 6), travel (Chapter 8), sound (Chapter 9), and time (Chapter 10).

Point de mire was published in 1921 by Jacques Povolozky under the series title 'Collection Z' in a print-run of two hundred, with an additional five deluxe copies. Already, Arnauld confounds us by beginning her collection, designated as 'poèmes', with a text that is something quite other than a poem. 'Jeu d'échecs' is a dialogue for two characters that was discussed at the end of Chapter 2. It is followed by twenty poems, fourteen of which would later be included in Arnauld's 1936 anthology. Four were also published in journals, 'Périscope' [Periscope] (*391*, 14, November 1920), 'Surnom' [Nickname] (*Ça ira*, 16, November 1921), 'Jeux d'anneaux' [Quoits] (*Action*, 9, October 1921), and 'Fête' [Festival] (*Action*, 12, March-April 1922). A literal translation of 'point de mire' as a target calls to mind one of Francis Picabia's favourite icons, which appears repeatedly in his artworks and journals, and the title may well be a nod to him. My translation 'Focal Point' emphasises this visual possibility and ties in with Arnauld's frequent references to visuality and more specifically to film. It also connotes more figuratively. In this case it could be read as gesturing to an ongoing quest to find a means of expression, to bring an idea into focus, to get to the meaning(s) of a word.

The first poem in *Point de mire*, excepting the prologue-dialogue 'Jeu d'échecs', is 'Jeux d'anneaux' (*OC*, pp. 109–10). Unusually a protagonist can be clearly identified in the first four-line stanza:

> Traversant les anneaux des vagues
> Au désir presque enfantin
> Il songeait les mains jointes en avions stellaires
> Pleines de rayons soupirs d'orvet

[Crossing the rings of the waves | With almost childlike desire | He reflected, hands clasped as stellar aeroplanes | Filled with rays slow-worm sighs]

This sort of fecund collision of images is typical of Arnauld's formal strategies. The referents, too, are favoured leitmotifs. The word 'anneaux' offers an immediate echo of the title, with circles here suggesting the ripples on an expanse of water. Stars and aeroplanes bring together modernity and the natural world, as our protagonist, hands clasped, seems to look up in thought or prayer. Sunrays point to vision and projection; the slow-worm is one of the creatures that pepper Arnauld's non-human landscapes; and sighing offers a non-verbal but vocal expression of feeling that resists capture.

While this incongruous accrual of nouns from the natural human and insect worlds contains magic and spirituality, an air of very real threat is nevertheless present. A second, five-line stanza brings to the fore the uncertainty intimated in the first:

> Tandis que la meute des soupçons
> Enveloppe l'incendiaire
> Là-bas les tombes s'ouvrent comme des lys.
> Et se referment sur un bourdon
> Paresseux et sage curé liseron[3]

[While the pack of suspicions | Envelops the incendiary | Over there the tombs open like lilies | And close again on a bumblebee | Idle and wise bindweed parish priest]

The scene evoked is surely the battlefields of the First World War, the man praying, perhaps, in the midst of chaos and death. The sighs of the slow-worm in the first stanza now seem hopeless rather than hopeful, as the open tombs — like lilies, a flower often associated with death — threaten, beckon, and consume. The last line offers another telescopic snapshot. This thumbnail sketch might be read as a delayed identification and concise judgement of our protagonist, an upright religious figure who is nevertheless lazy and insidious.

A third, seven-line, stanza introduces a new subject 'elles' ('they', feminine). The ground beneath the reader's feet shifts with this sudden change in pronoun.

A group of women are described as having set off 'dans la barque du bourdon' [in the bumblebee boat], encouraging or underscoring an association of the 'bourdon' with the pastor. They were looking for a mysteriously-designated 'moine chapelier' [hatter monk], perhaps the same pastor. Having found him, they carried him away; 'Sur les épaules fragiles | Elles l'ont porté au cimetière des tonneaux défoncés [On their fragile shoulders | They carried him to the cemetery of bottomed-out casks]. Sight and sound are conflated here, for example in 'les sons de brume' [the sounds of mist]. An eerie sonic landscape is reinforced in a fourth stanza, with the jarring screech of glass, marked by the wailing of a musical bow, depicted as crashing against, but not reaching the moon. Repetition prolongs this dreadful procession:

> Elles l'ont porté au cimetière
> Des tonneaux défoncés comme des lys
> Sur les épaules des fillettes

[They carried him to the cemetery | Bottomed-out casks like lilies | On their young girls' shoulders]

The shoulders, last time fragile, are the shoulders of young girls.

Still, it is the man, the subject of the fifth stanza, who is again associated with the childlike. The child's desire introduced at the beginning of the poem is reprised. Another phrase from the first stanza recurs in amended form. This time, his hands are characterised as 'jointes en fougères stellaires' [clasped in stellar ferns]. 'Stellar aeroplanes' become 'stellar ferns' as the mechanical and natural worlds are alternately evoked by this repetition. Alone, he turns away from temptation — 'les charmeurs serpents' [snake charmers] — and returns to the convent to build his life 'vers un désert de rire' [towards a desert of laughter].

The next, sixth, stanza is printed in italics and presents the reader with a tale or song that he creates:

> *Le marchand de magie*
> *Jongle avec les anneaux*
> *Et l'on saute à la corde*
> *À travers l'échelle d'eau*

[*The merchant of magic | Juggles with rings | and they skip | Over the ladder of water*]

The first line might suggest a conflation of storytelling and magic, of a merchant and religious man. Are these tales magical in an innocent way, or are they harmful? The third line, 'et l'on saute à la corde', hints at believers following the power of the storyteller. A term from the fourth stanza is relevant here, 'Leur imagination souriait au mensonge' [Their imagination smiled at the lie]. Lying, storytelling, and religion are dangerously aligned.

The final two stanzas reveal no more of the characters present in the earlier stanzas. The four-line refrain was, perhaps, the pastor's last words, or tale. The penultimate stanza is devoted to sight and sound and returns us to a precarious reality. At the edges of evening and shadows, weeping combines with the cawing of trolley cars. In the final stanza, another ray of light appears and comes to rest.

'New', 'ardent', and 'gay' sounds are born around the oriflamme, or banner of war, offering a measure of hope, but a far from certain rebirth.

Each reading of this poem opens new interpretations. It appears to suggest a nebulous and treacherous environment in which suspicion, lies, and death are never far away. A hazy protagonist might be read as representative of religion, in possession of a dubious leadership and following. He entices and is enticed, finally retreating from reality and the women who look to him. Narratives are magical and powerful but fail to provide a solution to the circumstance of war. This ambivalent attitude towards religion is another example of in-betweenness in Arnauld's work. As Sjöberg points out, the avant-garde is known for its rejection of organised religion, yet different forms of religious and spiritual thought were variously explored by its participants. He also proposes that the tension between tradition and religion, on the one hand, and innovation and modernity, on the other, were a particular area of enquiry for European Jewish avant-gardists. Drawn to anti-nationalism, as a result of diaspora, and anti-traditionalist in their attachment to the avant-garde, they were doubly-bound.[4] Arguably, they were also in a unique position to critically interrogate the spaces between continuity and change.

In 'Apothéose' [Finale] (*OC*, pp. 115–16) tensions between beginnings and endings, reality and dreams, belonging and isolation, and life and death are also played out. A first-person narrator shifts in and out of view, speaking to conceptual addressees such as 'Mes jeunes ans sur la colline' [My early years on the hill]. This past self is exhorted, 'Ayez pitié de ma lumière' [Have pity on my light]. The poem seems to be a call for freedom for the visionary. A striking third stanza exalts imagination:

> Rire voleur spirituel
> Ostensiblement repose dans la mémoire du poète
> Ne crains-tu pas d'être pendu
> Au cou de la réalité

> [Witty thief laughter | Apparently at ease in the poet's memory | Do you not fear being hanged | Around reality's neck]

This resistance to the menace of hanging will be repeated in another poem in this collection, 'Somnambule' [Sleepwalker], as 'Ne crains-tu pas ô rêve | D'être pendu un jour' [Do you not fear oh dream | Being hanged one day] (*OC*, p. 124). In both instances the imagination-fuelling dream state offers a counterpoint to reality.

In the next two stanzas of 'Apothéose' grief, solitude, cruelty, mortification, and silence accumulate. As villages collapse into voids we may not be surprised, as readers of Arnauld, by the appearance of a procession, 'Le cortège lyrique de moi seule entrevu' [The lyrical procession glimpsed only be me]. 'Inclinez-vous — riez — dansez' [Take a bow — laugh — dance] is the imperative to all. A ghostly return is described 'Tous en celluloïd', the reference to the filmic a sudden intervention of modernity. The past, present, and future come up against one another, their boundaries porous. These points of emphasis, coalescing around tensions between tradition and modernity, memory, presence, and projection, chime, again, with Apollinaire's writing, not least in his poem 'Cortège'.[5]

The subject of Arnauld's poem, too, shifts with dizzying alacrity, throwing into question the fixity of identity in dynamic time. Is the celebrated yet threatened seer the narrator, the feminine 'moi seule'? It is also 'le musagète le forain le revenant' [the master of muses the carnie the ghost]. The lack of punctuation only encourages the blurring of these categories. A listing strategy gives ample room for mutations:

> La vierge en rapolin
> Les papillons en cristaux
> Une muse en chiffon
> Un amour en carton
> Don Quichote en satin

[The virgin in ripolin | The crystal butterflies | A muse in chiffon | A cardboard Cupid | Don Quixote in satin]

Materials, textures, human, insect, fictional, and conceptual overlap. This will be his, or her finale and we should all look out ('Mettez-vous en garde'). A homage to 'le météore le plus haut de la roue' [the highest meteor on the wheel] ends with a four-line stanza. Typeset in italics, it offers a song-like plea from a 'musarde' [wastrel] to never die, to be able to love, to be lifted up to see. This is romantic, rhetorical, and yet slippery poetry; it expresses interior doubts yet projects visual marvels; fears persecution and yet insists on living.

In the poem 'Porte-peine' [Pains-taking] (OC, p. 122) a giddying world of motion is evoked. From possible translations as 'laborious, painful, or pains-taking' I have chosen the latter for its retention of two elements, linked by a hyphen, and since it too is a term, in that form at least, that has fallen out of use.[6] That outdatedness in language is in stark contrast to the poem's first line, which locates us near the modern metropolis, 'A la lisière du métro station de l'Arc-du-cœur' [At the outer edge of the metro station l'Arc-du-cœur]. We are on the fringes, the outskirts again, neither here nor there. The station is an invented one, moreover, a familiar signifier of twentieth-century Paris given a dreamlike name, and only a figment of the imagination. Rails modulate and hum like bees (*bourdonner*), in the first stanza, there is a twittering, the term 'gazouillement' one that will appear again in the final poem in this collection, 'Point de mire'. Sound is paramount, the cacophonies of nature transposed to the urban environment.

All is in motion, ever-changing haptically and visually, and it transpires from pieced-together fragments that the location is a fun fair. There is a moving pavement, a slide or toboggan, and a Ferris Wheel. In the second stanza the reader is addressed, we are travelling:

> Si des vertiges vous accablent
> Les compartiments se vident — mugissent
> Les vitres se transforment en regards fiers et fabuleux

[If you are suffering from vertigo | The compartments empty — bellow | The windows are transformed into proud and fabulous looks]

The carriages roar like beasts or howl like the wind ('mugissent'). The views flash by; one is observed, as well as observes, in this giddying trajectory. Questions of memory and forgetting permeate the poem. People come here to escape. A cataclysm carries everything away, 'Pour toi il ne reste rien | Pas même le poème de l'autre' [There is nothing left for you | Not even the other's poem]. Within three lines *vous* has been honed down to *tu*. The reader is drawn into an experience that mixes exhilaration and fear. The ending offers a different kind of balm:

> Mais je connais une chanson qui guérit
> les pîqures d'abeilles
> [...]
> Je te la chanterais [...]
> Pour te faire oublier

[But I know a song that cures | bee stings | [...] | I would sing it to you [...] | To make you forget]

Song, like poetry, offers healing, where the park has provided extremes of experience and emotion.

The collection takes its name from the final poem, 'Point de mire' (OC, pp. 133–34). It, too, partakes in the modernist fascination with leisure and transport. The first stanza begins with an expression that immediately brings together the apparently conflicting elements of the natural world and modern technology in a succinct collision. 'Le gazouillement du train' [The train's twittering] gives the sound qualities of a bird to a piece of moving machinery and recalls that same noun in 'Porte-peine'. Opening one black, sleepy eye the train heads to a tunnel, crushing the horizon with its noisy new sound. A pile-up of nouns offers up more facets of this anthropomorphised beast intervening in the landscape, 'Des phonographes bouches ouvertes | des lampes postillons '[Open-mouthed phonographs | spitting lamps]. The machinery is loud, bright, intrusive; an amalgam of sound and vision. As it disappears into the tunnel the sound is strangled and dies. The personification 'Les rails en folie', at the end of this first stanza, recalls the madness associated with this incursion of a system of speed into everyday life that was so effectively evoked in the telescopic lines of 'Avertisseur' (Chapter 3), with its similar construction, 'Les rails en pleurs'.

In a second stanza we get the sense of human inhabitants. Loosely identified, only their mood is conveyed by a kind of collective corporeal gesture, 'Lâche on courbe les épaules | Devant le train fouillant la ville' [Lax shoulders slouch | Before the train rifling through the town]. The train assumes the menacing eye of Cyclops, projecting its light thought the night, dazzling the apathetic, even cowardly, crowd. Flaming light, sudden and angry, contrasts with an anthropomorphised sea that does not know whether to cry or laugh in the face of this assault. Sound, namely rhyme and assonance, dictates the development, as much as semantics, 'Une flamme dans un miroir se mire | La mer mime un sanglot qui n'était que rire' [A flame is reflected in a mirror | The sea mimes a sob that was only laughter]. Ahead of daybreak, which will dazzle like the artificial light, is a proclamation, 'Je suis le point de mire' [I am the focal point]. Who is this 'I'? It is the only instance of the first-person in this poem. This incursion of a narrative voice nevertheless evades stable identification, a relentlessly moving target itself, perhaps.

In the next stanza *je* becomes *nous*, inviting the reader to share this unsettling experience. This 'we' beholds the rushing past of time and lights, is weary, has lost everything. Hatred lies in wait at every turn. Perhaps the subject is on the train, aligned now with other passengers, rushing headlong who knows where, past people and through the landscape. 'La foule acclame le mourant' [The crowd cheers the dying one], the third stanza declares. This dying thing could be the train as it hurtles past, lights powerful but necessarily elusive, finally only reflections, in a mirror, in the water, never stopping long enough to be grasped. Recurrences punctuate the poem. 'Lumière' and 'flamme' each appear twice; 'éblouie' is backed up by 'éblouissant'; 'écrasant' by 'écrasement', twice repeated; 'la foule' is twice invoked; 'le mourant' by 'la mort'. Repetitions and variations build a tone. Isolating them in this way conveys a message: light, dazzling light, a crowd, crushing, a dying away. These things are only glimpsed in the speed of travel. Light disappears as soon as it appears. Perception is altered by rapidity and movement.

There is also a refrain, singled out in italics, and appearing twice, '*C'était l'unique sans lyre | Le point de mire*' [*It was the only one without a lyre | The focal point*]. The poem ends with this rhyming couplet. The penultimate line is this, 'Puis plus rien que des mots' [Then nothing left but words]. One has the sense that the only hope for longevity and permanence in the march of time and progress is language. The lyre symbolises creativity, song, lyricism, writing, hanging on as this mechanical monster, devoid of its own lyrical inspiration, crashes on. Here is a poem in which both the mechanical and the human come off badly. Between the unthinking train with its cargo of passengers, the dazzled inhabitants of the landscape, and the natural environment can there be something productive and comprehensible? Words are the best hope, it would appear, just as they are in the song in 'Porte-peine'.

The poems sketched out here demonstrate the difficulty of a narrative reading. A review by Jean Bouchary of *Point de mire* concludes, 'La réalité est transposée, tout semble vivre dans un autre monde où tout n'est que parfums, sons et couleurs' [Reality is transposed, everything seems to live in another world where everything is only perfumes, sounds and colours'.[7] This acknowledgement of the multisensory and otherworldliness bears witness to Arnauld's liberal use of linguistic invention to approach themes that are nevertheless mired, in some cases, in reality, from transport to religion to war. There are no didactic messages and semantic clarity is muddied. Representation cedes to abstraction. As readers we are left to form our own impressions, to clutch and grasp at verbal fragments that have been defamiliarised. Unstable signifiers, lack of punctuation, and slippery syntax disallow easy legibility. We are always at the borders of things, from 'au bord des soirs' [at the evenings' edges] ('Jeux d'anneaux'), to 'au bord des étangs' [on the banks of the ponds] ('Surnom'), to 'au bord du croissant de la lune' [on the edge of the crescent moon] ('Périscope') in the first three poems alone. In two brief reviews of Arnauld's writing by Élie Richard, the poet and editor of *Les Images de Paris*, this tension between challenge and reward for the reader is palpable. He emphasises the novelty of Arnauld's metaphors as well as the dedication required as a reader to interpret them.[8] More apparent sentiment would have wider appeal, affect and audience, he proposes. His conclusion, though, is that it is for the reader to make an effort.

Perhaps the most markedly experimental of the texts in *Point de mire* is 'Périscope' (*OC*, p. 112), which was also published in Picabia's *391*.[9] Formally it is especially inventive, exemplary of Arnauld's attempts to liberate language from semantics and syntax. A text of approximately 170 words, divided into only six sentences, it scarcely uses punctuation, and resembles prose rather than verse. The driving force behind the selection of words appears to have been their material qualities, as demonstrated by the first sentence, 'La rapière s'est plantée dans le limon tatoué de la taupinée maison faite à tâtons avec l'aide du violon après le solstice la mort des chanteurs des buissons et des javelles cathédrales séchées par des chansons' [The rapier sank into the lemon tattooed with the molehill house made gropingly with the violin's help after the solstice the death of the singers the bushes and the swathes cathedrals dried up by songs]. Words such as 'rapière', 'javelles', and 'taupinée', standing alone, are striking in their sound quality, as well as having less than common meanings. Combined, they produce even more remarkable and unexpected effects, such as 'Affolés les criquets pèlerins se posèrent à trois au bord du croissant de la lune descendue par sympathie sur les seins d'Argine' [Panic-stricken the pilgrim crickets lined up in threes at the side of the crescent moon come down out of sympathy on the Queen of Club's bosom].

The title of this piece, too, is an explicit reference to ways of seeing. It features birds, symbols of freedom and flight, and makes numerous references to light, lanterns, morsels of light, stars, the solstice, lightning, and the moon, to suggest the primacy of the visual. In an analysis of Edgar Degas, Linda Nochlin writes of his use of iconic elements, 'connected only through the relation of specularity — and it is really our position of spectatorship, reiterating the original viewing position of the artist, that holds the elements together'.[10] Arnauld's signified objects, observed in her imagination, are likewise loosely-held, relayed like juggling balls to the reader who must try to keep them all in the air.

The formal approach apparent in 'Périscope' can usefully be positioned within the broader context of the historical avant-garde, and its evolving views on semantics and syntax. Marinetti, in 1913, had theorised his vision of language using the term 'imagination without strings', which he defines as, 'By the imagination without strings I mean the absolute freedom of images or analogies, expressed with unhampered words and with no connecting strings of syntax and with no punctuation'.[11] From 1916 Dada in Zurich gathered writers who experimented with sound and simultaneous poetry, encompassing their love of chance, random juxtapositions, and liberated linguistic signs. An extract from 'la couille d'hirondelle' [the swallow's ball] by Arp, which appears on the same page of *391* as Arnauld's 'Périscope', reminds us of his extensive innovations from the 1910s, through Dada and Surrealism, in liberating syntax and semantics.[12] Last but by no means least, as a way of setting this particular piece of prose by Arnauld in context, we might look to 'automatic writing', a key surrealist technique developed by Breton and Soupault. Having much in common with Freud's free association method, automatic writing promotes the unfettered outpouring of words unchecked and hindered by prior conscious thought. Arnauld's 'Périscope' can justly be considered a forerunner of this experiment.[13]

Together with *Poèmes à claires-voies*, this second volume offers a fecund set of texts that are revelatory of modernist and avant-garde preoccupations at a flashpoint of literary activity in Paris. An interest in technologies of transport and communications, for example, will be seen to mark instances of texts in the second part of this book, the focus of which will be collaborations with avant-garde groups. Film, especially, will come to the fore. Formally, there are collisions, neologisms, and free associations. We can think back to Apollinaire and ahead to Surrealism. As Goll will state in his 'Manifeste du surréalisme' in 1924, 'Les plus belles images sont celles qui rapprochent des éléments de la réalité éloignés les uns des autres le plus directement et le plus rapidement possible' [The most beautiful images are those that bring together elements in reality that are estranged from each other in the most direct and rapid way possible].[14] Other aspects, emerging here, include the natural and fantastical worlds, dreamscapes, and twilight worlds. These interests will dominate in Arnauld's work of the late 1920s and 1930s, post-Dada, in which the provisional and incomplete are foregrounded. For now we see a giddying eclecticism, a willingness to embrace topics and techniques that, as Artaud stated, can scarcely be confined. An epigraph added to selected texts from *Point de mire* in Arnauld's 1936 anthology, insists on freedom. 'Pourquoi plonge-t'on des mains impures dans cette âme d'enfant?' [Why plunge impure hands into this child's soul?], she asks, citing her own words from *L'Apaisement de l'éclipse*.[15]

The instability and contingency of Arnauld's work, both formally and thematically, places her firmly in her modernist context. She gives us snapshots, impressions, images that cannot quite be pinned down, landscapes that are vaporous, people half-glimpsed or cropped. In a 1932 interview Arnauld herself offers a rare illumination of her writing:

> Mes images ne correspondent guère à ce qu'on entend d'ordinaire par ce mot. Au lieu d'être picturales, de tracer une ressemblance plus ou moins directe, elles consistent comme l'a écrit un critique philosophe, 'en rapports affectifs et sensibles entre des réalités multiples fort éloignées les unes des autres'. C'est ce que j'appelle mon incohérence.[16]
>
> [My images scarcely correspond to what we ordinarily understand by this word. Instead of being pictorial, or tracing a more or less direct resemblance, they constitute, as a philosophical critic put it, 'affective and sensitive relations between multiple realities at great distance from each other'. It is what I call my incoherence.]

Here we are reminded of the surrealist love of juxtaposition. We also come full circle to Artaud's appraisal of coherence as out of reach. And yet there is also a 'compensatory dynamism and flow, a sometimes centrifugal and often random organization'.[17] I have borrowed these words from Nochlin, again, who uses them in relation to modern painting and sets this aspect up as counterpoint to a fragmentariness associated with modernity and Modernism. But the contrary forces she identifies apply to writing too. The repetitions and refrains that emerge in Arnauld's work produce vivid chains of emotive signification and memorable imagery in fluid circumstances.

The extent to which Arnauld's work intersects with Modernism, Dada, and/or Surrealism, is an inescapable point of discussion and poses traps of assimilation and difference. What are the characteristics of this work, taken as a body of output? Does it change over time? Does Arnauld develop a style that can be identified for herself as an individual, and in relation to others? In the next part of this study the intersections of her work with Dada and relationship with Surrealism will be the focus. A third section will return to her individual outputs that, as we will see, continue the interrogation of some core themes and techniques in the box of treasures that is her early work and that mark her out as an individual writer of significant invention and experiment. Although this study of Arnauld is divided into three parts, along these lines, it is apposite to note that the borders between them are blurred. Questions of definition, moreover, are not only a matter of controversy for today's critic or scholar. Here is Dermée responding hotly to an association made by a reviewer, 'Votre note sur *Point de mire* est d'un crétin et d'un goujat. La poésie de Céline Arnault [*sic*] n'a rien de Dada (car il n'y a pas d'esthétique Dada) ni rien de Tristan Tzara' [Your note on *Point de mire* is that of a cretin and a boor. There is nothing of Dada in Céline Arnauld's poetry (since there is no Dada aesthetic) nor of Tristan Tzara].[18] Doubtless an effort at distancing — and it can be taken with a pinch of salt, after all — this riposte from as early as 1922 warns us to take care nearly one hundred years later lest we try to categorise either our poet or Dada too readily. At the risk of being boorish in the next chapter I will underscore Arnauld's Dada credentials. This will be followed, though, by a contextualisation of her shifting allegiances and emphases that point to more expansive possibilities.

Notes to Chapter 4

1. Antonin Artaud, 'Livres reçues: *Point de mire*', *Action*, 12 (March-April 1922), [n.p.]; repr. in Antonin Artaud, *Œuvres Complètes*, 26 vols (Paris: Gallimard, 1956–1994), 11, 227–28 (*OC*, pp. 483–84).
2. For five poems from this volume, in French and in translation, see Sarah Hayden, 'Céline Arnauld, Six Poems Translated by Sarah Hayden', *Translation Ireland*, 20.1 (2017), 139–51. The poems are 'Dans l'abîme' [In the Abyss], 'Surtout ne regarde pas' [Above All do not Look], 'Symphonie' [Symphony], 'Tempête' [Tempest], and 'Fête' [Fete].
3. I am respecting the layout of the printed versions in both *Point de mire* and *Action* rather than the altered one in *OC*, in which the first two stanzas are conflated.
4. Sjöberg, 'Any Other Transnationalism', p. 49.
5. For more on these themes in Apollinaire's work, including some analysis of 'Cortège' (published in *Alcools*, 1913), see Charles Russell, 'The Poets of Time: Apollinaire and the Italian Futurists', in *Poets, Prophets and Revolutionaries: The Literary Avant-garde from Rimbaud through Postmodernism* (New York & Oxford: Oxford University Press, 1985), pp. 62–95. The topic of time in Arnauld's work, including further notes on Apollinaire, will be a focal point in Chapter 10 of the present study.
6. Guy Miège, *A New Dictionary: French and English, with Another English and French*, (London: printed for Thomas Basset, 1679).
7. Jean Bouchary, 'Point de mire', *La Vie des lettres et des arts*, n.s. 11 (August 1922), 345 (not repr. in *OC*).

8. Élie Richard, 'Le Jardin des supplices' [review of *Point de mire*], *Les Images de Paris*, 34 (September-October 1922), [n.p.]; 'Le Jardin des supplices' [review of *Guêpier de diamants*], *Les Images de Paris*, 48 (December 1923), [n.p.] (not repr. in *OC*).
9. Céline Arnauld, 'Périscope', *391*, 14 (November 1920), [n.p.]. For the poem as it appears in the journal see the full edition reprinted in *Francis Picabia et 391: revue publiée de 1917 à 1924 par Francis Picabia*, ed. by Michel Sanouillet, 2 vols (Nice: Centre du XXè siècle; Paris: Eric Losfeld, 1960–1966), I, 89–96.
10. Linda Nochlin, *The Body in Pieces: The Fragment as a Metaphor of Modernity* (London: Thames & Hudson, 2001), pp. 43–45.
11. Marinetti, 'Destruction of Syntax', p. 99.
12. For a thorough discussion of Arp's poetry, as well as his work across the visual arts, see Eric Robertson, *Arp: Painter, Poet, Sculptor* (New Haven, CT, & London: Yale University Press, 2007).
13. While this is an excellent example it is not the only one. A collection of reprinted handwritten texts includes Arnauld's 'Levée d'écrou' [Release from Prison]. A single page made up of two sentences, it reminds us of what is so easily forgotten, that is the manual production of writing and its attendant spontaneity; see Céline Arnauld, 'Levée d'écrou', in *Le Cahier des muses: textes autographes de Juliette Adam, Céline Arnauld et autres*, ed. by Charles d'Éternod and Élie Moroy (Geneva: Eggimann, 1922), p. 8 (not repr. in *OC*).
14. Goll, 'Manifeste du surréalisme'. The explosive potential of bringing together apparent oppositions will be further articulated in Breton's *Second manifeste du surréalisme* (1930).
15. Arnauld, *Anthologie Céline Arnauld*, p. 39.
16. Céline Arnauld, in 'Céline Arnauld nous dit ... Mystère de l'image', interview with P. L. Flouquet, *Le Journal des poètes*, 2.21 (30 April 1932), 1 (*OC*, p. 443).
17. Nochlin, *The Body in Pieces*, p. 25.
18. Dermée's letter was printed in *L'Œuf dur*, 9 (April 1922), 16. The original review note appeared in *L'Œuf dur*, 8 (March 1922), 16; consulted in BnF (*OC*, pp. 482–83).

PART II

Avant-Garde Collaborator

FIG. 5.1. Photograph of the Paris Dada group (c. 1920)
By kind permission of the Prodan Romanian Cultural Foundation

CHAPTER 5

Dada Actions:
Magazines and Manifestos (1920–21)

In a 1924 letter to Tristan Tzara, the 'father of Dada', Céline Arnauld wrote:

> Mon cher ami, Je suis très étonnée que dans votre historique du Mouvement Dada — où vous vous montrez assez généreux même pour vos adversaires actuels — vous oubliez mon effort tant dans le lyrisme que dans l'action.[1]

> [My dear friend, I am very surprised that in your history of the Dada movement — where you show yourself to be fairly generous even towards your current enemies — you forget my efforts both in lyricism and in action.]

This letter acted as an injection of adrenaline on my lengthy quest to bring attention to this poet and I claimed it in *Dada's Women* as a paradigm for the omission of women's names from accounts of the avant-garde and the erasure of their contributions. I want to come back to it now for the terms 'lyricism' and 'action' which, I propose, offer a tension between Arnauld's individual poetic output and her participation in polemical group activities.

Where the first part of this book focused on Arnauld's early single-authored volumes, the next chapters will consider her interventions in the Dada collective. Arnauld was profoundly implicated in the journal culture of her Parisian literary circle. Her name, and occasionally photographic image, left numerous indexical traces in journals, pamphlets, and programmes. She published work in celebrated magazines associated with Dada including *Cannibale*, *391*, and *Le Pilhaou-Thibaou*, all founded by Picabia, Tzara's *Dada* and *Le Cœur à barbe*, and the long-running *Littérature*, through which Aragon, Breton, and Soupault dabbled in Dada and spearheaded Surrealism. In 1920, the year of Dada's highpoint in Paris, Arnauld's work appeared in no fewer than eight separate publications.[2] She was also listed as one of Tzara's seventy-five 'Présidents and Présidentes de Dada', a summary of Dada affiliates and occasional inspirations that was published in *Bulletin Dada* in February 1920. I have used this list elsewhere as a trigger for a discussion of gender, fortified by its non-hierarchical approach, its inclusion of the feminine in the title, and of women in the list.[3] Her name appears, too, on Picabia's 1921 *L'Œil cacodylate* [The Cacodylic Eye], his groundbreaking artwork made up of visual icons and signatures. Last but not least, the group photograph of the Dadaists in Paris (Fig. 5.1) has turned out to be indelible and inspirational. This image, in which Arnauld looks back at the camera cheerfully and confidently, places her convincingly in the Dada club. She is the only woman among eleven men. The photograph endures, outlasting gripes and grievances, and offering an antidote to effacement.

This chapter will consider six of Arnauld's contributions to journals in 1920 and in 1921, in which inventiveness with language is apparent, as well as the attempt to access experience that lies beyond the established boundaries of language. None of the texts selected here appears in her single-authored volumes or anthology and can thus most aptly be discussed within the framework of avant-garde journals. Though more prolific in the writing of poetry Arnauld produced numerous short prose pieces and, as we will see, the characteristics separating poetry and prose prove fluid in her work. The same level of play with words and interest in the fabric of language is evident throughout her texts. These short pieces combine deconstruction and iconoclasm with lyricism and invention. While in some cases there is a recognisable narrative structure the focus is still on textuality, surprise sound qualities, vibrant images, and a mix of the ordinary and extraordinary. Most importantly, together they provide indexical traces of Arnauld's active participation in Dada as a collective. The tension between lyricism and action will be brought out as I seek to maintain a recognition of that nuance in her work.

In Chapter 4 an exposition of 'Pérsicope', published in *391* (November 1920), underscored an almost-automatic style of writing. Two more short texts, in another of Picabia's magazines, the one-off *Le Pilhaou-Thibaou* (July 1921), demonstrate a likewise ludic approach to language and also some familiar themes.[4] The short text 'Envoi du Japon' [Consignment from Japan] (*OC*, p. 454) takes a relatable narrative form that mimics a Japanese folktale. It recounts the story of an autopsy, performed on a butterfly, that uncovers an incongruous collection of objects hidden beneath its wings, including a locomotive, a barley sugar, a bottle of aspirin, a star, a sheep, a snake, an umbrella, a moon, and eight suns. In the list, too, are human figures: a parish priest, an emperor, four martyrs, and a man. Taken together they represent 'an entire court', Arnauld writes, seemingly representing civilisation, or society. The burden of objects having been removed, the butterfly is free to fly away, to the 'great joy and great chagrin' of the people who thought it dead. Here is a fantasy of flight, escape, or metamorphosis, in a form akin to a moral parable.

Like 'Périscope', Arnauld's prose here shares common ground with principles of Surrealism. In its imaginative juxtapositions, it recalls the celebration of *objets trouvés*. As well as the human figures, the unlikely collection of objects under the butterfly's wings ranges from the animate to the inanimate, the everyday to the intangible. It can be read as the verbalisation of a dream, in which fragments of reality and memory collide. Joyful, fun, and fanciful readings and reactions are invoked. That edge of humour begins with the rhyming name 'D' Li-ti-pi,' Arnauld's invention of a Japanese name. It is a richly visual piece, humorous and accessible, and a rare example of a short avant-garde text in which narrative accessibility combines with linguistic invention and imaginative freedom.

A second text, 'Extrait de Saturne' [Extract from Saturn] (*OC*, pp. 453–54), falls somewhere between poetic prose and manifesto. It begins, 'Un mot, cela court plus vite qu'un champion de course, on s'en empare et l'on en fait ou une histoire personnelle ou même une œuvre. Méfiez-vous des voleurs de bribes d'intrigues' [A word, it runs more quickly than a running champion, you grab it and make of it a personal story or even an entire work. Watch out for thieves of plot snatches]. This first short paragraph at once suggests the positive potential of language as well as warning against its misuse. It comments on the arts and philosophises about the power of language.

A second paragraph includes a cast of characters at a forest fair: a thief, loyal man, rich man, poor man, and merchant, each playing their expected parts. Arnauld writes, for example, 'Le marchand se drape dans ses tapis et ses couvertures et devient le roi' [The merchant drapes himself in his carpets and becomes the king]. This brief section echoes Arnauld's experimental novel *Tournevire* and recalls her dialogue 'Jeu d'échecs' (see Chapter 2) in its use of types to thematise social relations. Even at a fair, she concludes explicitly, the individual follows patterns and acts out roles according to their status and level of social ambition. In a third paragraph Arnauld outlines how poetry, on the other hand, offers the chance of freedom:

> La poésie ne pense pas au lendemain; elle n'aime pas les gros habits de bourgeois; elle est en maillot, elle est transparente. C'est plutôt un papillon — Mais il y a des amateurs qui lui piquent une épingle dans le corps.
>
> [Poetry doesn't think about tomorrow; it doesn't like coarse bourgeois clothes; it wears a bathing costume, it's transparent. It's more like a butterfly — But there are amateurs who stick a pin through its body.]

Another metaphor for poetry evokes speed and movement again, 'Vous prenez la poésie pour un match de boxe ... c'est plutôt une course de chevaux, une course cycliste et même une course à pied' [You take poetry for a boxing match ... it's more a horse race, a cycle race or even a running race]. Arnauld here calls up boxing, beloved of the Dadaists, but expands her frame of reference. As in the metaphor of the butterfly, poetry is set up as mobile, forging ahead, escaping adversaries.

Finally, Arnauld launches a more explicit attack. If bad (or conventional) poets are anathema to the avant-garde, silence and complicity are even worse, 'Ce silence de bourreau sur vos figures nous fait honte. Quelle accumulation de haine, de rancune et de méchanceté derrière ce calme!' [This executioner's silence on your faces shames us. What an accumulation of hatred, of rancour and of evil behind that calm!]. Arnauld would prefer free expression at any event, 'Croyez-moi, vomissez tout cela en paroles mauvaises, écrivez-le, criez-le devant tout le monde et vous serez soulagés. On a besoin de purger son esprit comme son corps. On peut tout dire dans la colère et garder le cœur pur' [Believe me, vomit all that up in bad words, write it, shout it in front of everybody and you'll be relieved. One needs to purge one's mind like one's body. One can say anything in anger and keep the heart pure]. Finally, she warns critics, '"Connais-toi toi-même" c'est-à-dire: "Savonne-toi toi-même avant de savonner les autres"' ['Know yourself' in other words: 'Soap yourself before soaping others']. This may be a play on the ancient Greek 'know thyself' (in French 'connais-toi toi-même'). Together these violent, cleansing metaphors convey a powerful passion about the need to resist hypocrisy and the necessity of unimpeded expression.

While 'Extrait de Saturne' shares characteristics with the Dada manifesto, it is also distinctly Arnauld. Her anger at criticism and complacency are vehemently and colourfully expressed and place her within the context of Dada attacks on the cultural and social status quo. However, the text is also characterised by the subverted tropes of myth and fantasy that are common to many of Arnauld's prose pieces. Moreover, there is a forceful strand of faith in language and literature made new, and the potential that the poet offers. Nihilism is balanced by both her revelry in the material of language and declarations of its power.

These texts, published in Dada journals, evidently have much in common with the group's creative production. Arnauld's testing of style and genre, and her texts' resistance to narrative coherence, challenge the presumption that women writers of the avant-garde were not as innovative with form as men. A related misconception is that women were mimics rather than pioneers, that they followed trends rather than forged them. If the desire to revolutionise literature is implicit in Arnauld's work, the question might yet be asked whether she also made it explicit. Dada is characterised by its provocative manifestos and statements, which disseminated radical ideas about the arts even as they resisted fixed meaning. At times inflammatory, they articulated and conveyed newness and novelty to other writers, critics, and wider audiences. Arnauld, like her male colleagues, participated in this maelstrom of manifestos, adding to the tumult of the times first with her declarations of Dada, and later with her more individual fledgling theories.

Here is the question of 'action' that Arnauld claimed for herself in her letter to Tzara. From acerbic one-liners to short pieces of prose some of the texts she published in Dada journals can rightly be likened to manifestos. For her husband Dermée's journal Z, for example, published in March 1920, she wrote three phrases (*OC*, p. 455). The first, 'Le cafard est cubiste' [The cockroach is cubist], is impishly derogatory. A neatly concise slogan, it is tempting to read it, too, in reverse. The idea of the cockroach as cubist is visually immediate, triggering, consequentially, an association of the cubist as a cockroach. 'Cafard' also means melancholy or depression. In either reading, Arnauld's appealing, alliterative association means that Cubism comes off badly; it is at best apathetic, at worst a pest.

The term *cafard* recurs in Dada texts, a favourite because of its associative abundance. One month after Arnauld's phrase in Z, for example, Picabia's *Cannibale* included a poem 'Cafard' by Ribemont-Dessaignes.[5] Explicit references to Cubism, too, are numerous. In a typically avant-garde attitude, the Dadaists rejected their predecessors, consigning them to a heap of worn-out art movements. In the third issue of *Proverbe*, published in April 1920, Picabia, Ribemont-Dessaignes, and Cocteau printed several insults aimed at the Cubists. *Cannibale*, 2, published in May, also attacked them, including in the spoof column 'Cabinet du Docteur Aïsen'; and Tzara's broadsheet *Dada soulève tout*, published 15 January 1921, declared, 'Le cubisme construit une cathédrale en pâté de foie artistique' [Cubism constructs a cathedral out of artistic liver pâté].[6] In the same vein, Picabia announced almost two years later in *La Pomme de pins* (February 1922), 'Le Cubisme est une cathédrale de merde' [Cubism is a cathedral of shit], and in March 1922 produced a tract named *Plus de cubisme* [No More Cubism].[7] This public sparring, falling somewhere between jest and judgement, was designed to draw attention to the freshness of the Dada project. This sort of reiteration of words and phrases was common in Dada, pointing to an intertextual self-reflexivity, as well as to a plumbing of vocabulary that built layers of connotations and suggested richness and slippage in language. This technique was discussed in Chapter 4 as a strategy within Arnauld's own work. In this instance we see her use it to participate in a Dada web of production.

The confrontational aspect already evident in Arnauld's first phrase in *Z* is reprised in two subsequent sentences. Where the first was published under the heading 'PHRASE', these are listed as 'RÉPONSES' [replies], mimicking the practice of journal editors to address correspondence from their readers. The first phrase reads, 'à P. R. — Le mépris, voilà ma réponse' [to P. R. — Scorn, that's my reply]. Although the identity of 'P. R.' is not specified, it almost certainly refers to Pierre Reverdy. As noted in Chapter 2, he and Dermée had fallen out. In this instance Arnauld is taking up the case, and the cause, of her husband.[8]

The second 'réponse' is likewise aimed at a perceived enemy, but this time its target is more general, 'La plus basse littérature, c'est la littérature de vengeance. A ceux qui ne sont pas mes amis: "Suivez la foule, troupeau d'imbéciles"' [The lowest form of literature is revenge literature. To those who are not my friends: 'Follow the crowd, you bunch of imbeciles']. The offence is direct and deliberate, not least in the imperative final note. Any critics, real or imagined, present or future, are dismissed as idiotic, unoriginal adherents to popular opinion. But the expression has a second, ironic aspect, which lifts it from mere vitriol. Even as it dismisses a vengeful attitude in the first sentence, it goes on to rebuke opposition and dissent in the second. It is self-contradictory, then, refusing to be taken at face value, throwing doubt upon its own integrity and credibility, and even that of the written word. Arrogant and dismissive, it can be said at the same time to satirise the egoism of journal editors.

Z, the publication in which Arnauld's phrases appear, was one of many short-lived journals produced by the loose grouping of Dada in Paris. Like other publications at this flashpoint, it occupied a tense position, suspended between serious literary endeavour and satire, between Dada ideology and individual self-promotion (in this case for its editor Dermée), and between convention and resistance (its tall, thin format alone sets it apart). Arnauld, a couple of months later, would produce her own journal with an equally unusual format (in her case, landscape), and a pronounced ambition for new direction (see Chapter 6). In the meantime, she was proving herself an avid contributor to the key journals of Dada in Paris.

Another notable contribution is to Tzara's *Dadaphone* (March 1920). This document, the seventh issue of *Dada*, is special because it includes both an image of her and a poem by her.[9] A small photographic portrait is one of eight distributed through the pages of the journal. She is the only woman. The name of the poem she contributes, 'Énigme-personnages' [Enigma Figures], aptly relates to the portraits of the Dada troupe (*OC*, p. 400).[10] This text reveals distinctly Dada characteristics, abandoning narrative coherence in favour of a series of enigmatic images. The images it produces, centring on transport and travel, carry the poem along intriguing and digressing paths, both temporally and spatially. The poem addresses the informal *tu*, who is imagined at the wheel of a car. The action moves through a bus, to a rambling bicycle, to the side of the road, and finally to the railway. These fragments of daily transport are like flashes in time or momentary sights glimpsed by the traveller or commuter. The concise nature of the language reflects the speed at which an image might be captured, such as 'Bicyclette en divagation lunettes noblement remontées' [Rambling bicycle spectacles nobly put back on], which leaves out any main verb altogether, but which produces a vivid visual impression. Other imagery is equally evocative, such as the staggered lines:

> le chemin de fer railleur
> montre ses dents neuves
> au dernier train

[the mocking railway | shows its new teeth | to the last train]

Both phrases evoke striking images: in the first, the glasses, made up of two circles and a metal frame, remind us of the shape of the bicycle. In the second, the tracks of the railway are likened to teeth.

The journey in the poem evokes, on the one hand, a physical displacement and, on the other, a mental voyage, stimulated by so many sights. Arnauld seems to be challenging the reader to free his or her thoughts from the evidence of physical reality. At the very start she makes the accusation 'Pas assez mystérieux au volant de ta voiture' [Not mysterious enough at the wheel of your car] and later of being 'pas assez Dada' [not Dada enough]. Her object of critique is apparently the failure to perceive anything beyond everyday logic and external appearance. Then, repeating the 'énigme' of the title she declares, 'Tu ne trouveras jamais la clé de | D à l'envers énigme en autobus M' [You'll never find the key to | D back-to-front enigma on bus M]. 'La clé de D' might have arisen simply from the rhyme, or from its visual shape. Alternatively, the 'D' might stand for Dada. Martin-Schmets points out that the bus lines in Paris were formerly referred to by letter (*OC*, p. 400, n. 2). This use of 'D' and 'M' as signifiers is an example of language broken down into its smallest component, the letter, the arbitrary sign. In this case it has denotations for the contemporary metropolitan reader (the bus lines) while remaining open to connotations. In any case the reader is challenged, indeed directly taunted, to discover or impose semantic coherence on the poem. Instead, though, the poem celebrates the 'feu follet' [will-o'-the-wisp] and 'rire du délire enfantin' [laugh of childish delight] that come with fantasy rather than rationality.

'Énigme-personnages' revels in free-flowing thought, the collision of images, and language play. Some images are fantastical, such as 'Raccrochée par une étoile l'échelle renversée' [Hung up by a star the overturned ladder]. The alliterative 'envers', énigme', 'étoile', and 'échelle' in the third and fourth lines of the poem play as much with the visual and sound quality of the words as with their meanings. In 'le chemin de fer railleur' the word 'railleur' [mocking] has lexical as well as visual associations, pointing to, or emerging from, the term *rail*. Grammar is partially abandoned, with the subject of a phrase often unspecified or unclear. The 'énigme-personnages' of the title seem to haunt the poem and evade identification. The result is the fusion of an actual physical journey and the sights it produces, with the visions and mental meanderings that pervade the mind if it is allowed to wander. The poem is playful, but wilfully rejects authority, logic, and the imposition of answers. It advocates the liberation of imagination and of language and identifies Dada as an agent.

The poem 'Mes trois péchés Dada' [My Three Dada Sins] (*OC*, pp. 397–98) can likewise be considered a Dada intervention thanks firstly to its title, and secondly to its place of publication; it appeared in Picabia's *Cannibale* in 1920.[11] The three Dada sins of the title are echoed by the poem's tripartite structure. The first scene suggests a journey and measure of conflict, 'En remontant la colline | la roue cassée, prunelle amère' ('Climbing up the hill | broken wheel, bitter pupil').[12] The suffering subject ends that section with the dramatic proposal, 'Pour me punir j'irai m'immoler dans le cellier'. Kamenish's translation, 'To punish myself I'll banish myself to the storeroom', fails to convey the more dramatic meaning of 'm'immoler'. The verb points to suicide, to a sacrifice of oneself, most usually as a result of religious motivation. The second section appears to be a transition, as the subject falls asleep, still tormented, by 'ma trahison envers moi-même' ('my betrayal of myself'). In the third section s/he rails against this apparent state of suffering, against judgements made by herself and by others. The poem may be taken as the expression of a tortuous, painful, moral conflict, in which the stakes are life and death.

As in 'Énigme-personnages', Arnauld addresses a second person, 'you', this time using the polite or plural form 'vous', who might be her opponent, observer, or reader. She declares, 'Vous n'êtes ni Dieu, ni mantille | ni ombrelle, ni mécanisme de réveil' ('You are neither God nor mantilla | nor parasol, nor alarm clock'). This list initially appears nonsensical and random. Each object, however, has the potential to exercise some power or effect: God, as authority, the mantilla (a traditional scarf, worn by women, which covers the head), the umbrella as shelter, and the alarm clock as rousing. (The alarm clock appeared in 'Avertisseur' too, discussed in Chapter 3.) Arnauld declares that her addressee is none of these, and so pronounces them ineffectual. Instead, she writes, 'Vous êtes l'amphitryon d'Amphion sans lyre | Sire se mirant sans lyre' ('You are the amphitryon of Amphion without lyre | Lord gazing at your reflection without lyre'). The language play is evident in the combinations of 'amphitryon' and 'Amphion' as well as the rhyming of 'Sire,' 'se mirant', and 'lyre'. In Greek mythology, Amphion was the son of Zeus who, together with his twin Zetheus, built a wall around Thebes by charming the stones with his magical lyre. Without his lyre, as he is imagined here, he would be powerless: hence, this can be read both as an insult to the mythological figure and a provocation to the reader, who is compared with him. Since the lyre is also associated with Orpheus, the musician and poet of Greek myth, this might also be a provocation to the poet.[13]

The poem's narrator rejects any opposition with vehemence, but beneath the bravado there is a sense of guilt and self-conflict. 'Mes trois péchés Dada' appears to represent the poet's uncertainty about her role, her status and purpose. She seems torn between freedom and convention, personal liberty and social expectation. At the end of the poem she finally demolishes 'l'édifice bâti sur une roue et un clou' ('the structure built on a wheel and a nail'). Institutions of authority and religion are rejected. More broadly, physical, external reality is destroyed in favour of escapes into language, imagery, and vision. 'Mes trois péchés Dada' enacts a battle between guilt and liberation, restriction and freedom, authority and self-determination. The Dada sins, it turns out, will triumph in the end.

Nevertheless, there is no clear linear narrative or outcome, and in this sense structure and content complement one another. In particular, the circle is a recurring motif. Eyes, wheels, sunflowers, marbles, and headlights proliferate. A broken wheel, or broken circle, appears in the second line, and again in the eleventh line, appearing to represent disharmony or a break in continuity. Arnauld returns to this broken wheel in the third paragraph, 'Et c'était toujours cette roué cassée | qui me tourmentait' ('And it was still that broken wheel | that was bothering me'). When she tries to repair the damage, the result is 'mes yeux comme beau langage' ('my eyes like beautiful language'). Vision, represented by the eye, is all-important. The choice of the number three is also interesting, appearing in the title and acting as structure to the poem. It could be seen as a disruption of binary oppositions, or a disruption of order, in the sense that it scarcely conforms to the tripartite methodology in which a tension is partially resolved in the third part.

Finally, it is once again the language material that takes centre stage in Arnauld's poem. References and images are extraordinarily eclectic, verging on surrealist in their apparently unconscious and bizarre juxtapositions, such as, 'La marelle accouche d'un tournesol' ('Hopscotch gives birth to a sunflower'). Words are brought together to create visual, fantastical conundrums, as well as for their pure linguistic assonances or discord, such as in 'les yeux de perroquets sont des billes billevesées' ('Parrots' eyes are nonsense marbles'). Though we can draw meanings from it, this is not, after all, a narrative poem.

Arnauld's most explicit pronouncement of Dada, arguably, is the text 'Ombrelle Dada' ('Dada Parasol') (*OC*, p. 448). Referring to itself as a manifesto from the outset — its very first phrase is 'Vous n'aimez pas mon manifeste?' ('You don't like my manifesto?') — it adheres to Dada in title, style, and context.[14] 'Ombrelle Dada' was one of the 'Vingt-trois manifestes du mouvement Dada' [Twenty-Three Manifestos of the Dada Movement] printed in *Littérature*, 13 (May 1920), subsequent to public readings in previous months at the Salon des Indépendants, the Club du Faubourg, and the Université populaire du Faubourg Saint-Antoine.[15] Founded by Aragon, Breton, and Soupault in March 1919, *Littérature* had featured a broad range of avant-garde writers, and would go on to act as an important vehicle for literary Surrealism, but this issue's pages were filled with Dada messages. Here, twelve contributors made their Dada declarations: Picabia, Aragon, Breton, Tzara, Arp, Éluard, Soupault, Walter Serner, Dermée, Ribemont-Dessaignes, W. C. Arensberg, and Arnauld. This group of twelve names, as featured on the cover, offers a verbal parallel to the group photograph discussed earlier, in which Arnauld's face is the only female one. Here hers is the only woman's name, and even then it is mis-spelt 'Arnault'. More positively, the order of publication, at least, was apparently decided by random selection, an appropriately aleatory and democratic gesture.[16]

Georges Hugnet wrote of the *Littérature* manifestos, 'Nous connaissons déjà les manifestes de Tzara. Comme ceux-ci, les autres rivalisent d'insolence ou d'absurdité, de lyrisme, de gratuité ou d'humour' ('We are already familiar with Tzara's manifestos. These others, just like them, vie for insolence or absurdity, lyricism, gratuity or humour').[17] How far does this statement apply to Arnauld's contribution? Insolence, to begin with Hugnet's first term, is evident from the very first lines, which address, engage, and potentially enrage the audience, 'Vous n'aimez pas mon manifeste? | Vous êtes venus ici pleins d'hostilité et vous allez me siffler avant même de m'entendre?' ('You don't like my manifesto? | You've come here full of hostility and you're going to boo even before hearing me?'). Rhetorical dialogue, based on an anticipation of hostility, continues throughout, with questions launched like missiles at the audience, 'Êtes-vous contents maintenant?' ('Are you happy now?'). The fact that 'Ombrelle Dada' would have been written to be spoken aloud, rather than printed and read, is clear from its declarative style.

Absurdity, Hugnet's second term, is also in evidence. Arnauld asks her audience or reader, 'Avez-vous déjà vu au bord des routes entre les orties et les pneus crevés, un poteau télégraphique pousser péniblement? | Mais dès qu'il a dépassé ses voisins, il monte si vite que vous ne pourriez plus l'arrêter ... jamais!' ('Have you ever seen on the sides of the road between the nettles and the flat tires, a telegraph pole painfully growing? | But as soon as it has outgrown its neighbours, it climbs so fast that you can no longer stop it ... never!'). This fantastical dreamlike scene can be read as a metaphor for the Dada of the title: a new, unexpected, and unstoppable force outgrowing the rubbish around it. In the next lines the telegraph pole opens out, lights up, and swells, recalling the parasol of the title, which is mentioned again: 'c'est une ombrelle, un taxi, une encyclopédie ou un cure-dent' ('it's a parasol, a taxi, an encyclopaedia, or a toothpick'). The same collection of words re-appears just a few lines later, this time in relation to poetry, 'Poésie — cure-dent, encyclopédie, taxi ou abri-ombrelle', thus making an association between Dada and poetry, both of which embrace and include an eclectic array of everyday objects, transforming and revitalising our impressions of them. The odd mix of objects revels in the absurdity to be found in connections between disparate objects.

As for lyricism, it is the quality of the words, their acoustic materiality, that drives their selection, as much as their semantics. This is attention at the level of the individual word, foregrounded, rolled on the tongue, pronounced, and experienced afresh. The unusual, playful words interfere in any excess of seriousness or didacticism. 'Ombrelle' (umbrella or parasol), in the title, recalls a phrase by the comte de Lautréamont, the alter ego of the writer Isidore Ducasse, who was celebrated by the Dadaists and Surrealists. His famous formulation, 'beau comme ... la rencontre fortuite sur une table de dissection d'une machine à coudre et d'un parapluie' ('as beautiful as ... the chance encounter of a sewing machine and an umbrella on a dissecting table'), evokes the joy in incongruous linguistic, imagined, or even real meetings between ordinary but unrelated objects, with mysterious or even menacing effects.[18]

Nevertheless, this text is distinct from others by Arnauld in that it is a more 'legible' attack on the culture of convention, which is always implicit in her work but here is made more overt and accessible. She decries stagnation, 'C'est parfait!! Continuez donc, la roue tourne, tourne depuis [f]eu Adam, rien n'est changé, sauf que nous n'avons plus que deux pattes au lieu de quatre' ('That's perfect!! So just go on, the wheel turns, turns since Adam, nothing's changed, except that we have only two feet instead of four').[19] With her reference to Genesis she locates us in Western Christian civilisation and in invoking human invention and development she mocks the accepted notion of progress. The turning wheel suggests cyclical movement rather than linear, ever-improving change.

The manifesto then targets the arts more specifically, 'Mais vous me faites trop rire et je veux vous récompenser de votre bon accueil, en vous parlant d'Aart, de Poésie et d'etc. d'etc. ipécacuanha' ('But you really make me laugh and I want to pay you back for your nice welcome by speaking to you about Aart, about Poetry etc. etc. ipecacuanha'). And towards the end she sums up, 'c'est tout ce que j'avais à vous dire. C'est la Poéésie, croyez-moi' ('Oh well, that's all that I had to say to you. That's what Poeetry is, believe me'). Her subtle play with the vowel sounds in 'Aart' and 'Poéésie' ridicules the pretensions and self-importance of art and literature. As Dermée writes in Z, 'Dada est irrité de ceux qui écrivent "l'Art" "la Beauté", "la Vérité" avec des majuscules' [Dada is irritated by people who write "Art" "Beauty", and "Truth" with capital letters]. Rigid definitions of poetry and art are rejected; poetry is the Dada parasol, words-in-the-mouth, the lowly toothpick. This distrust of intellectual posturing is expressed in an observation in Proust's fiction, 'nous en avons trop vu de ces intellectuels adorant l'Art avec un grand A' ('we have seen more than enough of these intellectuals worshipping Art with a big A').[20]

The last lines of Arnauld's manifesto continue her rhetorical attack on her listeners and/or readers but the ending adds an unusual twist, 'Et si vous n'êtes pas contents ... | A LA TOUR DE NESLE' ('And if you're not pleased ... | TO THE NESLE TOWER'). The tower of Nesle was one of four on the old city walls of Paris, constructed in the thirteenth century. It is often associated with a scandalous historical event turned legend. The story centres on the alleged adultery of two women, Marguerite and Blanche, daughters-in-law of Philippe IV. The knights with whom they were consorting were executed and they were confined. The tale was reworked over time, the tower evoked as a site of depravity in various lurid iterations of female debauchery.[21] Arnauld may have been drawn to these myths, to immorality beneath the veer of civilisation and women's subversions. More simply, she casts judgement on her accusers, assumes power, and metaphorically sends them down.

An analysis of one more text will aptly take us to our next chapter. 'Dangereux' [Dangerous] was published in Picabia's Cannibale in April 1920, the height of Dada activity in Paris (OC, p. 397).[22] It is a marvellously vitriolic manifesto that sets itself apart for the way in which Arnauld puts herself firmly centre-stage and omits any direct mention of Dada. What makes it distinct, moreover, is its proclamation of the author's own name, and this time there is no spelling error. It reads:

> Pour mettre fin à la stupide comédie de ceux qui se croient les défenseurs d'une nation qu'ils empoisonnent avec leur art fait de commérages, j'ai inventé une chanson filmée, une chanson qui tue, une chanson qui étrangle et qui désinfecte les regards en épluchures d'oignon; c'est le dernier film-fusée insecticide, visible au *Cinéma Céline Arnauld*, à Montmartre.

> [To put an end to the stupid comedy of those who believe themselves to be the defenders of a nation that they poison with their art, made up of gossip, I've invented a filmed song, a song that kills, a song that strangles and that disinfects gazes into onion peelings; it's the last rocket-film insecticide, screening at the *Céline Arnauld Cinema* in Montmartre.]

'Dangereux' is derisive of other artists, who are seen to be upholding national authority and power through their complacent contributions to culture. It is a Marxist-inspired acknowledgment, too, of the culture industry as hegemonic. Arnauld's alternative is not appeasement, not slow change, but revolution. Her envisaged attack takes the form of a filmed song, destructive and murderous. She draws on vivid metaphors of strangulation, disinfectant, and insecticide to counter the poison of the present state. Such images recall Tzara's cleansing metaphors from an early Zurich 'Dada Manifesto' (*Dada*, 3, December 1918), 'Que chaque homme crie: il y a un grand travail destructif, négatif à accomplir. Balayer, nettoyer' ('Every man must shout: there is great destructive, negative work to be done. To sweep, to clean').[23] It also ties in with the often-violent rhetoric employed by the Futurists, in whose texts half-measures for transformation were scarcely conceived. The rhetoric of rage, though, is mixed with inventiveness and unique visualisations. Arnauld's rejection of the hostile gaze, reduced to onion peelings, has a sharply sensuous edge.

Compelling, too, is her proposed response: a 'rocket-film'. This neologism points to the new technologies of travel and exploration, and pairs its inherent ideas of movement, transport, and rapidity with the potential of film. Arnauld's imaginary new art form, a fusion of word and image, will have the power to strangle and kill belief in the 'stupid comedy' of the status quo. She, the writer, is the inventor of this new cross-genre, multi-media weapon, suggesting a will to break through the restrictions of literature and expand its possibilities, above all in the light of new technologies that allow for movement and sound. Her fantasy of the Céline Arnauld Cinema, a venue in her name, is also strikingly assertive. In opposition to stagnation, the culture that she envisages proposes a powerful new way of seeing.

As we have seen in this chapter, Arnauld's Dada-era texts are indeed notable for their combinations of both action and lyricism. The first texts we discussed (albeit not chronologically) bore witness to the verbal play evident in her early collections of works. The manifesto-style texts, meanwhile, share ideological and stylistic concerns with other Dada interventions. Their pre-emptive rejection of criticism is typically Dada, as is their play with words, their self-reflexive irony, and their gratuity and humour (to complete Hugnet's list). Arnauld appears to be enmeshed in the Dada network, contributing to the tone and objectives shared for at least a short time by its protagonists and publicists in Paris.

However, it is the free and playful use of images, fantastical qualities, and privileging and highlighting of the language material that are crucial to her Dada texts. They present a conviction of the power of visual perception, sometimes explicitly but more often implicitly. Arnauld's free use of language sets itself against semantic logic, and her images aim to enlarge the scope of what can be thought and experienced. A statement by Dermée in *Z* applies to the spontaneity and freedom in her work, 'Dada ruinant l'autorité des contraintes tend à libérer le jeu naturel de nos activités. Dada mène donc à l'amoralisme et au lyrisme le plus spontané, par conséquent le moins logique. Ce lyrisme s'exprime de mille façons dans la vie' [Dada's shattering of the authority of constraints tended to liberate the natural playfulness in our activities. Dada led, then, to amorality and to the most spontaneous — and consequently least logical — lyricism. This lyricism expresses itself in a thousand ways in life]. Here, vitally, action and lyricism combine. Arnauld's belief in Dada has been demonstrated. But her belief in herself too, as suggested in 'Dangereux', offers an absorbing vision that belies total Dada absorption. In the next chapter I will pick up on this self-assertion as we consider Arnauld's founding of her own journal *Projecteur*.

Notes to Chapter 5

1. Céline Arnauld, letter to Tristan Tzara, 24 October 1924, Tristan Tzara archives, Bibliothèque littéraire Jacques Doucet, Paris.
2. Many of these are available online at the Digital Dada Library at the International Dada Archive, University of Iowa Libraries, <http://sdrc.lib.uiowa.edu/dada/index.html> [accessed 1 March 2020], or at Monoskop <https://monoskop.org/Avant-garde_and_modernist_magazines> [accessed 1 March 2020].
3. See, for example, Ruth Hemus, 'Céline Arnauld: Dada Présidente?', in *The French Avant-Garde*, ed. by Stephen Forcer and Emma Wagstaff (Nottingham: Nottingham French Studies, 2012), pp. 67–77. Arnauld is one of fifteen women included in the list.
4. Céline Arnauld, 'Envoi du Japon' and 'Extrait de Saturne', *Le Pilhaou-Thibaou* (July 1921), [n.p.]. For a full reprint of *Le Pilhaou-Thibaou*, see Sanouillet, *Francis Picabia et 391*, I, 97–110. This magazine is widely perceived as a manifestation of a growing estrangement on Picabia's part from both Dada and Breton. For a brief account see 'Francis Picabia et 391' in this same publication, pp. 14–15.
5. Georges Ribemont-Dessaignes, 'Cafard', *Cannibale*, 1 (April 1920), [n.p.]. Reprinted in Georges Hugnet, *L'Aventure Dada (1916–1922)* (Vichy: Seghers, 1971), p. 201. Or for the full journal see Sanouillet, *Francis Picabia et 391*, II, 188.
6. Tristan Tzara, *Dada soulève tout* (15 January 1921). Reprinted in *Documents Dada*, ed. by Poupard-Lieussou and Sanouillet, pp. 52–53. Cubism is at the top of a list that includes expressionism, simultaneism, futurism, unanism, neo-classicism, paroxysm, ultraism and creationism.
7. Francis Picabia, *La Pomme de pins* (February 1922). Reprinted in Sanouillet, *Francis Picabia et 391*, II, 221–24; Francis Picabia, *Plus de cubisme* (March 1922). Reprinted in *Documents Dada*, ed. by Poupard-Lieussou and Sanouillet, pp. 80–81 (document 48).
8. For more on these publications and protagonists see Simon Dell, 'After Apollinaire: *SIC* (1916–19); *Nord-Sud* (1917–18); and *L'Esprit nouveau* (1920–5)', in *The Oxford Critical and Cultural History of Modernist Magazines*, ed. by Peter Brooker and others, 3 vols in 4 (Oxford: Oxford University Press, 2013), III, 143–59.
9. Céline Arnauld, 'Énigme-personnages', *Dadaphone*, 7 (March 1920), [n.p.]. The full edition is reprinted in *Dada: réimpression intégrale et dossier critique de la revue publiée de 1917 à 1922 par Tristan Tzara*, ed. by Michel Sanouillet and Dominique Baudouin, 2 vols (Nice: Centre du XXe siècle, 1976–1983), I, VII, 1–8.

10. Céline Arnauld, 'Enigma Figures', trans. by Ruth Hemus, in *Burning City*, ed. by Rasula and Conley, p. 350. For an analysis of this poem as a critique of the Dada group see Forcer, *Dada as Text, Thought and Theory*, p. 18.
11. Céline Arnauld, 'Mes trois péchés Dada', *Cannibale*, 2 (25 May 1920), [n.p.]. For a full reproduction see Sanouillet, *Francis Picabia et 391*, II, 201–20.
12. Arnauld, 'My Three Dada Sins', trans. by Paula Kamenish, in *Mamas of Dada*, pp. 78–81. *Prunelle* can also mean 'sloe'.
13. By plumbing intertextual references, Forcer reads in this poem loaded references to Picabia and Tzara (*Dada as Text, Thought and Theory*, pp. 29–31).
14. Céline Arnauld, 'Dada Parasol', trans. by Kamenish, in *Mamas of Dada*, pp. 82–84.
15. 'Vingt-trois manifestes du mouvement Dada', *Littérature*, 13 (May 1920). For a detailed account of these readings see Michel Sanouillet, *Dada à Paris* (Paris: Flammarion, 2005), Chapter 7.
16. Hugnet: 'L'ordre de leur publication a été tiré au sort' (*L'Aventure Dada*, p. 93).
17. Ibid.
18. Isidore Ducasse, '*Les Chants de Maldoror*', in *Œuvres complètes*, ed. by Maurice Saillet (Paris: Livre de Poche, 1963), p. 322; cited by Willard Bohn, *Marvelous Encounters: Surrealist Responses to Film, Art, Poetry and, Architecture* (Lewisburg, PA: Bucknell University Press, 2005), pp. 121–23.
19. The original published version reads 'depuis eu Adam'. In the *OC* it has been changed to 'depuis feu Adam', the meaning of 'feu', here, being 'departed', 'deceased', or 'late'.
20. Proust, *A la recherche du temps perdu*, III, 346; *Remembrance of Things Past*. Vol. 3, *The Guermantes Way*, trans. by C. K. Scott-Moncrieff (London: Chatto & Windus, 1927), p. 141.
21. Further intertexts include the story of a queen, Marguerite de Bourgogne, who disposes of her lovers after nights of passion. Versions were relayed, for example, in: François Villon's fifteenth-century poem *Balade des dames du temps jadis*; the nineteenth-century play *La Tour de Nesle* written by Frédéric Gaillardet and rewritten by Alexandre Dumas; and a 1901 short film made by Albert Capillani. One more reference is irresistible and puts an entirely different perspective on events. When I undertook a tour of Arnauld's known addresses in Paris, I noted a café near one of them called 'La Tour de Nesle'. Quite simply, the sights of the contemporary city may have been her inspiration. This semi-arbitrariness, the clash between past, present, and future held in tension in verbal signs, would become dear to the Surrealists.
22. Céline Arnauld, 'Dangereux', *Cannibale*, 1 (April 1920), [n.p.]. See Sanouillet, *Francis Picabia et 391*, I, 184, to view it in the magazine.
23. Tristan Tzara, *Lampisteries: sept manifestes Dada* (Paris: Pauvert, 2001), p. 30; *Seven Dada Manifestos and Lampisteries*, trans. by Barbara Wright (London: Calder, 1992), p. 12.

CHAPTER 6

Founding a Journal: Ambition and Vision in *Projecteur* (1920)

> *Projecteur* n'insère aucune rectification, aucun droit de réponse, aucune publicité!¹
>
> [*Projecteur* will not include any rectification, any right of response, any advertising!]

As we have seen, Arnauld was an avid contributor to avant-garde magazines and a persistent presence in Paris Dada. Her contributions to others' magazines now established, what surprises and promises to reveal yet more about her place in this period of literary history is the fact that she started up her own journal. *Projecteur*, appearing in May 1920, both underscores Arnauld's co-operative efforts with her Dada peers and reveals her individual ambition.² Given the propensity in some histories of Paris Dada to rank women as only adjuncts or assistants to the radical experiments of the male literati rather than as drivers or instigators, it is gratifying to find evidence of an attempt by Arnauld to drive her own agenda.

In the context of Paris Dada, the editorial ventures of contemporaries such as Picabia and Tzara are well-documented. Reproduced, analysed, and lauded, they have shaped narratives of the avant-garde.³ Women were rare even as contributors to these journals, let alone as editors. Arnauld is apparently the only woman to have started up a journal within Dada circles. This venture belies any lazy categorisation of her as a follower rather than an instigator and marks her out as unique.⁴ In the following analysis of Arnauld's little-plumbed magazine, *Projecteur*, I will outline what is known of its origins and briefly sketch out the contributors and content of the magazine, with a view to relating it to the Dada group and its abundant journal activity. Beyond emphasising Arnauld's place in that context, however, I want to demonstrate how this necessarily collaborative publication paradoxically bears witness to an emerging schism between its author and the collective. I will do this by close readings of the format, title, prospectus, and choice of texts, to show how Arnauld was attempting here to negotiate her allegiance to Dada alongside her independent thinking about literature, above all in relation to film culture.

Arnauld's nascent plans for a journal are illuminated to a limited extent in surviving primary materials. A 'Mouvement Dada' letterhead printed by Tzara in the early part of 1920, for example, lists Dada journal titles together with their directors' names: Tzara (*Dada*), Ribemont-Dessaignes (*Dd O⁴ H²*), Aragon, Breton, and Soupault (*Littérature*), Arnauld (*M'Amenez'y*), Éluard (*Proverbe*), Picabia (*391*), and Dermée (*Z*). The document can be read as an unambiguous signal of the inclusion of Arnauld and her title (the publisher is specified as 'dépositaire de toutes les revues Dada'). But where we might expect to see the title *Projecteur* in the list of seven publications we instead read '*M'Amenez'y*'.

Further textual clues indicate that this was the title originally planned for Arnauld's journal. Tzara's *Dadaphone* of March 1920 includes *M'Amenez'y* in a list of five forthcoming Dada reviews, with Arnauld named as director. A flyer for *Littérature*, dated January 1920, printed only shortly after Tzara and Breton began collaborating, also advertises Arnauld's new venture. And the review of Arnauld's *Poèmes à claires-voies* by Renée Dunan, discussed in Chapter 3, refers to her as 'La directrice de *M'Amenez'y*'. This trail of references is revealing. Firstly, it tells us that Arnauld was firmly located in a prolific and active Dada network of advertising and publicity that was promoting this title among others. Secondly, it points to a fast-moving set of circumstances. Between January and April 1920, at least, it seems that plans were in place to use one title for her journal. By the time of its publication in May that title had been abandoned and replaced.

The original title takes its place linguistically within a network of associations, the phrase having been used and re-used by more than one Dadaist in various contexts during the early months of 1920. The most well-known of these are Picabia's oil painting on cardboard *M'Amenez'y* (1919–1920), and his re-deployment of the phrase in his celebrated verbal-visual artwork *Le Double Monde* [The Double World], first exhibited at the Dada *matinée* of 23 January 1920. The term also recurred in written texts. Picabia, once again, included it in a poem 'Le Rat circulaire', published in Éluard's *Proverbe* on 1 February 1920. Picabia's three-time use of this one phrase within such a short timeframe, as well as its deployment by more than one individual, highlights the Dada tendency to adopt and recontextualise uncommon or reworked fragments of language in esoteric interplay.[5]

The phrase itself is grammatically incorrect. The nearest accurate rendering would be 'Amenez-m'y [Take me there]. In the reordered phrase 'M'Amenez'y' the 'M' could be read aloud separately as *aime/s* [like/s], while the 'Amenez'y' calls to mind *amnésie* [amnesia]. It thus combines a sense of familiarity (the components are recognisable to the French speaker) with a strangeness (the ordering is unexpected) that makes the reader stumble. It is exemplary of a playful breakdown of the conventional language system. Like the term 'Dada', this 'readymade verbal' (to use a term employed by Fernand Drijkoningen), acts as a brand or slogan that connects the group's artists and writers.[6]

A letter from Dermée to Tzara provides some background to Arnauld's planned use of the term, suggesting a selection process that was discursive and to some extent collaborative. He writes, 'Il est inutile de changer "M'Amenez'y" jusque c'est déjà sur les prospectus de *Littérature*' [There is no point changing 'M'Amenez'y' since it's already on the prospectus for *Littérature*]. He goes on, 'C'est que Céline Arnauld avait trouvé un bien beau titre: *Ipéca* ou *I.P.K.*, vomitif extrêmement puissant! Ce sera pour une autre publication ou forme de pamphlet' [The point is Céline Arnauld had found a really great title: *Ipéca* ou *I.P.K*, an extremely powerful vomiting agent! This can be used for another publication or some type of pamphlet].[7] Dermée's letter implies that the title *M'Amenez'y* had been chosen for her, rather than by her, and that in fact she had in mind a different title altogether. Compounded by a situation in which Dermée and Tzara correspond about her, it is perhaps unsurprising, albeit disappointing, that her presence and participation in Dada have too often been omitted from narratives.[8]

'Ipéca' (ipecacuanha, or 'ipecac' in American English) refers to a medicinal preparation made from a low-growing tropical American shrub and is used, as Dermée indicates in his letter, to induce vomiting.[9] Like 'M'Amenez'y,' it appeared in more than one Dada text. Ribemont-Dessaignes used it in a poem 'ZA', published in Dermée's magazine *Z* in March 1920, 'Coffre-fort à mot ipéca' [ipecac word safebox]. Tellingly, Arnauld herself also used the unabbreviated form 'ipécacuanha' in her manifesto 'Ombrelle Dada'. While this was not published until May 1920, alongside twenty-two other manifestos in the thirteenth issue of *Littérature*, these had been read aloud at the Salon des Indépendants months earlier, on 5 February. Instead of assuming Arnauld borrowed the word from Ribemont-Dessaignes, we might assert — given both the timings and Dermée's notes to Tzara about its meaning and assignation to Arnauld — that she was the first to come up with it. The word's connotations, a radical purging agent, and its unusual sound and appearance, which Arnauld intended to render phonetically as a pseudo-acronym 'I.P.K.', make it ripe for Dada (re)invention and underline its adopter's credentials as a Dada wordsmith.

Finally, neither *M'Amenez'y* nor *Ipéca* transpired. Instead, Arnauld realised her plans for a journal in May 1920 with the radically different title *Projecteur*. It was printed by Sans Pareil, led by René Hilsum. Concerns about prior publicity for the original title, had, it seems, been either allayed, superseded, or overruled. Humour, in any case, prevails, in the form of references in the final publication to Arnauld's initial choices. In a short text 'Signalement' ('Particulars'), Dermée chooses a few lines to refer to each of the contributors to the journal.[10] Of its editor he writes, 'Céline Arnauld a déjà tué deux revues: "M'Amenez'y" et "Ipéca" aujourd'hui introuvables. N'insistez pas M. Doucet ... introuvable, introuvable' ('Céline Arnauld has already killed off two reviews: *M'Amenez'y*: and Ipéca are totally unobtainable. Do not press the point, Mr. Doucet ... they are utterly unobtainable').[11] The extract is noteworthy for its self-referentiality (noting its own coming-into-being) as well as its refusal to take too seriously the path to publication. It also neatly evokes the twin poles of destruction and production so characteristic of Dada.

Arnauld's publication appeared at an intense point of journal production in Paris. That same month saw the appearance of *Littérature*, 13, edited by Aragon, Breton, and Soupault, Éluard's *Proverbe*, 5, and Picabia's *Cannibale*, 2. The simultaneous appearance of these journals is a material manifestation of the multiple and complex web of collaborations at that time. Bohn writes of an 'interlocking directorship', especially in terms of reviews, that facilitated cohesion and 'unprecedented collaboration'.[12] Arnauld's decision to launch her own journal puts her at the heart of this activity. It also, though, points to a desire for leadership and the exploration of a different direction, as evident in her ultimate choice of title. If intertextual links are discernible in Arnauld's first two proposals, the final title is very much her own. Considerably less esoteric than the Dada puns discussed, it is more recognisable to a wider readership. Importantly, it suggests new thinking about literature beyond Dada, marked by Arnauld's persistent preoccupations with film culture.

The prospectus on the front page of *Projecteur* (OC, p. 451) sets out its editor's vision and makes particular recourse to the visual. Under a bold, upper-case, underlined heading that occupies a third of the page in height and extends the full width of the page, it reads:

> *Projecteur* est une lanterne pour aveugles. Il ne marchande pas ses lumières, elles sont gratuites. *Projecteur* se moque de tout: argent, gloire et réclame — il inonde de soleil ceux qui vivent dans le froid, dans l'obscurité et dans l'ennui. D'ailleurs, la lumière est aussi produite par une pullulation madréporique dans les espaces célestes.
>
> [*Projecteur* is a lantern for the blind. It doesn't begrudge its lights, they're free of charge. *Projecteur* mocks everything: money, glory and advertising — it bathes in sunshine those who live in the cold, in darkness and in ennui. Moreover, the light is also produced by a madreporian proliferation in heavenly spaces.]

The term 'prospectus' is a surprising choice. More often used commercially, it suggests the promotion of an emerging enterprise with a view to winning over investors or partners. It can be used in the same way to signal a publishing project, but in either case the way in which the editor insults her potential buyers or readership privileges irony over courtship. The journal is presented as a 'lantern for the blind', alluding to a metaphorical blindness, or ignorance. In its claim to reject advertising, meanwhile, the text is at odds with itself. After all, the prominent title *Projecteur* is invoked and repeated twice within the prospectus on the front page, lodging itself in the reader's mind. It proposes to reject glory but paradoxically makes grandiose claims at enlightenment. These lofty claims, too, are at least in part ironic. The final line, with its alliterative quality ('produite par une pullulation madréporique'), introduced somewhat glibly by 'd'ailleurs', puts paid to a strictly serious tone and propels the reader into imaginative thinking.

Metaphors of enlightenment are also saved from cliché in that they relate not only to natural, celestial light but also to new visual media. The description of the journal as a lantern indicates man-made light ahead of sunshine and recalls the *Lanterne magique* of Arnauld's first publication. The projector or lantern can be read as having the potential to provoke thought and effect change, just as in Proust. But the actual and ideological illuminating power of these apparatus are here wished upon the written text. The projector of the title, most notably, explicitly refers to and privileges the potential of film. One contemporary reference that it calls to mind, I would argue, is *Monument to the Third International* (1919–1920) by Vladimir Tatlin. Planned but never realised, this symbolic, aspirational project would have resulted in a tower, with searchlights to illuminate its surroundings, a radio transmitter, and a projector at its top to beam slogans into the clouds on overcast nights.[13] Arnauld's prospectus evokes the impact of projected light, alludes to a spectacular celestial display, and shares to an extent a utopian vision that binds electric light and language.

The format of the journal is also of note. Unlike many of the more visually complex and arresting Dada journals of the time that incorporate visual images, Arnauld's might at first be considered disappointingly reactionary. It does not include any images, nor does it experiment typographically beyond the front page. Its unique experiment, however, is its material format. Set out in landscape, it is twenty-three centimetres wide and ten and a half centimetres high. Arnauld's original, groundbreaking choice of size and orientation might be said to recall the 'window on the world' of the framed canvas in painting but the connection flagged by the title is rather between the page and the cinema screen. On each page, texts are set out in two columns, which could be read as a succession of filmic frames generating a sequence of mental images. Instead of confronting a format that echoes a conventional newspaper or journal, the reader is treated to snapshots of texts, one or two to a page.[14] Like her precursors and her peers, Arnauld experiments with material ways of presenting literature that draw attention to the process of reading.[15] But she is less interested in the graphic than in the cinematographic.

The journal includes contributions by key Dada writers, constituting an impressive, albeit predictable line-up of the key men associated with Dada that aligns with the list of journal editors above. More unusually, it showcases work by two women writers, Arnauld herself and Renée Dunan.[16] The balance of texts is notable. In every case the ratio is one contribution per writer, with the exception of Dermée, Arnauld, and Dunan, who are each represented by three texts. We might conclude that Arnauld is maximising the unique opportunity she has created in order to provide a platform for these three individuals orbiting the Dada centre.

The first page following the title page features two short prose texts. 'Julot', by Éluard, sketches out a red-cheeked, overdressed, puffed-up character introduced as 'l'invité de Charlot' [Charlot's guest]. A contrast is set up between the ridiculousness of this bourgeois man 'Julot' (a synonym for 'Jules' meaning a bloke, a pimp, or even a chamber pot), and the wisdom of 'Charlot', the fond name for Charlie Chaplin, who was greatly admired by the Dadaists. Indeed, Arnauld would go on to write a review of the film *The Kid* the year following the publication of *Projecteur* (see Chapter 7). The placement of Éluard's piece as a first text, at the front of her journal, points again to Arnauld's emphasis on the medium of film and her recognition of its potential.

The second text, 'L'Un pour l'autre' [For Each Other] by Dermée, depicts a dramatic moment: the death of a man under a train, and the indifference of the crowd. Thematic connections with Arnauld's poem 'Point de mire', discussed in Chapter 4, are apparent. Futility and absurdity characterise this brief vignette, not least as a proto-surrealist hand clad in a white glove scatters notes on the tracks where the dead man lies split apart. Both these first texts are relatively accessible mini-narratives, which foreground themes of modernity (film and travel) and the chance encounters and happenings of the everyday. Side-by-side they might be read as two filmic scenes, tying in with an interpretation of the journal's layout as reminiscent of a cinema screen.

Picabia's poem 'Handicap' hints at the absurdity of the human condition. In the face of confusing emotions and arbitrary social conventions his uncertain and unhappy protagonists seek answers at the town hall. The only shared and appropriate ambition in the face of the unknown, he concludes, is 'partir le dernier et arriver le premier' [leave last and arrive first]. Tzara's subsequent early poem 'Le Cierge et la vierge' [The Candle and the Virgin], dated 1914, is a collage of seemingly random concepts and visual impressions in which juxtaposed leeches, brambles, hanged men, frustrated sailors, and centipedes form a nightmarish landscape. Above all, it plays with lexical and sonorous invention, combination, and repetition.

If the term 'Dada' risks being forgotten (thus far it has not appeared), it surfaces at the foot of this fourth page in the form of two four-line stanzas authored by Dunan. 'Les Méditations du saladier' [Meditations of a Salad Bowl] and 'Dadaphysis' add yet more threads to the tangle of Dada definitions in other journals and statements by refusing clarity in favour of negation and language play. The first text begins by telling the reader what Dada is *not*, 'Dada n'est pas une gigogne | A douze pattes dont un pied' [Dada is not a stork | With twelve legs, one a foot]. The second is pure rhyme and assonance reminiscent of a tongue-twister:

> C'est l'infusoire et l'infusé
> Qui refuse la mort infuse
> Le néant fuse
> du chef usé.

[It's the infusoria and the infused | Refusing infused death | The fused nothingness | of the used-up leader.]

Her comedy is counterbalanced by a simple, meditative poem 'Salutations distinguées' [Yours Sincerely] by Soupault. In nine sparse lines beginning 'Bateaux lanternes sourdes' [Boats lanterns muted] the text gently rocks its reader with a refrain:

> tout cela encore
> tout cela
> tout

[all this once more | all this | all]

A refrain which echoes the cry of birds and pulls in the reader, 'Vous êtes là | moi aussi' [You are there | me too]. The images evoked in Soupault's poem — a boat, lantern, birds, and train stations — remind us exactly of those themes favoured by Arnauld in her substantial body of poetry.

Dermée's second contribution, 'Signalement', touched on above, is Dadaist in format and tone. It lists the contributors to the journal together with comical tags, drawing on a recurring Dada journalistic technique.[17] Paul Éluard, for example, is 'le père de Paul Draule' ('Paul Draule's father'), employing an anagram of his name that Éluard used repeatedly. 'Tzara n'a jamais, jamais, jamais le cafard' ('Tzara is never down in the dumps') employs another popular turn of phrase (*avoir le cafard*) that had been exploited before.[18] Dermée's playfulness borders on acerbic critique, however, when it comes to his qualifier for Breton, 'André Breton devient le moraliste du mouvement Dada. Qui en sera l'esthéticien?' ('André Breton is becoming the moralist of the Dada movement. Who will be its aesthetician?'). Here is an early warning about the literary figure who would soon dominate the avant-garde in Paris, and with whom Arnauld and Dermée would break acrimoniously.

Despite Dermée's criticism, Breton is also represented in Arnauld's journal. 'Parfums d'Orsay' is a scarcely punctuated, breathless vignette with a fast, filmic quality. The reader is plunged directly into a scene that might have been lifted from a longer narrative but instead exists alone. Visual, momentary details and drama replace context and frustrate closure. It is followed by the longest text in the magazine, Aragon's 'Café crème', a dialogue between two men that hovers between philosophy, irony, romanticism, and satire.[19] Next to it is Dermée's third text 'Philosophie de l'histoire', another dramatic snapshot, in this case narrated in the first person, that begins with a white bonnet blowing away and an express train. Ribemont-Dessaigne's double-column poem 'Pneumatique' completes the line-up of Dada men in irreverent fashion. Each line adds a dimension to a collage that appeals to all the senses. Bodily functions are rife: a couple make love in a threesome, having rested their ears on a night-table where their urine sleeps; the memory of spasms on the bidet is like sadness; and the temperature is so fine that its thermometer lover possesses it only via the nostrils. Even God and the mess of the body are brought together in blasphemous form: 'Rien ne pousse sauf eczema divin'; 'Intimité de Dieu cochon châtré' [Nothing grows except divine eczema; Intimacy of God castrated pig].

As well as her prospectus, Arnauld prints two of her own poems, 'Luna Park' and 'Les Ronge-Bois' (The Wood-Gnawers) (*OC*, pp. 451–52).[20] The first, occupying the halfway point, can be said to reprise ideas evoked by the title of the journal itself. For contemporary readers the funfairs that began in Coney Island, New York, in 1903 and proliferated across the USA and Europe, including in Paris (Porte Maillot) from 1909, would have been familiar and thrilling. The parks' towers, Ferris wheels, and rides, lit up in stunning displays of electric lighting, were exemplary of modern leisure pursuits enabled by new technologies. Throughout the poem, references to the natural and the artificial environment collide, with light as a recurring reference. From 'glace optique' ('optical mirror'), to 'photophore horoscope' ('photophorous horoscope'), and 'éclairs fuyants' ('rapid lightning'), light and imagination are linked. The poem evokes a landscape of visual tricks and fantasy, where the lines between real and unreal are blurred, and where the narrator seeks to grasp elusive experience, 'Au Luna Park on jongle | avec les cœurs en cristal' ('In Luna Park one juggles | with hearts of crystal'). In her reading of the poem, Kamenish stresses this and other elements of fleetingness as an opposition to permanence and fixity that ties in with Dada aims.[21] While I do not disagree with this reading, I would link that sense of rapidity (in movements and sounds and visions) more firmly to an experience of the world that is informed by new modes of entertainment including fairground rides and film. These were at once amusing and alarming. Forcer, meantime, points eloquently to Arnauld's rendering of the park's 'unreal, transformative possibilities to figure a space in which memory and the future combine', proposing that her interest goes beyond only the ludic.[22]

In the last stanza there is a direct echo of the journal's title:

> Ne vous méfiez pas
> je ne suis que le reflet éphèmère
> du projecteur
> aubade à porte-voix
>
> Do not distrust me
> I am only the fleeting reflection
> of the projector
> morning song with a megaphone

In a more conciliatory and less aggressive tone than that of the prospectus, and the warnings of the poem 'Avertisseur' (discussed in Chapter 3), the poem's narrator draws in the reader to a world of imagination. The 'sinistre étalage' ('sinister display') that opened the poem, the 'mauvais jours' and 'tristes réservoirs' referred to in the first stanza, have been superseded by reverie and escapism that should be embraced rather than treated with suspicion. The subject, 'je', could be read as the park itself, offering a projection of lights and illusions, or as the poet, gathering and transmitting fleeting visions with words. The latter interpretation is underpinned by a reference to the verbal as well as visual, and sound as well as sight, in the very last lines, in which the megaphone pairs with the projector in a powerful verbal-visual transmission. Like Arnauld's text for her prospectus, which suggests insight via film, entertainment and enlightenment go hand in hand in 'Luna Park'.

On the last page of creative texts Arnauld's second poem 'Les Ronge-Bois' sits alongside a block of prose 'Hyper Dada' by Dunan. That the final word is granted to two women writers who have taken their place among this group of men is no coincidence. The first stanza of Arnauld's 'Les Ronge-Bois' brings into collision crazed mosquitos and a dying bird in an atmospheric maelstrom of anguish, rain, and a light-bulb, around which this natural scene coalesces. Another juxtaposition is drawn between two geographical snapshots, Argentina (Mendoza) and Paris. Where the former permits mandoras, elephants, wheels, and wooden horses in an uncanny procession, the latter offers only apathy and boredom, 'Au Collège de France ils s'endorment sur les bancs' ('At the Collège de France, they fall asleep on the benches'). This mockery of patriarchal, institutional learning and prestige as a poor substitute for imagination and free association is typically Dada. The poem ends with another self-conscious declaration from its narrator, 'Moi je ne sais rien que maudire | et divaguer contre l'hypothèse …' ('Me I only know how to curse | and ramble on against hypotheses …'), which reads as a riposte to critics, whether real or imagined.

If we as readers had forgotten all about Dada, it is another woman, Dunan, who adds grist to the mill of Dada definitions in her third and final text 'Hyper Dada'. But in contrast to her linguistically playful short texts that appear earlier in the magazine — and indeed to all the other contributions — this prose is semantically coherent and appears to offer a relatively meaningful explanation of Dada. Dunan pronounces against logic, rationality, stupidity, and routine. Particularly interesting are her comments rejecting the concept of fixed identity as a 'monstreuse blague' [monstrous joke]. Her phrase 'Le moi est un centre de polarisation' offers an echo of the uncertain 'moi' that concluded Arnauld's 'Les Ronge-Bois' and the ephemeral 'je' of 'Luna Park'. The final line of Dunan's text, meanwhile, recalls the linguistically playful style of the last line of Arnauld's 'Prospectus Projecteur', 'Quant au logicien, ce pithécoïde, il sera utilisé à sa propre reliure en sous-veau' [As for the logician, this pithecoid, he will be used for his own *sous-veau* book-binding]. A note of humour adds levity to this manifesto also, avoiding its own descent into too much logic.

On the very final page of the journal there is an advertisement for the Festival Dada of 26 May at the Salle Gaveau, the next major event in Paris. It is indexical of *Projecteur*'s part in a proliferation of magazines that was intended to maximise publicity for Dada. Though few of the texts in *Projecteur* mention Dada explicitly, their authors were well-known for their affiliations, and the writing is typically Dada in style. Dunan's texts, moreover, explicitly foreground the term, with Arnauld arguably providing her fellow woman writer with an opportunity to get more profoundly involved in the group. In a further textual twist: a pink page insert was added to *Projecteur* on which the handwritten text of 'Ombrelle Dada' was reproduced. This was the manifesto Arnauld had read at Dada soirées and which was printed in *Littérature*, 13.

The semi-presence of that insert points to an oscillation in *Projecteur*, however, whose editor, I argue, had a firm eye on future possibilities. Arnauld's chosen journal title and manifesto-style prospectus make no mention of Dada. The magazine's front page advertises a twelve-edition subscription, suggesting its editor's intentions for a longer future. Moreover, past and planned volumes by Arnauld and Dermée are publicised on the back page as 'Editions de "Projecteur"', a clear indication of the ambitions she had for the title she finally chose and for leadership. *Projecteur*, then, can be said to sit between intense group networking and a new conceptual turn. It points to a double allegiance on the part of its editor.

Arnauld's one-off journal builds on a set of references to film that run through her *œuvre*. Throughout her work she draws on the vocabulary of light, from the natural (sun, stars, and moon) to pre-cinematic apparati (the magic lantern and diorama), to the cinematic projector. She was intrigued not by the possibilities of mimesis but by the opportunities to create alternative worlds, to visualise fantasies, and to offer escape from external reality. She was an avid viewer and passionate spectator of film, recognising it as a form to be celebrated. In the 1920s she would write a number of film reviews for journals including *L'Esprit nouveau* and *Action*.

The next chapter of this study will pursue and develop two key strands that have emerged from an analysis of *Projecteur*. The first is Arnauld's focus on film. Out of *Projecteur* would come a concept, *projectivisme*, announced by her as a new movement. That idea will be analysed as a working-through of the challenges posed to writers in modernity, not least the advent of film, most famously outlined by Breton, 'l'invention de la photographie a porté un coup mortel aux vieux modes d'expression' ('The invention of photography has dealt a mortal blow to old modes of expression').[23] Goll's manifesto of Surrealism also signalled this trend. Noting how poetry had been 'ruled' by the ear, he claims, 'Depuis une vingtaine d'années, l'œil prend sa revanche. C'est le siècle du film. Nous communiquons davantage par de signes visuels. Et c'est la rapidité qui fait aujourd'hui la qualité' [For some twenty years now, the eye has been taking its revenge. It is the century of film. We increasingly communicate via visual signs. And it is rapidity that makes for quality today].[24] Arnauld's plundering of filmic vocabulary, as well as her formal experiments that relate to visual and modern culture, as discussed in the first part of this book, will coalesce in this resolute attempt to theorise the place of the poet in the early twentieth century.

Secondly, *Projecteur* can be considered as a signal both of the loosening of her ties with Dada and of her relationship with emerging Surrealism. Close attention to relevant texts will illuminate her insistence on her own independence in the dynamic and volatile landscape of the avant-garde that develops over the next few years. In a text 'Les Faux Managers', for example, published in Dermée's 1924 pamphlet *Le Mouvement accéléré*, she will launch a caustic attack on Breton. Meanwhile, in a preface to her next, post-Dada single-authored volume, *L'Apaisement de l'éclipse*, she will assert that her work should not be too closely aligned with any group or movement. Arnauld's resistance to assimilation gives weight to a contention that it is time to posit her not only as an energetic participant in the avant-garde's confrontation and subversion, but also as an agitator and innovator working on her own terms.[25]

Notes to Chapter 6

1. Céline Arnauld, 'Prospectus Projecteur', *Projecteur* (May 1920), [n.d.] (*OC*, p. 451).
2. For a scanned copy of the entire magazine see the International Dada Archive <http://sdrc.lib.uiowa.edu/dada/index.html>.
3. See Ruth Hemus, 'Dada's Paris Season', and Raymond Spiteri 'What Can the Surrealists Do?', both in *The Oxford Critical and Cultural History of Modernist Magazines*, ed. by Brooker and others, III, 180–202 & 219–43.
4. A rare exception relating to Paris Surrealism is Lise Deharme, who produced *Le Phare de Neuilly* (1933). For a detailed exposition and analysis that likewise seeks to restore the reputation of this neglected review and its author see Marie-Claire Barnet, 'To Lise Deharme's Lighthouse: *Le Phare de Neuilly*, a Forgotten Surrealist Review', *French Studies*, 57.3 (2003), 323–34. Happily, Deharme includes a text by Arnauld in the first number (1933). This text, 'Griffes de Lumière', would later be published in *La Nuit rêve tout haut* (1939). Beyond Dada and Surrealism there are more instances of women editing long-running modernist magazines in English, especially in the USA. These include: Margaret Anderson and Jane Heap, *The Little Review* (1914–1929); Harriet Monroe, *Poetry* (1911–1936); Marianne Moore, *The Dial* (1925–1929). See Jane E. Marek, *Women Editing Modernism: 'Little' Magazines and Literary History* (Lexington: University Press of Kentucky, 1995).
5. There seems to be agreement amongst critics that the phrase originated with Marcel Duchamp. See Jacquelynne Bass, *Marcel Duchamp and the Art of Life* (Cambridge, MA: MIT Press, 2019), p. 171. She cites Jacques Lebel (*Marcel Duchamp*, trans. by George Heard Hamilton (New York: Grove Press, 1959), as well as Michel Sanouillet, in support.
6. Fernand Drijkoningen, 'Un tableau-manifeste de Picabia: le double monde', in *Marcel Duchamp*, ed. by Klaus Beekman and Antje von Graevenitz (Amsterdam: Rodopi, 1989), pp. 97–112.
7. Paul Dermée, letter to Tristan Tzara, [1920], Tristan Tzara Archives, BLJD; repr. in Sanouillet, *Dada à Paris*, p. 188, n. 43.

8. For example Kamenish (*Mamas of Dada*, p. 84) notes that the scholar Henri Béhar wrongly ascribes *Projecteur* to Dermée in Tristan Tzara, *Dada est tatou: tout est dada*, ed. by Henri Béhar (Paris: Flammarion, 1996), p. 357. This apparently minor mistake is typical of the passing-over in academic histories of women's inputs and outputs.
9. It is also used as a cough expectorant but Dermée's letter suggests that its emetic function was its draw for Arnauld.
10. Paul Dermée, 'Particulars', trans. by Ian Monk, in *The Dada Reader*, ed. by Dawn Ades (London: Tate Publishing, 2006), p. 250. Oddly, it is attributed to Arnauld rather than Dermée, even though the initials 'P.D.' appear underneath it in the original journal.
11. Jacques Doucet was a fashion designer and collector of art and literature whose donated papers form an archive held in Paris. Dermée rightly presages the significance of such a collector in transmitting history and his ironic words taunt the curious scholar in search of documents even now.
12. Bohn, 'Introduction', in *The Dada Market*, ed. by Bohn, p. xiv.
13. A later comparison is Deharme's *Phare de Neuilly* from 1933 (four numbers). Its cover depicts a pared-down drawing of a lighthouse issuing two beams, with the names of the magazine's contributors printed down its column. Accessible at <https://monoskop.org/Le_Phare_de_Neuilly> [accessed 1 March 2020].
14. Xavier Rey notes that the layout of one text per page becomes progressively less rigid. See his brief entry, 'Céline Arnauld: *Projecteur*', in *Dada*, exhibition catalogue, 5 October 2005–9 January 2006 (Paris: Éditions Centre Pompidou, 2005), p. 88.
15. Stéphane Mallarmé's views on the column of the printed page as monotonous and almost tyrannical, especially in newspapers, are pertinent here. See Stéphane Mallarmé, 'Le Livre: instrument spirituel', in *Œuvres complètes*, ed. by Bertrand Marchal, 2 vols, Bibliothèque de la Pléiade (Paris: Gallimard, 1998–2003), II, 373–82.
16. Dunan wrote under a dozen or so pseudonyms, as well as her own name. She produced writing in genres including science fiction and erotic literature.
17. Disappointingly Dermée omits Dunan from his list.
18. The English translation offered in *The Dada Reader*, ed. by Ades, p. 250, is: '*Tzara* is never, never, never in a brown study'. I have given my own since this does not convey the idiomatic meaning of the phrase.
19. See *The Dada Reader*, ed. by Ades, pp. 251–52, for an English translation, 'White Coffee'.
20. An English translation of 'Luna Park' by Ian Monk appears in *The Dada Reader*, ed. by Ades, pp. 250–51, and my own in *Burning City*, ed. by Rasula and Conley, p. 238, that I am using here. Kamenish produces another, in *Mamas of Dada*, pp. 85–87, together with a close reading. 'Les Ronge-Bois' is also reprinted together with an English translation, 'The Wood-Gnawers', in *The Dada Market*, ed. by Bohn, pp. 16–17, used here, and another version by Hayden, in 'Céline Arnauld: Six Poems Translated by Sarah Hayden', pp. 150–51.
21. Kamenish, *Mamas of Dada*, p. 87.
22. For more detailed analysis see Forcer, *Dada as Text, Thought and Theory*, p. 28.
23. André Breton, 'Max Ernst', in *Œuvres complètes*, ed. by Marguerite Bonnet, 4 vols, Bibliothèque de la Pléiade (Paris: Gallimard: 1988–2008), I, 245; *What is Surrealism? Selected Writings*, trans. by Franklin Rosemont (New York: Pathfinder, 1978), pp. 8–9.
24. Goll, 'Manifeste du surréalisme'.
25. See Barnet for similarly assertive conclusions about Deharme ('To Lise Deharme's Lighthouse', p. 325).

CHAPTER 7

Battles with Breton: 'Les Faux Managers' (1924) and Projectivism

Je ne veux aucun maître.¹

[I want no master.]

Journals and reviews have been our focus in this section on Arnauld's collaborations. Their vibrant, unmediated history of the avant-garde allows us as readers to experience something of the passion, immediacy, and invention of the Parisian literary scene in the 1920s with its amorphous groupings. As Hubert Juin puts it:

> Nul ne peut prendre une exacte mesure des mouvements d'hier, des propositions qui se firent, des sursauts qui eurent lieu, de l'étrange mélange de ce qui est occupé à se faire avec ce qui se fait, sans recourir à ces documents fondamentaux que sont les publications collectives.²
>
> [No one can get an exact measure of the movements of yesterday, the propositions that were made, the leaps that took place, the strange mix of who was getting up to what, without returning to the fundamental documents that are collective publications.]

As Dada began to disintegrate in Paris, and as notorious leadership disagreements between Picabia and Tzara, Picabia and Breton, and then between Tzara and Breton intensified, many individual writers and artists struggled with their allegiances to one or other figure. Arnauld was no exception. She demonstrated her allegiance to Picabia by collaborating with him on his July 1921 pamphlet *Le Pilhaou-Thibaou*, an expression of his schism with both Tzara and Breton. On 25 February 1922, she attended a meeting at the Closerie des Lilas arranged by Albert Gleizes, to support the resolution against the Congress that backed Tzara in the face of Breton's attack on him. Her name appears, indelibly, on Picabia's subsequent pamphlet *La Pomme de pins*.³

Far from dissipating, her antipathy towards Breton would become more pronounced over the next couple of years, becoming evident — publicly, passionately, and in print — in late 1924. *Le Mouvement accéléré* [The Accelerated Movement], a tract produced by Dermée, appeared in November 1924. It included texts by Erik Satie, Picabia, Goll, René Crevel, François Kupka (aka František or Frank), Vincente Huidobro, Ribemont-Dessaignes, and Arnauld. The publication was a weapon in the battleground to gain control and lead the next front of the avant-garde in Paris, with Dada in retreat and Surrealism on the advance. Dermée was at war with Breton. Arnauld's contribution, 'Les Faux Managers' [The False Managers] (*OC*, pp. 450–51), is a lengthy, unadulterated criticism of the surrealist leader.

Her inference that Breton considered himself a deity was scarcely subtle in the following iconoclastic claim:

> Le Christ, qui était un vrai poète et qui a fait des miracles parce que certains de ses admirateurs ont voulu qu'il en ait fait, était aussi surréaliste. Et avant lui, Dieu, et avant Dieu, les animaux et les arbres et les astres, et peut-être d'autres avant eux. (*OC*, p. 450)

> [Christ, who was a true poet, and who performed miracles because some of his admirers wanted him to, was also surrealist. And before him God, and before God the animals and the trees and the stars, and perhaps others before them.]

Arnauld's rebuke to Breton is that a surrealist way of thinking existed before it was 'invented' by the group and can be found in nature and in antiquity. Without a doubt her objection was to Breton's tendency to accept certain poets as legitimate and to reject others as insufficiently surrealist.

If there were any doubt as to her specific target, she continues, 'M. André Breton votre corbeille de précurseurs surréalistes était-elle donc si pleine que vous avez oublié ceux-là? Vous voulez substituer le mot surréalisme au mot poésie, mais la poésie est vaste et ce mot sous vos doigts s'effrite déjà' [Mr André Breton, was your basket of surrealist precursors so full that you forgot these? You want to substitute the word Surrealism for poetry, but poetry is vast, and the word is already crumbling in your fingers] (*OC*, p. 450). Decrying what she sees as Breton's selective neglect of precursors to Surrealism and his will to over-define a new poetics, she suggests that the term's profundity and the movement's longevity were already in doubt.

In the next paragraph Arnauld metaphorically sharpens the knife, making the following attack:

> Serait-ce au cours d'un de vos sommeils 'merveilleux' qu'une puissance occulte est venue vous dicter que tel et tel n'existent pas? Serait-ce au cours de ces rêves où le poète oublie toute réalité que vous faites justice froide d'excommunication? N'êtes-vous pas encore écœuré de toutes ces vieilles histoires? (*OC*, p. 450)

> [Was it during of one of your 'marvellous' naps that an occult power came to tell you that so and so does not exist? Was it during one of these dreams where the poet forgets all reality that you carried out the cold justice of excommunication? Are you not yet sick of all these old stories?]

Turning the great surrealist invention, automatic writing, against its creator and exponent, she criticises what she sees as Breton's selective and exclusive hold on Surrealism — and on poetry — and his lack of acknowledgement of other poets. Her approach constitutes a forceful and impassioned rejection of the policing proposed by Breton, that is his proposals, in his manifestos, to excommunicate those artists and writers who might diverge from the movement's rules. Arnauld's stance brings out the paradox of the surrealist love of free imagination, on the one hand, and the will to authorisation, on the other.

If Dada had inspired Arnauld to adopt the manifesto form in inventive, largely humorous ways, with an edge of critique, in this case it gives way to pure antagonism. Wit is replaced by acerbic satire. 'Faux Managers' is the most vitriolic example of Arnauld's critical work. Where other texts mixed critique and comedy, seriousness and irony, this prose text is an unambiguous declaration of disgust at institutionalisation. As a piece of literature, it lacks the inventiveness and intrigue of Arnauld's other work. It does, though, demonstrate a directness hitherto unseen in her writing.

But there is another element in this text that illuminates the tension between criticism and creativity so prevalent in Dada — and the tension between action and lyricism in Arnauld's work — and which takes us beyond denigration to invention. Arnauld ends her text by announcing her own manifesto. She addresses Breton, 'Malgré vous, [...] il y a une élite qui a fait son choix. C'est à cette élite que j'adresse mon *Manifeste du Projectivisme*' [In spite of you, [...] there is an elite which has made its choice. It is to this elite that I am addressing my *Manifesto of Projectivism*] (OC, p. 450). The term *projectivisme*, introduced in the previous chapter, now becomes a call for a splinter movement.[4] The term 'élite' calls to mind a conception of artists as leaders in a new social order, voiced at the end of the nineteenth century by Henri de Saint-Simon in his vision of an artistic avant-garde. On the other hand, an insistence on art for art's sake was still at the fore of thinking about the role of the artist from the nineteenth century into the twentieth. Should art be pure and free, or at the vanguard of social change? Arnauld's letter to Tzara cited in Chapter 5, with its beacons of lyricism and action, comes to mind.

Although the bold and intriguing 'manifesto' declared in this text remained at the level of a promise, the term *projectivisme* would reappear in print again the following year. The 1924 text 'Diorama' will be more fully discussed in the next chapter but its relevance to the question of Arnauld's ambitions and seriousness of intent is vital here, since *projectivisme* and associated terms pepper the text. In the following passage, for example, there are three instances:

> Alors nous projeterons nos lumières lyriques [...]. Ce sera la vraie révolution mondiale: une révolution projectiviste. [...] Les mains des poètes et des artistes seront aussi nouvelles et fragiles que cette fleur qui est le réveil-matin de l'aurore. Nous ferons toute une chaîne solide, la chaîne projectiviste. (OC, p. 180)

> [Then we will project our lyrical lights [...]. This will be the true world revolution: a projectivist revolution. [...] The hands of poets and artists will be as new and as fragile as the flower that is daybreak's alarm-call. We will all form a solid chain, the projectivist chain.]

Arnauld here employs metaphors from the natural world to conjure up a utopia of writers leading the way to revolution. This echoes Saint-Simon's conception of the avant-garde, with its ideal of social harmony. The visual metaphor of a chain might also be compared to the pyramid conceived by Wassily Kandinsky in his essay 'Concerning the Spiritual in Art', in which artists are posited as the forward-thinking elite.[5]

Meantime, even as Arnauld refutes Surrealism, she refers directly to Freud, the unconscious, the marvellous, and states of dreaming. Her notion of projectivism follows swiftly:

> Le projectivisme dégage le rêve de la lumière sourde d'une lampe mourante et le lance devant lui comme un phare. Les poètes projectivistes marchent sur la réalité sans l'apercevoir, plongent dans leur silence au milieu même d'une assemblée, promènent leur rêve partout comme un éventail de la fantaisie. (*OC*, p. 180)

> [Projectivism releases the dream from the faint light of a dying lamp and launches it in front of itself like a beacon. The projectivist poets march on reality without noticing it, plunge with their silence into the very middle of a gathering, trail their dream everywhere like a fan of fantasy.]

In this extract, electric light is evoked as well as natural light. In other places, birds are invoked symbolically for freedom and travel, yet the opening passage is dominated by the image of the aeroplane. Frequently Arnauld is drawn to the more familiar literary terrain of the natural even as she points to the possibilities of new technologies. That expansiveness is apparent too in her exaltation of both poetry and film, situating her on the cusp of modernity.

In a further layer of intertextual complexity, Arnauld prefaced 'Diorama' with an 'Avertissement aux lecteurs' [Note to Readers] (*OC*, pp. 177–78). Here she discusses her writing and the term 'projectivism' in plainer, more explicit terms. She first acknowledges the specialist nature of her poetry, noting that its appeal is really for those who are interested in 'poésie ultra-moderne'. In so doing she locates herself firmly within the experimental Parisian literary scene. She also, however, makes clear her distance from both Dada and Surrealism:

> Si on voyait tenté de rapprocher maintenant mon inspiration et mon esthétique de celles de certaines écoles modernes qui font quelque bruit aujourd'hui, je prie que l'on considère combien ma poésie est restée elle-même. [...] Je ne voudrais pas que ceux qui ignorent mon œuvre me rattachent arbitrairement à l'un ou à l'autre de ces mouvements. (*OC*, p. 177)

> [If anyone should be tempted now to align my inspiration and my aesthetic to those of certain modern schools that are making the headlines today, I would ask them to consider the extent to which my poetry has remained the same. [...] I would not like those who don't know my work to attach me arbitrarily to one or other of those movements.]

If this declaration smacks of defensiveness, it can be explained in part by the dissolution of Dada and advance of Surrealism. Arnauld shows herself either reluctant, or unable, to align herself with either one of the two dominant avant-garde groups. Written in October 1924, her statement points to a complete disenchantment with Dada which, by this point, had fallen prey to dogma and competition and was ceding the ground to Surrealism, and from which she clearly felt squeezed and marginalised.

Her solution is to revive projectivism:

> Je voudrais que mes lecteurs ne se trompent pas sur ce que j'appelle *Projectivisme*.

Non, c'est ni une école ni un mouvement. C'est une poésie que je prétends unique parce que, rentrée en moi-même, j'ai cherché d'où me vient l'inquiétude, l'amour et la souffrance. Et cette vie profonde que j'ai découverte en moi, je l'ai projetée dans mes œuvres avec toutes ses irisations, tout son imprévu et ce qu'elle peut avoir de déconcertant pour notre raison. Cette 'projection' de notre vie profonde, dans des œuvres, est selon moi la poésie même. (OC, p. 177)

[I would like my readers to make no mistake about what I call *Projectivism*. No, it is neither a school nor a movement. It is poetry that I claim to be unique because, looking deep inside myself, I have sought out the source of my worry, love, and suffering, and I have projected it into my work with all its iridescences, all its unexpectedness and whatever might be disconcerting to our reason. This 'projection' of our innermost life into works is, for me, poetry itself.]

Arnauld's conception of the writer might appear at odds with the anti-romantic and anti-esoteric stance asserted by Dada but it does have something in common with Surrealism, namely its emphasis on the inner workings of the mind, or subconscious, and on the unexpected and disconcerting. It might be more aptly related, though, to a longer trajectory in French poetry. Its emphasis on inner subjectivity, for example, recalls the language and precepts of symbolist poets and that movement's precursors. The extract from Proust (discussed in Chapter 1) also comes to mind. Arnauld's 'worry, love, and suffering' recall the 'thoughts, and feelings, [...] such sad things' described by Proust's narrator. A page earlier, too, he had described the magic lantern, 'Elle substituait à l'opacité des murs d'impalpables irisations, de surnaturelles apparitions multicolores' ('It replaced the opacity of the walls with impalpable iridescences, supernatural multicoloured apparitions').[6] The fact that both Arnauld and Proust use the term *irisation* is striking. We recall, moreover, that Proust also used the term *projection*. Both writers share concerns with perception and expression, evoked through visual metaphors.

In her sketching out of a notion of projectivism in this passage, Arnauld's emphasis is on her identity not only as a modern subject, but as an expressive subject, and in particular as a poet. She uses the verb *projeter* to describe the process of poetic expression. In this respect, her choice calls to mind theories of communication developed by linguists in the early decades of the twentieth century. Ferdinand de Saussure's 'Circuit de la parole', expressed diagrammatically as well as in words, for example, sought to demonstrate the combination of psychological and physical processes involved in any act of communication from one person to another.[7] In his diagram, curved lines drawn from the brain via the mouth represent phonation and audition in a visually comprehensible form, demonstrating the transmission of a 'concept' to 'une image acoustique'. Such analyses of communication coincided with new technologies allowing the transmission of sound waves that were fascinating to the contemporary citizen.

Arnauld was of course interested in the link between thought and written expression. In her communicative model the writer 'projects' her thoughts. If we extrapolate from the notion that the poet projects and take into account references including the title of her journal, we might aptly conceive of the writer as a projector. That concept, I would argue, has something in common with Breton's later concept of writers as 'modestes *appareils enregisteurs*' [modest *recording instruments*].[8] Appearing in his 1924 'Manifeste du surréalisme', it calls on the metaphor of a sound-recording instrument to expound the surrealist notion of automatic writing. The writing subject, in transcribing their thoughts unmediated to paper, is rather a conduit for the expression of the unconscious than a creator. Arnauld's notion, preceding Breton's, has an alternative edge. Instead of sound technology, she evokes the devices and technical apparatus of film. Where Breton establishes a link between hearing and writing, Arnauld points to that between seeing and writing. The word 'projection' implies not so much the communication of words, but the generation of images. Where Breton's human writer is presented as a sound recorder, Arnauld's is a projection machine. Like Breton's recording device, Arnauld's poet-projector is a transmitter. She is the lens, capturing and relaying whatever is happening in the moment. This conceit additionally brings to mind Henri Bergson's early philosophies. In his 1907 essay 'L'Évolution créatrice' [Creative Evolution] Bergson used the language of the cinematic apparatus to articulate how the mind approaches reality. The notion of projection is deployed to express the combination of intellect and intuition employed to apprehend (break down into static frames) and reconstitute what we see in the world.[9] Arnauld's application of the idea to literature is an 'ultra-modern' conceit, in this respect.[10]

Narrative and semantics are disrupted in Arnauld's poetry and prose, with precedence given to the word as material object, to be seen, read, heard, and understood as an 'acoustic image'. Like much avant-garde writing, her texts resist habitual reading strategies, and she draws attention to the role of the reader, not only as reader, but as a listener, and as a viewer. As a modern poet, she seeks to understand what the development and expansion of visual media might mean for individual, writerly expression. In fledgling theories of writing, namely her coining of the term 'projectivism', albeit unpolished and unfinished, she interrogates writing, and the writer, in a theoretical way. If she dismissed Breton, she nonetheless shared some of his concerns. The term seems to have been entirely her own, moreover, unused before her deployment of it, a mark of her independent approach.[11]

Arnauld's manifesto-style texts, analysed in this section of three chapters, demonstrate an affiliation to Dada shot through with a more individual approach. As well as her allegiances to Dada, there are indices of self-declaration that speak to her individual ambition and vision. Far from a linear trajectory, her relationship with Dada was as complex and nuanced as that of her peers. Like them, she was jostling for position and potential. Finally, the tensions between Dada declarations and self-declaration in her work are revealing of one woman's struggle to locate herself and her work against and within a rapidly-changing literary background, where the group provided support and/or excommunication, where literature was to be reviled and/or celebrated, and where the rules were constantly being rewritten. As Juin describes it, 'On invente l'instant à chaque instant. Tous les "ismes" possibles, et quelques autres encore [...] se côtoyent. [...] Rien n'est fixe; tout est mouvant' [The instant was being invented every instant. All possible '-isms', and more besides [...] were mixed up. Nothing was fixed; everything was in motion].[12]

Earlier we read Arnauld's plea that her work should not be confined to one or other movement. Before leaving this exposition of the writer as 'collaborator' it is worth respecting that plea by acknowledging her activities beyond the two poles, now behemoths, of Dada and Surrealism. Relationships at the time were tangled, after all, and networks intriguingly complex and international. Unsurprisingly, perhaps, Arnauld's work appeared not only in journals based in Paris, but in more geographically widespread journals, including several based in central or eastern Europe. One example is *Zenit*, the magazine founded in Yugoslavia by Ljubomir Micić, which ran to forty-three issues. The magazine was the manifestation of Micić's vision, and of the radical, anarchic group of the same name, which drew on aspects of other European avant-garde groups. It sought to overthrow aesthetic conventions but also aspired to effect socio-political change, to reach a 'zenith' of modern life. Even as its aims were sometimes confused and contradictory, its ambition and utopianism were unashamed, and tied closely to the local situation. It proclaimed:

> La revue ZENIT [...] réunit en art tous les ismes ennemis et si proches parents: Futurisme, Cubisme, Purisme, Expressionisme, Dadaïsme, Ultraïsme, e.t.c. ZENIT est internationale et interréligieuse. Etc.'[13]

> [The review ZENIT [...] reunites in art all the enemy -isms that are such close relatives: Futurism, Cubism, Purism, Expressionism, Dadaism, Ultraism e.t.c. ZENIT is international and interreligious. Etc.]

The double use of 'etc' reminds us of a similarly flippant deployment at the end of Arnauld's 'Prospectus *Projecteur*' (Chapter 6). Her affinities with it are more concretely shown by traces of her name. A poem, 'Souffrances d'émail' [Enamel Sufferings], was published in *Zenit*, 24 (1923). The review also advertised her publications between 1922 and 1925.[14]

Other contributions in the 1920s to the list of titles beyond Paris included texts in *Ça ira*, *Het Overzicht*, and *Le Disque vert*, published in Belgium, and *Creación*, based in Madrid. Another journal that clearly crossed borders was *Muba*, a magazine published in Paris in French and Lithuanian. In its first of two issues, from 1928, Arnauld and Dermée appear in a group photograph with its editor Juozas Tysliava (Lithuanian), Aleksander Rafalowski and Henryk Stażewski (Polish), Luigi Russolo (Italian), Michel Seuphor and Georges Vantongerloo (Belgian), Piet Mondrian (Dutch), and Ilarie Voronca (Romanian). The photograph was taken in front of 11 rue des Morillons in the 15th arrondissement of Paris, the building in which Arnauld and Dermée lived at the time, pointing to their roles as networkers.[15] We are reminded of the Dada group photograph in which Arnauld, likewise, was the only woman. In this latter instance the nationalities are more diverse, a sign of this publication's international flavour.[16] Its call for a transnational, interlinguistic, cross-movement and spiritual 'chain' of people reminds us of Arnauld's projectivist chain.[17]

As for the Romanian avant-garde, Arnauld contributed a text 'Les Cordes du rail' [The Railtrack Cords] to a May 1923 issue of *Contimporanul*. This was the start-up of Marcel Janco who had returned to Bucharest having played a significant part in Dada in Zurich, and a publication that kick-started the Romanian avant-garde scene. 'Le Bocage des cygnes' appeared in a successor, *Integral*, 13–14 (1927), edited by Max Herman, together with the sketched portrait of her by Louis Favre that had been published in *L'Apaisement de l'éclipse* in 1925 (Fig. 8.1). This issue was a small anthology of French (or French-speaking) and Romanian poets. Arnauld, interestingly, is included in the French grouping.[18] The spirit of integralism, that is its objective to synthesise all groups and art forms into one modern spirit, might well have been appealing to Arnauld.

Arnauld also collaborated extensively with Dermée on the journal *L'Esprit nouveau*, the review that he co-founded with Amedée Ozenfant and Le Corbusier (aka Charles-Édouard Jeanneret).[19] The extent to which she worked for him, or even wrote as him, is not clear, and that question remains a matter for speculation.[20] It seems likely that her contributions to and assistance with this journal were substantial, given the couple's close relationship. More clearly, a number of reviews were published under her name.[21] For the second issue of November 1920, for example, she wrote a review of Lautréamont's *Les Chants de Maldoror*, a text that was celebrated by many of her peers (*OC*, pp. 405–08). Her range was inclusive, from novels and poetry to spectacles and films. A piece on the circus, 'Le Cirque, art nouveau' (October 1920), demonstrates her interest in this popular venue of thrills as an artform worthy of critical attention (*OC*, pp. 403–05) and, as discussed in Chapter 2, doubtless a source of inspiration for her own work.

Of the greatest import, though, was Arnauld's enthusiasm for film, a passion that has already been discussed in relation to her creative writing, her notions of projectivism, and which also manifests itself in the form of film reviews. For example, in a film review of *The Mark of Zorro* (1920), featuring Douglas Fairbanks, Arnauld demonstrates her appreciation of 'lowbrow' culture. She writes, 'Le cinéma [...] n'est déjà plus un art muet; il réunit tout: visions, images, pathétique, tendresse, lyrisme etc. Tout y est vivant, ardent, actif, comme la jeunesse' [Cinema [...] is no longer a silent art; it brings together everything: visions, images, pathos, tenderness, lyricism etc. Everything in it is alive, ardent, active, like youth].[22] Arnauld embraces film as an art form, listing its multiple qualities. Her words, forward-looking, acknowledge the power of the 'youthful' new art of film, with its multi-sensory possibilities, not least the advent of sound, and its potential to rival literature. That element of comparison is made even more explicit in the next line, 'Le Signe de Zorro est aussi beau qu'un poème en prose. Le drame y est enveloppé d'un voile poétique' [*The Mark of Zorro* is as beautiful as a prose poem. Its drama is wrapped in a poetic veil]. This claim is not even made of an avant-garde or experimental film, but of a commercial film, produced for mass appeal.

These comparisons and contrasts are continued in a second example of a review, this time of Charlie Chaplin's *The Kid* (1921). Arnauld, finds a number of faults with the film, but enthusiastically praises the form once more:

> C'est à des artistes tels que Charlot que le cinéma doit d'être aujourd'hui un art vivant, varié, construit, lyrique, qui ne manque ni d'imagination, ni de spontanéité, ni de traits de psychologie fine et mordante, — enfin capable d'œuvres aussi bien construites qu'un poème ou un roman modernes.[23]

[It is to artists such as Charlie that cinema is indebted for being, today, a living, varied, constructed, and lyrical art, lacking neither imagination, nor spontaneity, nor qualities of fine and biting psychology — finally capable of works as well constructed as a modern poem or novel.]

Her recognition of cinema here extends to equating the power of the medium with that of a modern poem or novel. For a self-proclaimed 'ultra-modern' poet, writing about American cinema, this is praise indeed.

Arnauld's lionising of film is echoed by Benjamin in his essay 'The Work of Art in the Age of Mechanical Reproduction'. Here he points out that film has the possibility to go below the surface of the mimetic tradition, with special effects that are reminiscent of dreams.[24] Dadaists would inevitably build on performance experiments at soirées in cabarets and theatres by embracing film. René Clair's short 1924 film *Entr'acte*, for example, was made for the interval of Picabia's ballet *Relâche*. It features sequences of action that exploit film-making techniques from slow motion to inversion, cropping to *contre-plongée*. Among the cameo appearances by Picabia, Duchamp, Man Ray, and Satie, my colleague Chris Townsend is convinced that Arnauld appears, as one of the crowd in the funeral cortège. From motifs of wheels, lights, processions, coffins, and chess, to techniques of repetition and montage, it can surely be imagined how greatly this would have appealed to her.

Antics by avant-garde film-makers may have been received as esoteric, baffling, inaccessible; those by Chaplin were not. Arnauld was a champion of both. She assesses the audience's role and expectations as follows:

Le public ne veut pas rêver au cinéma; il veut voir des réalités, les vivre et en emporter à la fin du spectacle non pas l'oubli immédiat, mais un souvenir qui entrera dans sa vie comme un rayon qui se poserait sur le bord de sa fenêtre et y resterait éternel et immobile.[25]

[The audience does not want to dream at the cinema; they want to see realities, to live them, and to carry away at the end of the spectacle not immediate forgetting but a memory that will enter into their lives like a ray coming to rest on a window-ledge, to remain there eternal and immobile.]

Her viewer wants a rich, memorable, immersive experience. A view of the artist as connector between imagination and vision, as purveyor of transformational visions, is echoed in the title of a second text on Chaplin, 'Charlot, prince des rêveurs' [Chaplin, Prince of Dreamers], printed in *Documents internationaux de l'Esprit nouveau* in 1927 (*OC*, p. 402).

Arnauld praises Chaplin in both reviews, printed six years apart. The first, though unhesitating in its praise of the actor, is critical of certain aspects of *The Kid*. Blaming high expectations, in part, for her disappointment, she also criticises the sentimentality of a plot contrived to show that Chaplin, in saving a child, can also be tender and capable of paternal feeling. Although convinced by his performance, she sees this as a corny device. It is the fact that he is human and fallible (his first reaction is to dispose of the child), rather than humanitarian and sentimental (his redemptive actions), that renders him so convincing and pertinent.

Further criticisms include her dislike of the dream sequences, and aversion to the denouement in which the child's mother is shown to be deserted and in dire straits, a plot she describes as 'ce morceau détestable de roman feuilleton' [a detestable morsel of a popular novel]. These points show Arnauld to be an incisive rather than infatuated reviewer.

This second text is less a critical review than a celebration, an ode to Chaplin's expressive skills and to the ways in which he represents so many emotions and experiences for the viewer. The form of the text mimics an elegy with its lilting, lyrical build-up of qualities, 'Charlot violoniste, Charlot poète, Charlot chien, Charlot mondain' [Charlie the violinist, Charlie the poet, Charlie the dog, Charlie the worldly]. When Arnauld writes 'Charlot est l'ami de ceux qui comme lui ouvrent grands les yeux sur la vie, de ceux à qui l'angoisse et le doute ont tenu lieu de sommeil' [Charlie is the friend of those who like him open their eyes wide to life, of those for whom anguish and doubt have taken the place of sleep], she both captures the poignancy of his performances and suggests a heartfelt empathy with her own struggles as outsider and poet. Vocabulary describing him as persecuted, as a vagabond, and as a sleepwalker is recurrent in her later poetry, as we will see in the third part of this book.

Arnauld's appreciation for Chaplin was shared by many other avant-garde artists, such identification amply described by her words 'Charlot est le frère des révoltés, des grands âmes libres et fières' [Charlie is the brother of those who revolt, of great souls who are free and proud].[26] In homing in on certain elements the text is also apt to the aims of any creative artist but with arguable links to Surrealism. Phrases including 'superbe d'inconscience' [sublimely unaware], 'des merveilles de rêve' [marvels of dreams], and 'langage des illuminés, langage de la passion' [language of the inspired, language of passion], demonstrate the reasons for her own identification with him. In both texts, she also highlights the role of comedy, behind which are often more profound messages and sentiments. The 'fou du peuple' connects with the Dada will to see through so-called idiocy to wisdom. As Tzara writes, 'Dada travaille avec toutes ses forces à l'instauration de l'idiot partout' ('Dada is working with all its might towards the universal installation of the idiot').[27]

This prescient understanding of the power of film and popular culture came at a time when some were deriding the new medium. It is notable, too, that Arnauld embraces American culture, rather than rejecting it, as was the tendency of many at that time. In film, it seems, she saw a way out of the deadlock of the literary academy. Dermée, by now, was establishing a career in radio, a source of much-needed finance and doubtless impact.[28] Both evidently foresaw the appeal of new technologies and communications with mass appeal. Rather than retreat, threatened, they actively engaged with these new possibilities.

In 1927 Dermée published the magazine *Les Documents internationaux de l'Esprit nouveau* with Michel Seuphor, reviving and amending the title he had edited with Ozenfant and Le Corbusier up until 1925.[29] Arnauld contributed three texts to this publication, that is the review discussed above, and two poems that would later be included in *Le Clavier secret*, 'Avion' [Aeroplane] and Les Tournois du vent'

[Wind Contests] (*OC*, pp. 256, 261). Book publications by Arnauld, Dermée, and Seuphor are gathered and publicised with a note underneath in large, bold type, 'ces poètes se distinguent en ceci qu'ils n'ont été recueillis dans aucune anthologie de la poésie moderne' [these poets are distinguished by not having been collected in any anthology of modern poetry]. It is stinging humour, with maybe just a hint of bitterness.

On its first page this new review, which ran only to one issue owing to financial constraints, calls for 'Un seul esprit nouveau mondial — décentralisation' [A single new world spirit — decentralisation]. A list of geographical centres below, as well as a page which humorously advertises a visit of Paris, with thirteen languages and 'toutes les autres langues sur commande' [all other languages to order], remind us of aspirations by Dermée, Arnauld, and others to cross national boundaries. A desire for internationalism was coupled at this point with a will to escape the -isms, also listed on the front page, which, for some, had become alternately suffocating, limiting, or unfriendly.

In these three chapters I have traced a trajectory of Arnauld's affiliations via primary publications. The process has been revealing. Finding, looking at, and reading her texts in their original material context, in journals, is vital even where anthologies exist. It is an important, active counterpoint to the necessarily historicised summaries of the avant-garde that can result in thinned-down and ossified versions of a fertile diversity. As Juin states, 'Pour échapper à une sclérose dommageable, il faut sans cesse en revenir à ces miroirs que j'ai dits: les revues, les journaux et les feuilles diverses. Là, et là seulement, l'aventure se démasque et se saisit au vif' [To avoid damaging sclerosis, we must return again and again to these mirrors of which I have spoken: to diverse reviews, journals and pamphlets. There, and there alone, the adventure is revealed and most keenly grasped].[30] Proceeding in this way has permitted revelations about the activities of Arnauld that had lain dormant.

Arnauld and Dermée appeared to share feelings of being outside a centre. Their projects, post-Dada, looked increasingly to collaborations beyond the expected and in which they might find belonging. Following the demise of *L'Esprit nouveau* they would both be heavily involved in the Brussels-based *Le Journal des Poètes* in the 1930s, for example. One of the taglines for that journal is in keeping with Arnauld's inclusive approach to poetry, '*Le Journal des Poètes* ne défend pas une poésie; il defend la poésie' [*Le Journal des poètes* does not defend one poetry; it defends all poetry].[31] Indeed her battles with Breton, seemingly at least partially informed by that spirit, continued there. A rare but exhilarating note by José Pierre suggests this, at least, 'Plus vraisemblablement, l'idée d'un *Journal des Poètes* aura paru bouffonne à Breton et à ses amis et quelques-uns des noms du sommaire — par exemple celui de Céline Arnauld [*sic*] — contribueront à stimuler une verve exclusivement ordurière du plus bas niveau' [Most likely the idea of a *Journal des poètes* would have seemed farcical to Breton and his friends and some of the names in the summary — for example Céline Arnauld — would contribute to the stimulation of an eloquence of pure filth of the lowest order].[32]

From reviews to radio Arnauld and Dermée continued to seek a community of writers in the 1920s and 1930s. Certainly Arnauld's career as both a collaborator and a poet was far from over. In the next 'post-Dada' era she would go on to publish another five volumes of poetry, as well as be honoured by an anthology issued by the supportive Pierre-Louis Flouquet and his *Cahier du Journal des poètes*. That prolific and evolving single-authored output will be sketched out in the next section. It takes us from 1923, which I will set up as a turning-point for Arnauld, to 1948. Unsurprisingly, given the political upheavals to come, this period would prove to be both tumultuous and productive.

Notes to Chapter 7

1. Céline Arnauld, 'Avertissement aux lecteurs' (*OC*, p. 178).
2. Hubert Juin, 'Préface', in *Documents internationaux de l'Esprit nouveau*, ed. by Paul Dermée and Michel Seuphor, repr. with a preface by Hubert Juin (Paris: J. M. Laplace, 1997), p. 1.
3. For a detailed account of these events and publications see Sanouillet, *Dada à Paris*, pp. 280–304.
4. Dermée also announced *le Panlyrisme*, another short-lived attempt at seizing control.
5. Wassily Kandinsky, 'Concerning the Spiritual in Art', in *Art in Theory 1900–1990: An Anthology of Changing Ideas*, ed. by Charles Harrison and Paul Wood (Oxford & Cambridge, MA: Blackwell, 2001), pp. 87–94; first published as 'Über das Geistige in der Kunst' in 1911.
6. Proust, *Du côté de chez Swann*, p. 16; *In Search of Lost Time*, p. 13.
7. Ferdinand de Saussure, *Cours de linguistique générale* (Paris: Payot, 1972); a lecture series delivered between 1907 and 1911 and first published in 1916.
8. Breton, *Manifestes du surréalisme*, p. 39.
9. Henri Bergson, *L'Évolution créatrice* (Paris: Alcan, 1917).
10. Today we are also aware of the manifesto 'Projective Verse' (1950) by the American poet Charles Olson. In his theory of 'composition by field' he articulated an energy between source, poet, and text, advocated open verse as opposed to received structure, and prioritised sound over sense in creating form and syntax. Usually seen as a bridge between Ezra Pound and William Carlos Williams, its connections with ideas voiced by Arnauld surely deserve further reflection.
11. Martin-Schmets points to the use of *projectif*, but only much later, by Emmanuel Monnier, *Traité du caractère* (1946), and Jean-Paul Sartre, *Les Mots* (1964) ('Céline Arnauld, épouse Paul Dermée, poète dadaïste', p. 179).
12. Juin, 'Préface', p. 2.
13. *Zenit*, 12 (March 1922), 11. For reprints see <https://monoskop.org/Zenit> [accessed 1 March 2020].
14. This issue is erroneously listed as 'number 23 (September 24)' (*OC*, p. 153). The volumes that were listed in *Zenit* are: *Point de mire*, 12 (1922); *Guêpier de diamants*, 25 (1924); and *L'Apaisement de l'éclipse*, 36 (1925). I was alerted to these references by Irina Cărăbaş, a scholar of the Romanian avant-garde. I will discuss 'Souffrances d'émail' in Chapter 8.
15. The photograph is reproduced with this information in Michel Seuphor and others, *Une vie à angle droit* (Paris: Éditions de la Différence, 1988), p. 312.
16. Other contributors to this first issue included Huidobro, the Chilean editor of *Créacion*, and the Russian Kasimir Malewicz.
17. Juozas Tysliava, 'Marche contre la terre', *Muba*, 1 (1928), 3. Consulted in the BnF.
18. This instance of publication is not noted in *OC*. I am grateful, again, to Irina Cărăbaş.
19. The journal ran to twenty-eight issues between 1920 and 1925 and supported the publication of books, including some by Arnauld. Dermée left following differences with his colleagues, before reviving the magazine for a one-off edition. For a recent account see Dell, 'After Apollinaire'. See also Roxana Vicovanu, 'L'Esprit nouveau et les avant-gardes', in *Les Oubliés des Avant-Garde*, ed. by Meazzi and Madou, pp. 103–22. Other publishing projects by Dermée were *Interventions*, which ran to two issues (December 1923 and January 1923), and *La Revue mosane* (October 1908 to 1910; January 1929 to January 1931).

20. See Martin-Schmets, 'Céline Arnauld, épouse Paul Dermée, poète dadaïste', pp. 176–82, for some speculative notes on the nature of their collaborations, from claims that he used her name for his own ventures, to suggestions that she mainly worked on his behalf. Finally, he concludes the article with his conviction that the poetry in her name is unmistakeably hers but that she might have assisted him in his radio journalism (p. 182).
21. See the Bibliography for Arnauld's many contributions to these journals, only a few of which are touched upon here.
22. Céline Arnauld, 'Cinéma: *Le Signe de Zorro*', *Action*, 10 (November 1921), [n.p.] (*OC*, pp. 395–96). She was not alone in her admiration for Fairbanks of course. For a poem see Jean Epstein, 'Douglas Fairbanks', in *Burning City*, ed. by Rasula and Conley, pp. 215–16. I am grateful to Jennifer Wild for first drawing my attention to Arnauld's film reviews at a conference in 2006.
23. Céline Arnauld, 'Cinéma: *Le Gosse*', *Action,* hors série (December 1921), [n.p.] (*OC*, pp. 393–95).
24. Benjamin, *Illuminations*, pp. 211–44.
25. Arnauld, 'Cinéma: *Le Gosse*'.
26. For a section of thirteen texts dedicated to Chaplin by writers as diverse as Alexander Rodchenko, Guillermo de Torre, and Benjamin, see *Burning City*, ed. by Rasula and Conley, pp. 432–47. They include three sections relating to film entitled 'Cineland'.
27. From his 1920 'Dada manifeste sur l'amour faible et l'amour amer' [Dada Manifesto of Feeble and Bitter Love]. See Tzara, *Dada est tatou: tout est dada*, p. 231; *Seven Dada Manifestos and Lampisteries*, p. 42.
28. Martin-Schmets notes his participation in the first radio newspaper on 3 November 1923 ('Céline Arnauld, épouse Paul Dermée, poète dadaïste', p. 174).
29. For a full reprint see *Documents internationaux de l'Esprit nouveau*, ed. by Dermée and Seuphor, [n.p.]. The preface by Juin, cited earlier, gives an introduction to this magazine, the history of *L'Esprit nouveau* before it, and a lively exposition of the context of Parisian journals.
30. Juin, 'Préface', p. 1.
31. The *Journal des poètes* was a long-running journal from 4 April 1931 led by the poet and painter Pierre-Louis Flouquet. Original issues from 1931 and 1932, consulted in the BnF, list 'Arnaud' [sic] as a member of the 'Comité de lecture'. For authored contributions see the Bibliography. For an account see Laurent Béghin and Hubert Roland, 'La Première Série du *Journal des Poètes* (1931–1935) de Pierre-Louis Flouquet et son réseau de médiateurs', *Textyles*, 52 (2018), 93–110.
32. José Pierre, *Tracts surréalistes et déclarations collectives* (Paris: Le Terrain vague, 1980), p. 451.

PART III

Writing beyond Dada

Fig. 8.1. Portrait of Céline Arnauld by Louis Favre, in *L'Apaisement de l'éclipse, passion en deux actes; précédé de 'Diorama', confession lyrique* (Paris: Écrivains réunis, 1925)

CHAPTER 8

The Lyric Traveller: Longing and Belonging in *Guêpier de diamants* (1923) and 'Diorama' (1925)

> Je suis isolée au milieu de ma rêverie comme dans une plaine sans fin.[1]
> [I am isolated in the midst of my reverie as in an endless plain.]

Arnauld's uneasy alliances with the avant-garde groups of the early 1920s have been laid bare in Part II. In a number of texts for collaborative journals, including a manifesto, she promoted Dada loudly and clearly.[2] By the time of her 'Avertissement aux lecteurs', however, from which the line above is taken, she appeared to be taking a step back from group dynamics. As early as 1924 she was showing an acute awareness of her situation and remarkable foresight about her legacy. In pleading against being annexed to a group, she offers a warning not only to contemporary critics but also to future scholars. As Forcer puts it, 'if we assess the literary contribution of women writers to canonical homosocial Dada we run the risk of inadvertently legitimizing the self-selecting male hierarchy that was directly and indirectly complicit in their marginalization'.[3] Arnauld's journal *Projecteur*, I argue, represented a concerted transition in the direction of independence. She demonstrated close links to her peers in her inclusion of their texts but, in testing out a new project with a new concept, she made manifest a will to innovate. Her subsequent reactions to Breton, moreover, were unambiguous. Her text 'Faux Managers' counts as the most explicit and prosaic of any of her writings and rules out any alignment with the surrealist group.

Overt articulations either of her attachments or her ambitions are relatively scarce. They grant us valuable, albeit diffuse insights into her motivations. But questions of belonging, more broadly, are without a doubt a stalwart of many of her poetic narratives. It is that feature of her writing that I want to bring out in this chapter. Movement is frequently present, with individuals (sometimes vagabonds) or troupes (often cortèges) setting out on journeys of discovery. The journeys conveyed can be actual, across water, for example, with boats a recurring motif. The question of flight, too, is dominant. This is evoked by the motif of aeroplanes in the man-made, modern environment, and by insects and birds in the natural world. In Chapter

4 we considered a preoccupation with the edges of things, with in-betweenness, and liminal spaces. That applies to real or imagined environments, to the borders of villages, to the horizon, and to the shoreline. These are encountered alternately as barriers and obstacles, or as restrictions to be refused, and limits to be traversed.

Journeys may also be metaphorical; they are remembered from the past, imagined in the present, or projected into the future. The traveller is on a quest of discovery, seeking security or stillness, love or belonging, but above all liberty of expression. The figure of the poet is evoked, perhaps even the figure of this poet. The *flâneur*, observing and reading the city, is a familiar focus in modernist literature, first proposed so eloquently by Baudelaire.[4] But they are in a relatively carefree, privileged position that scarcely applies to the journeys signalled in Arnauld's writing. Rather, the notion of the outsider is relevant here; of someone always travelling, never settling, sometimes stung by rejection, criticism, or even persecution. Given Arnauld's émigré status the possibilities of biographical readings are undeniable. Diaspora was a feature of experience for Romanian Jews, to whom citizenship was granted only in 1923. Paris offered an escape but a necessarily complicated one. Monica Spiridon has underscored how, from the nineteenth century onwards, for many Romanian writers, 'the French metropolis became the starting point of a tortuous process of cultural projection'. Coining the term 'the Romanian Paris', she reflects on the French capital as a nexus of identification, with heterogeneous perceptions and experiences occupying spaces between myth and memory, fiction and reality.[5] Sjöberg, more recently, specifically tackles the context of the early twentieth-century avant-garde. He draws out transnationalism as a particular feature of Romanian Jewish francophone writers, one that seeks to exceed dichotomies in favour of nuance and ambivalence.[6] As we move through the two objects of study in this chapter, *Guêpier de diamants* and 'Diorama', we will see similarly complex instances of longing and belonging, across shifting time and unspecified spaces, as key areas of enquiry and emotion played out in Arnauld's writing. We will also consider how her border-crossing in terms of language, nationality, and culture feeds experiments in form and language.[7]

Guêpier de diamants [Diamond Trap], was published in 1923. Both timing and geography set it apart from Arnauld's first three volumes discussed in Part I of this study. Where these were published in Paris, in 1919, 1920, and 1921, this book was printed by the Belgian publishing house *Ça ira*. Based in Antwerp, it was headed up by Clément Pansaers, who had split from Dada in 1921. The book is made up of twenty-three texts, sixteen of which would be chosen for Arnauld's 1936 anthology. Additionally, six appeared in journals. They were: 'Chevaux de frise' [Chevaux-de-frise], *Bleu*, 3 (January 1921); 'La Lyre des toits' [The Lyre of the Rooftops], *Les Images de Paris*, 40 (April 1923); 'Les Cordes du rail' [The Railtrack Cords], *Contimporanul*, 41 (6 May 1923); 'Cavatine de marées' [Cavatina of Tides], *Het Overzicht*, 16 (May-June 1923); and 'Souffrances d'émail' [Enamel Sufferings], *Zenit*, 24 (May 1923). The selection of journals demonstrates already a diversification in Arnauld's affiliations and an expansion of her reach. The Dada titles are gone. Of the four titles cited here, only the first was based in Paris. The others were published in the former Yugoslavia (Belgrade), Belgium, and Romania. Arnauld, it seems, was extending her contacts across Europe.

Guêpier de diamants is designated by its author as 'poèmes' but as many as half are laid out like prose. We are reminded of Artaud's review of Arnauld, cited in Chapter 4, 'Avant tout, Céline Arnauld ne fait pas de littérature' [After all, Céline Arnauld does not do literature].[8] Instead Arnauld does literature, it seems, in any way she pleases. These texts are too short to be considered stories in a conventional sense and, in general, resist a clear narrative structure, with attendant characters, description, progression, and plot. In short, they do not adhere to expectations of fictional narrative. Neither, however, do they conform to some of the conventions of verse, in that the majority are not organised in stanzas, but rather as blocks of text. In either case, prose or poetry, the reader's expectation of semantic coherence is challenged, with linguistic freedom assigned the upper hand. Arnauld's citation of Friedrich Nietzsche as an epigraph sets the mood for pushing boundaries of language and imagination, 'Ainsi, moi aussi, je jetai mon illusion par-delà les hommes, pareil à tous les hallucinés de l'arrière monde. Par-delà les hommes, en vérité!' ('Thus I too once cast my delusion beyond the human, like all believers in a world behind. Beyond the human, in truth!').[9]

The title of the volume is typically perplexing yet generative. The literal sense of 'guêpier' is a wasp's nest. It can also mean a tricky situation or tight corner. The addition of 'diamants' turns something potentially threatening into a treasure trove. Both wasps and diamonds will recur as symbolic elements. Both are naturally-occurring elements that take on different resonance in relation to the human being, the former conventionally perceived as a threat, the latter co-opted as a symbol of wealth. As a book this 'Diamond Trap' harnesses and celebrates extraordinary new riches in the form of unexpected combinations of words and ideas. A review by the poet Frédéric Saisset reflects the book's qualities of surprise and reward. Referring to the book as 'son voyage dans la forêt de son Inconscient' [her voyage into the forest of her unconscious], he points to 'des images imprévues' [unforeseen images] and 'des rapprochements des mots inouïs' [the bringing together of unheard words]. Continuing his metaphor of a journey of revelation, and stimulated by the imagery in the book, he likens her process to the seemingly random discovery of precious stones plundered from an expanse of water.[10]

Recurring vocabulary and imagery thread their way through this set of texts, on the one hand gaining familiarity, on the other continually reinvented. Even in the titles of its component texts we can trace pathways. Thus 'Terrasse des songes' [Terrace of Musing] is followed by 'Travaux songeux' [Pensive Works]. Dreaming and reflection are foregrounded in the term *songe*, the French encapsulating creative brain activity either when sleeping or awake. 'Le Musicien des marées' [The Musician of the Tides] is echoed by 'Cavatine de marées' [Cavatina of Tides], itself a return on the earlier 'Cavatine de velours' [Cavatina of Velvet], and the latter a reminder of 'Le Velours de l'espace [The Velvet of Space]. Titles are shot through with music and musing, tides and time. We cannot be surprised, either, to see titles that project us backwards, 'Les Claires-voies du sommeil' [The Openwork of

Sleep], and forwards, 'L'Apaisement de l'éclipse' [The Appeasement of the Eclipse], in Arnauld's trajectory of book titles.

The title of a first text chosen for discussion, 'Dévidoir des songes' [Skein-Winder of Dreams], takes its place in this network of connections (OC, pp. 158–59). The word *songe*, we noted above, is a term that recurs in the collection. A *dévidoir* is a skein-winder, a wooden tool used to wind yarn. The framework-like structure ties in with Arnauld's strong visual motif of openwork structures. More specifically it might bring to mind the nest of this volume's title. The reader is drawn to notions of creative production, both the manual manipulation of material threads, and the mental crafting of thoughts and words. The fact that the text takes as its protagonist a carter ('roulier'), adds another dimension to this notion of the fabrication of a structure from component parts.

Set out in ten paragraphs, this text is as near to a narrative as Arnauld gets, seemingly relating a conflict between staying and leaving, stasis and escape. Nevertheless, the action proceeds only gropingly, and a story emerges through a slow build-up of connections. Our starting-point is a standalone sentence, 'Les mensonges des poètes déroutent les rêves des rouliers' [Poets' lies change the course of carters' dreams]. It introduces a dilemma between imagination, encouraged and peddled by poets, and reality, embodied in the worker. The environment, too, suggests the threshold of adventure, as the reader is presented with 'la portée crépuscule de la ville' [the crepuscular span of the town]. The town seems unformed, uncertain, on the cusp of time and space. Its inhabitants 'tissent des portées de secours d'une demeure à l'autre' [weave emergency exits from one dwelling to the next]. The verb *tisser*, here, ties in with the skein-winder of the title; the notion of emergency exits suggests a preparedness to leave at any time. The place is disorienting. Towns, now plural, are described as an endlessly turning carousel, accompanied by music that is as haunting as plain-song and as relentless as sniggering ('ricanement'). Skewed and hostile, it is reminiscent of an expressionist painting. The road, on the other hand, tempts and invites, 'La route ouvre ses bras nobles au voyageur' [the road opens its noble arms to the traveller].

It is not until the fifth paragraph that the carter beings to crystallise as a character, 'Chassé par la ville [...], le roulier a quitté la ville et sûr de sa majesté native est allé dominer la route de la fortune, où les maisons n'ont pas encore écrasé de leur poids l'audace du soleil' [Chased away by the townspeople [...], the carter quit the town and sure of his native majesty went to win over the road of fortune, where the weight of the houses had not yet crushed the sun's audacity]. The narrative makes the reader think of the fortune-seeking journeys of fairy-tale or mythical heroes, setting out alone, on a quest for a better life. In this case, moreover, the protagonist is motivated to leave not only by the tug of his imagination but also by the hostility of his neighbours. And where the hero more usually sets out towards the city to find himself, in this instance the unpopulated countryside is posited as an untainted place in which to reflect. There one can experience the magical spectacle of the rural; woodland enlivened by insects and birds, resounding with melody and music. Here is a place of visions and escape, offering possibilities for revelation.

A sudden change occurs, however, in this environment, 'Mais il y a un moment où l'homme, et toute cette usine d'insectes et de plantes, retiennent leur souffle' [But there is a moment when the man, and this whole factory of insects and plants, holds its breath]. The word 'usine' startles the reader from their romantic, pastoral stupor. References to telegraph wires and rail tracks amplify the built environment and encroach on the rural. The final paragraph offers a climax, signalled succinctly as 'Conséquence étrange' [Strange Consequence]. Nerves jangling, the carter lights a cigarette. In one sense banal, this gesture nevertheless encompasses a fantastic quality. The cigarette is lit on a star; the lyres of the hubbub of insects and birds still tremble. And it proves to be one small step from the harmonious possibilities of the countryside to the town, from the cigarette to 'la fumée des villes' [the smoke of towns]. The motif of smoke in Apollinaire's work comes to mind. In the calligram 'Paysage' [Landscape], for example, rising smoke is enacted verbally and visually in the phrase 'Un cigare allumé qui fume' ('A lighted cigarette that smokes'), the words drifting up the page like cigarette smoke.[11] The four iconic elements so powerfully set out in Apollinaire's poem — a house, tree, human, and smoke — are echoed in Arnauld's poem. The smoke suggests transformation, here signalled clearly as a metamorphosis. In the light of his briar cigarette the scene shifts, the carter perceives pain, reproach, and pity. He turns back to the town, described as an immense furnace opening ahead of him. The ending is unequivocally doom-laden, 'Et des gazouillements railleurs l'escortent, et cinglent sa volonté jusqu'à l'anéantissement' [And a mocking twitter escorts him, and lashes his will to oblivion]. Escape, it transpires, was temporary, dreams thwarted.

This text can indubitably be read through the lens of the alienating effects of modern life so vital to the modernist arts. The gaze and judgement of others is keenly evoked. The urban environment provides only a suspicious and fearful community. The natural world offers some sanctuary but to a limited extent, the human still the interlocuter whose demons, both internal and external, accompany them. More specifically we are bound to think of the migrant's experience, the outsider in a place that is foreign to them and to which they are foreign or other.[12] Finally, there is the perception of the maker as misunderstood outsider, living or working on the margins. Autobiographical or not, the reflections are apparent, and the resulting loneliness, the metaphorical endless plain described in the epigraph to this chapter, is manifestly painful.

A mental state of in-betweenness is often elaborated, in Arnauld's work, via spatial and temporal shifts. Another example, 'Souffrances d'émail' [Enamel Sufferings] (*OC*, p. 153), describes nocturnal experience, evoking differing, intense emotions felt in the uncertain hours between nightfall and daybreak. That state is described powerfully thus, 'Tout au fond de ma tristesse s'entrechoquent de grands mouvements de clair-obscur et de claire-joie' [At the very depth of my sadness clash great movements of twilight and joylight]. Arnauld's reworking of the prefix *clair-* is familiar by now, not least from her first volume of poetry *Poèmes à claires-voies* (Chapter 3). The half-revelation expressed by the term 'clair-obscur' is here echoed in the neologism 'claire-joie'. Joy remains semi-glimpsed, beyond full reach. Collage has been discussed as a literary technique within individual poems. Increasingly we see evidence of the poems themselves forming a collage, with repetitions facilitating connections for the reader from poem to poem and even book to book. The effect is cumulative, with repeated terms triggering different, layered associations.

'Souffrances d'émail' permits itself to be read as autobiographical in a way that is resisted by many of Arnauld's poems because they omit personal pronouns. Here, the plural 'nous' of the first two paragraphs is superseded by the singular 'ma tristesse' [my sadness] in the third, and 'ma portée de chagrin' [my scope of grief] in the fifth. Although the sixth includes 'nous' and 'nos', the narrator returns to the singular in the eighth paragraph, 'l'aube chaque fois me surprend' [dawn surprises me every time] and 'ma vie nocturne' [my nocturnal life], before ending with 'ma chanson' [my song] in the ninth and final paragraph. Loneliness and isolation dominate. Sadness is rife. A list of nouns makes the case: 'regret', 'tristesse' [sadness], 'chagrin' [grief], 'blessures' [wounds], 'la brise des cœurs' [hearts breaking], 'cœur blessé' [wounded heart], 'le péril' [peril], and 'la souffrance' [suffering]. This attention to subjectivity and the inner realm of feeling reminds us more of Symbolism than Dada.

In the first paragraph, the metaphor of a boat, travelling the tides ('les marées'), points to a journey. It is doubly described as 'bateau de givre' [ice boat] and 'bateau vert de lune' [green moon boat]. The first description can be read as a play on words, recalling Rimbaud's 1871 poem 'Le Bateau ivre' [The Drunken Boat], the second 'vert de lune' a rhyme with 'clair de lune' [moonlight] preceding it. A striking feature is the presence of glow-worms and silk-worms. They pepper the text, offering creative, natural, hopeful elements. The word *ver* [worm] is conjugated throughout in the plural, as 'vers', and is of course a homonym of 'vert', above. The link with *vers* as a line or verse of poetry or song must surely also be made in the reader's mind. These worms, generating silk and light, surely represent the poet's almost magical creativity. That reading is reinforced by references to music, including 'les guitares' [guitars], 'les pianos mécaniques' [mechanical pianos], 'un adagio de danse' [a dance adagio], and the last words 'ma chanson' [my song]. Light and music oppose the darkness and silence of the night.

Rhyme and assonance are vital drivers. In some cases sound is privileged over semantics. The following line is exemplary of the surprise and newness of the resulting imagery, 'Le ciel envoie son messager de nacre glissant sur ma portée de chagrin, vers le paradis du cassis et des boissons brûlantes et dévorantes comme des blessures' [Heaven sends its mother-of-pearl messenger gliding over my grief's span, towards the paradise of cassis and beverages burning and devouring like wounds]. The relative lack of punctuation; the pure pleasure of a rhyme 'le paradis du cassis'; the alliteration of 'boissons brûlantes' and 'blessures', together with the assonance of 'brûlantes' and 'dévorantes', the latter appearing for a second time in this text, together build an inescapably sensuous feeling of hellish despair. Textures clash, from soft wounds and fruits to the iridescent brittleness of mother-of-pearl and the enamel of the title.

The fantastical, dream-like nature of night is summoned up by vocabulary including 'l'inévitable drame féerique' [the inevitable fairy-tale drama], 'cortège de sortilège' [procession of spells], 'mystères' [mysteries], and 'fantaisies' [fantasies]. The vocabulary of religion is deployed. Terms include 'reposoir' [altar of repose], 'céleste' [heavenly], 'autels' [altars], 'le paradis' [paradise], and 'prière' [prayer]. There are also references to a messenger from heaven, to processions, and to pride and suffering that suggest the rituals and principles of faith. Rationality and logic take a back seat; the bizarre and incongruous are conjured. More broadly, Arnauld's writing refutes the misguided notion of Dada verse as only nonsensical. As Forcer writes, it 'offers not random parades of non-sequiturs but obliquely patterned, involuted *texts* capable of a fundamentally *poetic* compacting of dense cultural allusions or personal statements into singles lines and words'.[13]

In sum, this text is a poignant evocation of night-time anxiety and suffering that moves beyond cliché. Words, placed in new contexts and combinations, have renewed impact. The contrasts and strength of feeling are appropriately evoked by sequences of vocabulary and imagery that give the impression of never having taken place before. Linguistic conflicts and confusions reflect the conceptual wranglings of the experience evoked in the text, where thoughts cannot be arranged logically, and sentiments cannot be rationalised. Structure would be artificial; the system is abandoned. The mind cannot settle. The chinks that feature so often in Arnauld's latticeworks are scarcely apparent here. The narrator's sufferings are enamel. They are opaque not translucent, rigid and brittle.

It is worth lingering over the motif of the diamond, foregrounded in the title of this collection, which shares its name with a first text. Diamonds appear repeatedly in Arnauld's work, the repetition or recycling of this symbolic object typical of her strategies of layering. In this volume alone it is included in nine texts. With its multiple facets it embodies a multitude of perspectives. With its refractions of light, it also links to the focus on light and the visual running throughout her writing. Its combined qualities of solidity and transparency evoke conflicts between assuredness and doubt. A diamond is a precious object, something to yearn for, natural, but adapted and assigned new functions by humans.[14]

A review by Lacaze-Duthiers draws attention to the motif of the diamond as an encapsulation of ideas of travel and enquiry, entrapment and possibility, 'Le *Guêpier* est un voyage à travers l'Europe féerique prisonnière dans un aquarium de diamant. Céline Arnauld fait parler le diamant qui devient humain et pathétique' [*Guêpier* is a voyage across a fairy-tale prisoner Europe in a diamond aquarium. Céline Arnauld makes the diamond speak, rendering it human and pathetic.][15] The reader shares this journey to get to the essence of the object. Not to be understood in one go, it must be studied, looked at and through from every angle.

In 'Guêpier de diamants' (OC, pp. 137–43), the volume's eponymous opening text, the diamond is a central device. This intriguing, fantastical tale of quest and discovery is related by a first-person male narrator. The context is fluid, seemingly timeless; the place ever-shifting, with odd references that seem to offer signposts but evade certainty. The narrator recounts, 'J'ai traversé la fleuve indomptable que le progrès des hommes avait affermi dans son scepticisme, à travers les rires et les chants légendaires des architectes et des constructeurs' [I have crossed the indomitable river that man's progress has strengthened with its scepticism, via the architects' and builders' legendary laughter and song] (p. 138). The mood is one of impermanence and timelessness, as if the narrator were a time traveller through a modernising landscape.

In the narrator's garden there is a 'guêpier de diamants', from which he picks a diamond. This object has powers beyond the imagination which constantly shift, and are of dubious use. It has the power to keep away everyone the protagonist loves, for example. It is also 'le diamant aux souvenirs des caravanes, au souffle pleureur, la fantasmagorie des lyriques et le cynique équilibre!' [the diamond of memories of caravans, of a weeping sigh, the phantasmagoria of lyricists and cynical equilibrium!] (p. 139). It is described, too, as containing ever-changing waters into which the narrator can look and with which he can play. Designated as 'Source de lyrisme pour certains, danger de mort pour d'autres!' [Source of lyricism for some, danger of death for others!], one day it even crumbles in his hands. It had originated in the heart of a butterfly, we learn, 'un véritable bijou rafraîchissant' [a true refreshing jewel], but turns out to be 'faux et vide' [false and empty] (p. 140). Like the mirror in *Tournevire* discussed in Chapter 2, it offers so much magic but is only what it is made to be, what is projected onto it, by human intervention.

The narrator continues his journey of discovery, 'Alors je laissai tomber les rideaux sur les passerelles de tes amours de diamant, at aux sons d'un fanfare dévorant le calme de mes douleurs je m'affranchis' [So I let the curtain fall on the footbridges of your diamond loves, and to the sounds of a fanfare devouring the calm of my sufferings I freed myself]. This is finally a journey of self-discovery, it seems, as the narrator turns to himself instead of looking for others' love, approval, or representations. The final line reads, 'J'avance sans cesse, à travers tes paroles veloutées de brume vers la profondeur de mon cœur' [I carry on unceasingly, through your words softened by mist, towards the depths of my heart] (p. 141).

When this text is reproduced in Arnauld's 1936 anthology, it appears in altered form. The title is changed, from 'Guêpier de diamants' to 'Dialogue lyrique du guêpier'. Where the first version was a continuous piece of text, albeit with some breaks, in this subsequent version different parts are assigned to two speakers, 'lui' and 'elle'. This restructuring produces a quite different text. With one point of view replaced by two we are less certain of its veracity. It also returns us to the vocal over the written, a feature of Arnauld's work that both predates and surpasses her association with the performances of Dada. Two years later, for example, *L'Apaisement de l'éclipse* [The Appeasement of the Eclipse] is introduced on the book's title page as 'Passion en deux actes'.[16]

The complex make-up of this 1925 publication by Arnauld has already been signalled. The dialogue, 'L'Apaisement de l'éclipse', is prefaced by a prose text 'Diorama' which, in turn, is already preceded by an 'Avertissement aux lecteurs'. There is much for the reader to comprehend in negotiating these composite parts. For the Arnauld scholar it promises to be a textual treasure box, not only offering up three different genres of writing, but also potential clues to the author's position, approach, and point of view. Close textual readings of Arnauld's work, both in the context of Dada and beyond, are making it apparent that dismissals of this era of writing as nonsensical and nihilist are inadequate. Forcer is clear on this:

> The fine detail of individual poems presents not a monotonous semantic vacuum but a paradoxical type of writing in which experimental verse ('language dissection') proliferates semantic content in compacted, poetic form, even as it appears to close off meaning through the collapse of conventional linguistic discourse.[17]

Paradoxically, the compressed and dense nature of Arnauld's writing, its accumulation of words pressed tightly together, generates an intensity of potential meanings.

In style, the short text 'Guêpier de diamants' anticipates the longer trajectory outlined in 'Diorama', the text that has been singled out from the start of this study as a structuring device. Both texts are given a date, the first, 17 July 1922, the second, October 1924. Both begin with quotations, the first from Nietzsche, the second from Baudelaire. I would argue that Arnauld's twin employment of dates and epigraphs points to texts with a strong message and encourages readings of them as semi-autobiographical. They are pinpointed in time, supported by a thinker or writer, contextualised as Arnauld's writings — about writing — at a given moment. But this longer text, 'Diorama', is far more explicit in exposing the narrator as author. It clearly stakes out her trajectory as a writer, in that it signals each book publication like signposts on a journey. As discussed in Chapter 7, it also sets up and expands on the concept of projectivism. Within the framework of this chapter on longing, belonging, and travelling, I want to focus on 'Diorama''s evocation of a journey over land and sea, and the ways in which it offers fertile possibilities for interpretation of the author's sometimes ambitious, sometimes alienating experiences as an émigré.

Like *La Lanterne magique* and *Projecteur*, the title pays direct homage to visual media and the emergence of technologies of the moving image. A diorama is a three-dimensional model replica of a scene, activated by illumination. In a museum setting it might take the form of a miniature model, viewed through a peephole. As a form of mass popular entertainment it was pioneered by Louis Daguerre. Huge screens painted like stage backdrops were lit, sometimes animated with props and music, to form a theatrical show for large audiences. Similarly to the magic lantern, it can be understood as a predecessor to film. Its potential, to convey a narrative that combines verbal language, sound, and images to multiple viewers at once, is given a nod of acknowledgment through its adoption by Arnauld. The writing itself is rich in associations, encouraging the reader to engage the full range of senses, as if confronted with a multimedia experience.

Arnauld offers a quotation by Baudelaire as an epigraph. She cites his thoughts on how to respond to critics, 'J'avais primitivement l'intention de répondre à de nombreuses critiques, et, en même temps, d'expliquer quelques questions très simples, totalement obscurcies par la lumière moderne: qu'est-ce que la poésie? quel est son but?' ('I had intended, at first, to answer numerous criticisms and at the same time to explain a few quite simple questions that have been totally obscured by modern enlightenment: What is poetry? What is its aim?'). This impetus to explain is one that he rejects, however, as both an uncomfortable pressure and a futile task. Baudelaire's quotation ends with a conclusion that those who know him will understand him while for those who cannot or will not comprehend him, his explanations are fruitless in any case ('Ceux qui me savent me devinent, et pour ceux qui ne peuvent ou ne veulent pas comprendre, j'amoncellerais sans fruit les explications').[18]

Arnauld's chosen quotation ties into her own defensive-aggressive assertions about writerly autonomy. We can expect some illumination of her experience as a writer, her epigraph suggests, but should not be disappointed if our questions are not definitively addressed. Years later, asked about her approach to writing in a 1932 interview, she would repeat this same extract from Baudelaire, together with an objection of her own formulation, 'Excusez-moi, [...] mais je pense que la théorie ne peut servir d'introduction à la poésie' [I'm sorry, [...] but I don't think theory can serve as an introduction to poetry].[19] An admiring review of *Guêpier de diamants*, earlier, had identified its author's characteristically uncompromising approach, 'Son seul défaut, c'est de trouver un malin plaisir à masquer sa pensée. Mais cela lui passera bien, n'ayez crainte. Nous possédons là une poétesse d'avenir' [Her only fault is that she finds pleasure in masking her thoughts. But it will all work out, never fear. We have here a poet of the future].[20]

Tellingly, Arnauld calls 'Diorama' a 'confession lyrique'. The first word permits a biographical reading, encourages emotional identification, and also hints at an oral tradition of storytelling; it points tantalisingly to intimacy and revelation. The term 'lyrical', however, militates against any kind of plain soul-baring. 'Diorama' tells a dramatic tale. The author evokes her creative journey from adolescence, as she sets off in a boat made of ferns, to gain her freedom. Again, we are reminded of Rimbaud's 'Le Bateau ivre'. Arnauld indicates her book publications at various stages of her journey, weaving their titles into the narrative. The result is a genre-defying mix of fantasy, reality, and dreamlike narrative. It occupies a space between fiction and autobiography, finally escaping any clear literary genre.

We have already taken heed of some of the signposts in 'Diorama' in this study. In Chapter 1 the relation of *La Lanterne magique* to Arnauld's childhood was noted. Any misconception of it as idyllic is tainted by her conviction that life was elsewhere and that in leaving she would carry 'le sujet tragique de cette histoire' [the tragic subject of this story] (OC, p. 183). *Tournevire* (Chapter 2) was posited as the start of a journey, the metaphorical lifting of an anchor in her creative life. *Poèmes à claires-voies*, next, was eloquently profiled as a chapel constellated with poems, characterised by visions and melodies on the one hand, and morbidity and madness on the other (Chapter 3). The twin projections with which we have become familiar were noted in relation to *Point de mire* (Chapter 4). Lastly, in terms of specific book signposts, *Guêpier de diamants* was evoked using the vocabulary of travel, water, music, and fantasy, as the narrator pondered her 'royaume projectiviste' [projectivist kingdom] (OC, p. 185). At this point she described a more challenging fight to regain her ambitions. Questions abounded as she professed a determination to continue her trajectory in spite of doubts.

There are many aspects of 'Diorama' that recall the characteristics of Arnauld's works as sketched out in previous chapters. On her journey the narrator interacts with bands of bohemians and musicians, as well as natural living beings such as trees, wasps, and fireflies, reminding us of the cast of human and non-human characters in her novel *Tournevire*. In addition to a carousel of fantastic characters and mythical landscapes, many of the metaphors in 'Diorama' centre on the natural world, on birds, water, light, and flight. Their potential for flight likewise occurs in repeated reference to modes of transport including boats and aeroplanes. The sometimes-uneasy collisions of these references echo, or indeed convey, profound and conflicting feelings. At various points in her journey the narrator is either hopeful or despairing, finds comradeship or fears solitude, pursues freedom or finds herself trapped.

The experience and potential of travel are key, both on a practical level (her own relocation) and metaphysical (the will to keep moving forward). There is longing, optimism, a search for freedom, and investigation. She writes, for example, 'Le chemin de l'avion est libre, irréel et sans piste déterminée; ses investigations sont illimitées' [The aeroplane's path is free, seemingly unreal and has no set course; its investigations are unlimited] (*OC*, p. 180). Here is a fantasy of liberty encapsulated in the possibilities of the aeroplane. But there are also frequent tensions as she searches for her place in a foreign, modern, or hybrid world. These conflicts persist in and characterise 'Diorama', which includes contrasting moments of serenity and despair. In a rare allusion to a specific place, her adopted home city of Paris, Arnauld writes, for example, 'Durant des nuits longues comme des tourments je rôdai au bord de la Seine pour voler l'archet de l'aube' [During nights long like torments I roamed the banks of the Seine to steal the dawn's bow] (*OC*, p. 184).

Arnauld's frequent light metaphors evoke, on the one hand, the natural world (sun, stars, and moon) and, on the other, beacons, headlights, and film. Her struggle is exemplified by a recurring motif of two beams, as in, for example, 'Et toujours les deux phares lumineux de ma vie se renvoyaient mon image comme des forces ennemies' [And still the two luminous beacons of my life reflected my image like enemy forces] (*OC*, p. 183). These luminous beams, mentioned six times in the text, recall the lights of the diorama in the title, scanning across a condensed but expansive life. Their designation as twin beams suggests diametrically opposed visions, pressures, or conflicting identities. They can be read as relating to an individual torn between identities, cultures, and above all directions in her writing. Her circumstances as an émigré can be seen to underpin the life's journey described in 'Diorama', in which she escapes from one home but never quite finds another. Identifiable landscapes are replaced with unreal, unstable worlds, peopled by strange, itinerant characters.

It is appropriate to consider the notion of 'écriture feminine', conceptualised by Hélène Cixous, in relation to 'Diorama'. Cixous identifies it as flow and drift; as plural, spontaneous, and without closure; as tactile, passing through the ear, drawing on the symbolic and archaic, and against the constraints of reason and logic.[21] All are characteristic of Arnauld's writing in 'Diorama', and in much of her poetic work. In the next chapter, for example, the importance of the speaking voice and of hearing will be underscored, and in Chapter 10 emphasis will be placed on elements of the body which are closely aligned with nature. Arnauld's use of her own experiences to reflect on writing and the writer, not least her characterisation of 'Diorama' as a 'confession lyrique', likewise point ahead to Cixous. Both writers break formal convention to produce constructive alternatives. Cixous has written, 'ce que je dis a au moins deux faces et deux visées: détruire, casser; prévoir l'imprévu, projeter' ('what I say has at least two sides and two aims: to break, to destroy; and to forsee the unforeseeable, to project').[22] The combinations, contradictions, and contraflows within Arnauld's writing invite connections with Cixous. Here, the notion of two-sidedness, and also the term 'projeter', offer common ground.

Nochlin's work, although focused on the visual arts, offers another useful framework. In an analysis of pictorial cropping or cutting, for example, she puts forward three interpretations of its potency: total contingency, total determination, and play. The first designation underscores the artist's role in capturing 'the raw data of visual experience, [...] whether or not a unified composition resulted'. It emphasises spontaneity and liberty and reminds us of Arnauld's concept of the writer as projector or lens. The second term, 'total determination', insists on the artist's right to make aesthetic choices in what to represent and how, and the modernist tendency to draw attention to the *'signifier*, not a simulacrum of reality, however modern'. The third is all about playfulness, sometimes forgotten, and the productive oscillation between the first two ideas, between chance and choice. These three terms, albeit deployed in a different context, resonate with and articulate points of emphasis in Arnauld's approach.[23] Open to the contingencies of language she nevertheless produces remarkable compositions that insist on chasing down words and ideas. She is also vocal about the autonomy of the poet. Finally the seriousness of some thematic currents in her work do not entirely militate against the sheer jouissance for writer and reader alike in the material qualities of words.

'Diorama' appears to be an attempt by Arnauld to locate herself and her writing in the ever-changing cultural and intellectual landscape to which she had relocated. It can be argued that this state of being is keenly felt by avant-garde artists and writers, always at odds with the prevailing culture, disruptive in their writing and in their actions, and therefore vulnerable to rejection and isolation. In Arnauld's case her fragility is exacerbated by an uneasy relationship with the structures of power at play in Dada and subsequently Surrealism. She must either enter into allegiance with them or take her own course. In one section in 'Diorama' she describes herself stranded in a large unknown house, the ceiling crushing her. She describes how she has concealed the luminous twin beams in her eyes, as if to protect herself, perhaps. Uncannily, a rose bush sprouts from her head, and each time a rose opens, a character springs from it. She writes of these strange apparitions, 'Ces hommes avaient le désir d'un univers plus large; ils parlaient tous à la fois, longtemps, et ils pleuraient de rage quand l'aube venait semer ses pétales sur leurs inquiétudes' [These men desired a larger universe; they would all talk at once, at length, and they would weep with rage when the dawn came to scatter its petals over their concerns] (*OC*, p. 184). Arnauld's creativity is portrayed, metaphorically, as fecund and generative.

The men's talk, meanwhile, is dominant and competitive but finally unproductive. The final lines of the section bring out Arnauld's profound disappointment with the situation, 'J'attendais, éblouie, quelque chose d'imprévu; mais ce fut en vain que les phares lumineux fouillèrent de leurs griffes de lumière la fraîcheur d'un sourire' [I waited, dazzled, for something unforeseen, but my searching luminous beacons failed to alight upon the spontaneity of a smile]. Located between the markers of her 1921 and 1923 volumes, the passage can be read justifiably as a metaphorical evocation of Arnauld's fraught and occasionally hostile interactions with the male-dominated Dada group. Finally, she states prosaically, she sets off on her own path.

In this chapter I have focused on journeys. We have seen movements between geographical places, on foot, by train, or by boat. Transitions between dreaming, sleeping, and awakening have also been elaborated. Edges and thresholds, real and metaphorical, have recurred. The horizon, the line between land and sky, has been called up, as have rooftops, places from which the outsider can take a vantage point and observe. These elements are not confined to *Guêpier de diamants* and 'Diorama'; neither do they define them. They are aspects which occur as early as *Tournevire*, with its travelling troupe and persecuted outsiders, which persist in allusions to transport in *Poèmes à claires-voies*, and which coalesce as liminal spaces in *Point de mire*. Arnauld's situation is inevitably and powerfully brought into view. In terms of nationality, religion, and language she is on the margins. These questions of displacement and belonging, already a point of emphasis in her writing, come to the fore in very tangible and perilous ways when Arnauld and Dermée are forced into hiding during the Occupation of France, in 1941, as will be seen in Chapter 11.

Following *L'Apaisement de l'éclipse*, there would be a nine-year gap before Arnauld published another book, *La Nuit rêve tout haut et Le Clavier secret, poèmes (1925 à 1934)*. But clearly, for Arnauld, experiment did not begin and end with Dada. On the contrary, the five volumes that she published in the 1930s and 1940s, to be considered in the next three chapters, demonstrate a heightened engagement with the value and role of poetry, and a continued pushing at the boundaries of genre. The generative potential of marginalisation and the critical distance it entails becomes ever-more apparent. As Arnauld asserts in 'Diorama', 'Dans mon vol, rassurez-vous, [...] je captiverai l'azur en lui offrant au creux de mes mains les lumières inquiètes écloses au bord du matin' [In my flight, be reassured, [...] I will capture the sky by offering to it, in the hollows of my hands, the anxious, dawning lights of daybreak] (OC, p. 186).

Notes to Chapter 8

1. Arnauld, 'Avertissement aux lecteurs', in *L'Apaisement de l'éclipse*; OC, p. 178.
2. Forcer goes further than me in his readings of Arnauld's relationship with Dada as negative: 'Arnauld's poems [...] indicate that even in 1920 she was aware that she aroused anxiety and discomfort, and that Dada's men were not as open to her as they were to each other' (*Dada as Text, Thought and Theory*, p. 33). His conclusions arise from readings of critical and parodic references to her peers in some of her texts. I tend to read the provocations in her Dada-manifestos as being directed from within the group to those outside of it.
3. Ibid., p. 41.

4. Baudelaire, 'Le Peintre de la vie moderne'; 'The Painter of Modern Life'.
5. Monica Spiridon, '"Bucharest-on-the-Seine": The Anatomy of a National Obsession', in *Paris-Bucharest, Bucharest-Paris*, ed. by Quinney, pp. 23–35 (p. 23). This essay is extremely useful for its further exploration of questions of national identity, and feelings of 'time lag' and 'cultural belatedness' for Romanian artists and writers in Paris. It is also noteworthy for its broad focus that includes the women writers Marthe Bibesco (1886–1973) and Hélène Vacaresco (1864–1967), beyond the usual canon of men.
6. Sjöberg, 'Any Other Transnationalism'.
7. Sjöberg's recent ideas on Jewishness and transnationalism are fruitful and convincing in this respect. He suggests the likelihood that 'the avant-gardists found in the Kabbalistic corpus a repository of original and idiosyncratic conceptions of language, meaning production, and textual techniques, which went hand in hand with the avant-gardist tendency to subvert common sense and normalized logic' ('Any Other Transnationalism', p. 37).
8. Artaud, 'Livres reçues: *Point de mire*'.
9. Friedrich Nietzsche, *Ainsi parlait Zarathoustra*, trans. by Henri Albert (Paris: Mercure de France, 1924), p. 41 (reference taken from *OC*, p. 137); *Thus Spoke Zarathustra: A Book for Anyone and Nobody*, trans. by Graham Parkes (Oxford: Oxford University Press, 2005), p. 27.
10. Frédéric Saisset, 'Les Livres; Les Poèmes', *La Nervie* (September-October 1923), 225 (*OC*, p. 498). 'La forêt de son Inconscient' seems to speak both to the unconscious in Surrealism and Baudelaire's 'forêt de symboles'. See Baudelaire, 'Correspondances', in *Œuvres complètes*, ed. by Claude Pichois, 2 vols, Bibliothèque de la Pléiade (Paris: Gallimard, 1975–1976), I, 11.
11. Guillaume Apollinaire, 'Paysage', in *Calligrammes*, pp. 30–31 (in French and English).
12. Sjöberg considers the extent to which Romanians Jewish writers could be said to be assimilated in France. In a nuanced analysis, he uses the terms 'close other' and 'double outsider' to examine a sliding scale of acceptance and non-belonging ('Any Other Transnationalism', pp. 41–43).
13. Forcer, *Dada as Text, Thought and Theory*, p. 37. This claim refers to the inventive and meditative free verse of Arnauld, Buffet, and Buffet-Picabia.
14. Mary Ann Caws has written about the crystal as a motif in Surrealism, the qualities of which share common ground with Arnauld's diamond. See '"Tzara-Dada": The Crystal and the Image', in Mary Ann Caws, *The Poetry of Dada and Surrealism* (Princeton, NJ: Princeton University Press, 1970), pp. 95–104. She cites multiple instances of its appearance in writing by Tzara and Breton, underscoring, among other observations, how it represents 'freedom and clarity, purity and transparency', and the surrealist quest to perceive interior depths beyond the surface (p. 96). This book is an excellent resource for its identification of key themes, including polarity, ambiguity, doubling, madness, light, and reflection, in poetry by Aragon, Breton, Tzara, Éluard, and Desnos. I have been wary, though, of too much comparison of Arnauld's work to others', preferring instead to read it independently.
15. Lacaze-Duthiers, 'Céline Arnauld'.
16. I have not been able to deal fully with this text within the scope and structure of this book. It offers plenty of potential for close analysis.
17. Forcer, *Dada as Text, Thought and Theory*, p. 42.
18. Charles Baudelaire, 'Préface des Fleurs', in *Œuvres Complètes*, ed. by Pichois, I, 182; *The Flowers of Evil*, ed. by Marthiel and Jackson Mathews (New York: New Directions, 1989), p. xxvii. The source was established by Martin-Schmets.
19. Céline Arnauld, in 'Céline Arnauld nous dit ... Mystère de l'image'.
20. Henry Petiot, untitled review, in *La Critique et Céline Arnauld*, p. 11 (*OC*, p. 503).
21. For more on the relationships between 'écriture féminine' and the avant-garde see Susan Rubin Suleiman, 'Writing Past the Wall', in *'Coming to Writing' and Other Essays by Hélène Cixous*, ed. by Deborah Jenson (Cambridge, MA: Harvard University Press, 1991), pp. v–xii.
22. Hélène Cixous, *Le Rire de la Méduse et autres ironies* (Paris: Éditions Galilée, 2010), p. 37; 'The Laugh of the Medusa', trans. by Keith Cohen and Paula Cohen, *Signs*, Vol. I, 4 (Summer 1976), p. 875.
23. Nochlin, *The Body in Pieces*, pp. 37–38. Her object of analysis is the painting *Masked Ball at the Opera* (1873) by Édouard Manet.

CHAPTER 9

❖

Music and Madness in *La Nuit rêve tout haut et Le Clavier secret* (1934)

Following a period of prolific individual publication and complex group dynamics in the 1920s, it would be nine years before Arnauld published another book. *La Nuit rêve tout haut et Le Clavier secret* appeared in print at the beginning of February 1934 and is the first in a line of six publications in the 1930s and 1940s that includes a dedicated anthology. A survey of Arnauld's work by the poet Paul Fort, published in 1939, sets out the qualities of her writing in this period. He refers to a broader context of revolutionary and lyrical writing that constantly calls for the new and that reminds us of Arnauld's twin tensions of action and lyricism (Chapter 5).[1] More specifically he places her in an ecology of experimental writers that takes in Dada as part of a developmental past and that also looks ahead to her individuality. He calls *La Nuit rêve tout haut* 'un des plus beaux livres publiés depuis vingt ans' [one of the most beautiful books published in the last twenty years]. In an indictment of critical reception he elaborates, 'Et il est bien regrettable que la critique ne l'ait pas signalé davantage. Mais la critique? ... Cette œuvre, je l'affirme, restera et témoignera en faveur de notre époque' [And it is highly regrettable that critics have not drawn more attention to it. But critics ? ... This work, I maintain, will endure and bear favourable witness to our period].[2]

The genesis of Arnauld's 1934 publication spanned almost a decade. The book is made up of two very different elements. The first, *La Nuit rêve tout haut* [The Night Dreams Aloud], Arnauld calls a 'poème à deux voix' [poem for two voices] and is dated 'summer 1933'. The second, *Le Clavier secret* [The Secret Keyboard] comprises twelve poems written over the period 1925 to 1934. In this chapter I want to bring attention to matters of aurality in Arnauld's work. The association of poetry with music comes across strongly in many texts and certainly here, as signalled by the very titles of its two main components. Linked to this is the association of poetry as music and the performative qualities of words. Words are like music, deployed for their sound qualities as much as semantics. The former can signify where the latter is slippery. Claude Coste has written about the appeal of music for the avant-garde poet:

> Lieu vide prêt à tous les investissements, symbole de l'énergie vitale, la musique ne vaut jamais pour elle-même. Flottant entre réalité et métaphore, elle ouvre sur la richesse mystérieuse du monde. [...] Pour dire ou approcher l'au-delà des mots et du monde, la musique, système de signes non linguistiques, permet une approche séduisante de l'étrangeté de notre décor familier.[3]
>
> [An empty place ready for investment, symbol of vital energy, music is never just itself. Floating between reality and metaphor, it opens up the mysterious richness of the world. [...] Seeking to say or approach what is beyond words and the world, music, as a system of non-linguistic signs, allows us to get seductively near to the strangeness of our familiar surroundings.]

For Arnauld, in these two volumes, orality and aurality are key, and silence is anathema. Sounds by living beings are synthesised in myriad forms of expression, from the insect, to the avian, to the human. References to soundscapes conjure up the dreamlike, in some cases, but in others are rooted in the noise of the environment. The poet, in her formulations, is closely aligned to the musician, bridging imagination and expression. She is a performer and conduit of sound that must be activated and interpreted by the listener-reader. Sometimes represented as a prophet, she comes across at times as a solitary and tortured outsider, but also a determined communicator. We will also consider the notion of madness, which haunts some of the texts in this collection, as a motif of the poet's creative persona and, we might speculate, a part of her lived experience.

La Nuit rêve tout haut is prefaced by a brief note to readers consisting of two sentences. Its tone is more conciliatory than the sort of outspoken antagonism evident in earlier instances of Arnauld's direct addresses, such as in her 'Avertissement aux lecteurs' (Chapter 7). It begins with an apology, for dealing not with matters of justice, at a time of great drama, but for coming up instead with a love poem. In a footnote Martin-Schmets points out the economic crisis in France at the time with its associated instability in government that saw countless changes in political personnel (*OC*, p. 225, n. 1). Arnauld's allusion is an unusually direct reference to the world at large but she does not clarify further, and we can only read into it an awareness of politics. More interesting is her subsequent introduction of the text, 'Dans ce poème labyrinthine, où la désésperance, la passion, la nature, la vie et même la mort sont sublimisés, je signale, toutefois, une sortie sur le réel: la tubéreuse que Giavena pique dans ses cheveux pour charmer' [In this labyrinthine poem, where despair, passion, nature, life, and even death are sublimated, I signal, nonetheless, a sortie into the real: the tuberose that Giavena puts into her hair in order to charm] (*OC*, p. 223). This characterisation of form ('labyrinthine') and key themes ('despair, passion, nature, life, and even death') is in line with much of Arnauld's *œuvre*, as we have seen. The final note subsequently strikes an unexpected and humorous tone. Reminiscent of the prospectus for *Projecteur* (Chapter 6) it follows grand topics (in that case it was money, glory, and advertising) with something pleasing, sensuous, and seemingly superficial (there it was madreporian pullulation in heavenly spaces, here it is a flower). The blooms in Giavena's hair, she suggests, are just as much a matter of reality as the apparently more profound topics just listed. We can expect something with serious undertones, perhaps, but above all a romance.

A 'Révélation du poème' precedes a text that is organised into two sections, 'La Nuit rêve tout haut' and 'Légende de la nébuleuse' [Legend of the Nebula]. The 'Revelation' is a fabulous tale of the narrator's discovery of the story that will follow. It describes a train journey to the heights of the mountains, an encounter with a wise man from the hills, and the plentiful inspiration afforded by nature. The dreaming of the night is succeeded by the illumination of the day, a temporal transition prevalent in Arnauld's imaginings. In this narrative both night and day are full of promise. Birds, above all, are designated as the source of poetic power, transmitting stories and truths through their song to the poet. This passage brings to mind much of the vocabulary and imagery of 'Diorama', for example, but it is a more legible, less elusive narrative. Connections are more robust; symbolic meanings signalled more directly. The reader is asked less to decipher than to enjoy. The tone, too, is one less of menace and doubt than of revelation and celebration.

In the dialogue that follows, various extracts of which appeared in Arnauld's anthology (1936), there are two characters.[4] 'Giavena' and 'Giaveno' are invented names that sound Italian to the reader. As Martin-Schmets points out, Giaveno is a town near Turin in Piedmont, with Giavena a feminised form of this place name. These variations on a single name offer a gendered doubling. In a first lengthy monologue spoken by Giavena, she approaches her lover. The setting is night-time. Our heroine is agitated, slightly fearful but lovestruck. Her words are frequently formed into hesitant but optimistic exclamations and declarations. She is on the verge, it seems, of meeting the object of her affections. She is aligned with nature, with the night, the stars, and the birds in her quest for expression and harmony. Her speech is punctuated by verse, finally heard by Giaveno, prompting his first intervention 'Quelle est cette féerie? On rit, on chante, on rêve tout haut dans la nuit! […] Qui m'appelle?' [What is this extravaganza? There is laughter, song, dreaming aloud in the night! […] Who is calling to me?] (OC, p. 232). 'Féerie' encompasses ideas of magic as well as a visual (theatrical or filmic) spectacle. Giavena announces herself, come to share her love and sorrow once more, and recites to her beloved an ode of their remembered love.

In subsequent exchanges the question of seasons is tied to the progress of our protagonists' story. Giaveno expects her in the spring, he exclaims, not the winter, but Giavena has come in the darkness, with weariness and pain, to seek his company. This love is both requited and robust, it would at first appear, since his response is to welcome her to stay with him and even to lean on him, his shoulder proffered for comfort. But there follows a to-ing and fro-ing about Giavena's state and what should happen next. Giaveno expects singing from her, not words; he wants joy not sorrow. 'Es-tu ici pour parler ou pour chanter?' [Are you here to talk or to sing?], he demands, when she expresses an opinion about the limits of what a man can offer (comfort or pride) (OC, p. 234). She should sleep, he advises, but she does not want to be fobbed off or silenced.

Giaveno articulates his fears about falling in love that had at first caused him to hesitate and even reject her. Her reply sets out the adventures and suffering into which she retreated, while he was tempted and tested by other women. Giavana iterates the winding path of their courtship as they each searched out their feelings. It is she who has been the traveller, explorer, and philosopher. She has come to serenade him, she is the one with the power of discovery; the one to be alternately revered and feared. A digression takes her into musing about others' misunderstandings of her. These recall other poetic passages in Arnauld's work in which the poet is defended and exalted in the face of antagonism from those who fail to comprehend her. It also points to a feminist subversion of the romance narrative. Arnauld plays with conventions to facilitate a narrative that privileges her female protagonist's quest.

A long address follows, full of questions addressed to Giaveno and perhaps beyond, in which Giavena sets out a trajectory that is, again, reminiscent of 'Diorama'. It touches on childhood, escape, and conflicts that have been overcome. It ends with an elegy to a character, Nèle, and a request from Giaveno to recount her story.[5] The final line of this section lets the reader know that this story will follow, as we are exhorted to listen. The language is typical of Arnauld, not least in its recurring vocabulary of celestial landscapes, light, water, insects, and birds, by now familiar to us. But character, storyline, and structure are here far more conventional than in other examples of her work. The structure, for example, offers an unusually comforting literary set-up. The repetition of words and concepts over her *œuvre* continues to build towards understanding on the part of the reader. This text is like a culmination of many reiterative ideas, solidifying from a nebulous openwork into some clarity.

The next section, 'La Légende de la nébuleuse', is less than half the first in length. This story-within-a-story echoes the narrative of Giavena. Nèle wakes up in the night, rushes towards her love, appearing naked at his door, before fleeing at dawn. She wanders through time, suffering silences, seeking to regain her dreams and visions, trying to find her voice, and battling weariness. Fearing she is close to death she lies down, only for her dreams to return. This event reminds us of the character Luciole in Arnauld's novel *Tournevire* (Chapter 1), another heroine who looks for solace and restoration in sleep. Nèle, like Luciole, is saved. Crucially, she finds her voice again, and sets out to look for her love once more. A miracle ensues; she sings her last song; she is raised up to the clouds.

Giaveno's role in the telling of the story is to interject only relatively briefly. The first fragment is a question; could Nèle not be returned to her senses? On a second occasion he urges Giavena to continue. In two further interjections he switches his attention to Giavena, lavishing praise on her, exalting her otherworldly qualities, and declaring his love even as he accepts that she is beyond him. From a feminist point of view, it is notable that Giavena is given by far the lengthiest utterances. It is she who courts the man, not the other way around. Patrilinear culture is challenged. The writing is arguably a treatise to love but as much to the importance of thinking and expressing, of writing, as to a merely earthly relationship between a man and a woman.

The text, we recall, was qualified as a poem for two voices. That designation privileges the notion of reading out loud. Its form is certainly more akin to a dialogue, shot through with poems or songs. Again, Arnauld readily blurs the boundaries between genres, between written and spoken texts, and between words and music. The text is peppered with words and concepts relating to vocal and musical utterances, many recurring in multiple instances. Some describe a range of non-verbal human emotion and emissions, from *sanglot/sangloter* [sob/to sob], *cris/crier* [shouting/to shout], and *pleurs/pleurer* [weeping/to weep] to *rires/rire*, [laughter/to laugh], as well as the more elusive *murmure* [murmur], *sifflement* [whistling], and *plaintes* [groaning]. Others note verbal communications, from the nouns *langage* [language] and *dialogues* to the important repetitions of *paroles* [speech] and *voix* [voice]. Verbs are *appeler* [to call], *dire* [to say], *parler* [to speak], *conter* [to tell], *raconter* [to recount], and *implorer* [to implore]. References to the mouth and lips recur. Language and possibility are linked; the body and its utterances are crucial to the expression of emotions and concepts.

There is also language relating to religion. Vocabulary that expresses the earth-bound appealing to the divine is in evidence, including *prière/prier* [prayer/to pray], 'hymnes', 'incantations', 'méditations', 'exaltations', 'appels' [pleas], 'répons' [response], and 'profaner' [to swear]. More of an abstract spirituality than any indication of faith, it suggests the enduring appeal of making sounds. And then there is the vocabulary of making music, from instruments such as the accordion, the harp, bells, and the lyre, to *chanson/chants/chanteurs/chanter* [song/singing/singers/to sing], *chœurs* [choirs], *musique*, *mélodies*, *opéras*, *symphonies*, and *solos*. Verbs include *carilloner* [to chime or peal] and *réverberer* [to reverberate]. The occasional reference to modern technology stands out in this cacophony, namely *microphone* and *projecteur*. Other terms span the human and insect worlds, like *bourdonner/bourdonnement* [to hum/humming] and *clameur* [clamour]. These words are deployed both figuratively and metaphorically.

A sensitivity to the sonorous, a recognition of the various forms that sound can take, and a repetition of motifs, produces a rich and dense symphonic effect. In calling up sound, music, and a gamut of noise-making, Arnauld shows herself to be interested in the power of the non-verbal as well as the linguistic as an expressive force. We are reminded of Symbolism, both in terms of the collision of verbal language and music, and the density — and at times obscurity — of the text. Referring to the views of Mallarmé, Malcolm Bowie has written, 'poetry must be difficult of access, its meanings densely compacted and its music cut across by cacophony'.[6] Peter Dayan, who has written extensively on the importance of music for avant-garde poets and precursors, not least Mallarmé and Apollinaire, has recently exposed its vitality in Dada. His breadth of enquiry produces links that resonate, 'There has always been a stubborn body of thinkers, of poets and philosophers, who believed in an inaudible music whose divine rhythms might be discerning echoing in poetry, or indeed any art, as well as in sound; this faith in an unheard music was at the very root of the Symbolist aesthetic on which many of the Dadaists were raised'.[7] He goes on to consider the distinction, or rather interrogation of that distinction, between music and noise, that can be traced to the avant-garde. From Arnauld's 'silent keyboard' to her evocations of noises in nature, we can see how her enquiries range across the possibilities of sound-making that were at the heart of the emphases and experiments of the avant-garde.

The counterpoint to sound, in Arnauld's text, is oppressive silence or muteness. In a passage reinforced by repetition Giavena leaves no doubt as to the horror of this state:

> Silence dans la vie, silence dans la mort, l'ivresse dans le silence, la pureté dans le silence, le mystère de l'amour dévoilé, les pleurs dans le silence, tout était silence et vide et pourtant tout n'était pas perdu, car pour les élus il y a toujours l'aide apporté au dernier moment par les prophètes. (*OC*, p. 245)
>
> [Silence in life, silence in death, drunkenness in silence, purity in silence, the unveiled mystery of love, crying in silence, everything was silence and emptiness and yet all was not lost, since for the elect there is always the help brought at the last minute by the prophets.]

Where silence produces emptiness, sound-making offers a means of redemption, a bridge between material existence and spiritual discovery. Word and song are closely aligned. The term 'prophet' is repeated in this volume, as elsewhere, in relation to the poet. We recall Arnauld's idea of poets projecting into the future, of forming a fragile but visionary chain, as discussed in Chapter 7. There she referred to an 'élite'; here she refers, in similar vein, to 'les élus'. Her conception of poets as prophets builds on ideas articulated by predecessors, whom we know she admired, from Rimbaud's 'voyant' to Apollinaire's 'prophète'.[8] An extract from a letter by Rimbaud, for example, comes to mind for its congruent concerns and language, 'Le poète se fait *voyant* par un long, immense et raisonné dérèglement de tous les sens. Toutes les formes d'amour, de souffrance, de folie; il cherche lui-même, il épuise en lui tous les poisons, pour n'en garder que les quintessences' [The Poet makes himself a *seer* by a long, immense, and rational dissolution of all the senses. All the forms of love, of suffering, of madness; he searches himself, he consumes all the poisons in him, to only keep their quintessence].[9] We might read *La Nuit rêve tout haut* as a love story, in the first place, but also as a version of Arnauld's own story as a self-appointed pioneer or trailblazer, confronting the range of experience from love to madness, but insisting on her own voice and visions.

As the three parts lead us from a revelation by a narrator to Giavena's first-person narrative, to her recounting of Nèle, we come to appreciate the agent as the creative woman, singer, narrator, poet. Giavena and Nèle embody expressive, vocal forces that bridge the natural and human worlds. They are the powerful presences in the narrative. They suffer doubts and sorrows, banishment and exile, the passing of time and solitude. Their insistence on speaking and singing make of them the prophets of the imaginary and the profound. Intertextual references to other fictional or mythical figures reinforce that sense of an exaltation of female verbal and vocal creativity. The protagonist of the story is a woman, the action is performed by her, and her voice dominates. In places she is hailed as a magician, notably using the feminine form 'magicienne'. This is a neat reversal of what Forcer exposes as 'the male-orchestrated sorcery of Dada performances and texts'.[10] 'Je suis l'héritage des prophètes, la femme!' [I am the heritage of the prophets, woman!], Giavena asserts (*OC*, p. 235). The insightful visionary exalted by Symbolism and the avant-garde is expressly and radically female in this manifestation.

We might reflect further, here, on the potential impact of Arnauld's national and cultural background on her approach to writing. I noted in Chapter 2 Mansbach's proposal of a less purist approach by avant-garde groups in central Europe towards influences and idioms.[11] Sandqvist, too, writes of a cultural mobility or willingness to synthesise different movements and moments. He discusses a 'double belonging' or 'doubleness' for Jewish writers and artists, caught between assimilation and otherness that, in turn, 'promotes a specific social, intellectual, and emotional competence and a system of values supporting the multilingual capacity and the cultural mobility between many cultures'.[12] By extension this results in an openness to form, genre, and style that should not be dismissed as a retreat from progress but as an acknowledgement of paradox. Rather than sweep away the past Arnauld draws on intertextual references; instead of dismissing what is beyond national boundaries she picks out inspirations from other cultural and historical contexts, moulding them to her own vision. The conventions of serenades and aubades, for example, are brought into the twentieth century, formulated by a woman writer and articulated by women characters.[13]

The title of the second part of this book, *Le Clavier secret* [The Secret Keyboard], draws heavily, once again, on the performative, spoken aspect of poetic language. Aligning poetry with music issuing from an instrument chimes with many of the instances we have seen so far of the author collapsing and conflating poetry and song, writer and musician. The secret keyboard might also make us think of the piano music accompanying silent film, the added soundtrack that creates moods and emotions alongside visuals. Kandinsky's close alignment of visual art and music also comes to mind, 'Color is the keyboard. The eye is the hammer. The soul is the piano, with its many strings. The artist is the hand that sets the soul vibrating, by means of this or that key'.[14] In the next chapter we will also elaborate on how Arnauld, too, refers to the body parts that Kandinsky identifies here — the eye and the hand — as encapsulations of creative agency.

There are twelve texts in *Le Clavier secret*, five of which are included in Arnauld's 1936 anthology, and an extraordinary ten of which were published in a range of journals, in some cases in more than one place. This is surely an indication of a will on the poet's part to extend her reach. The first text is 'Je me suis serrée très fort contre la folie' [I gripped myself tightly against madness] (*OC*, pp. 251–52). This first-person narrative of a journey of adversity and discovery offers a hybrid landscape of the familiar and unfamiliar, made marvellous and at times frightening. From birds of prey to 'la fourrure électrique des léopards' [the electric coats of the leopards], which light up the forest, it mixes nature and technology, and militates against a clear geography or temporality. The vocabulary of madness is conspicuous here: 'Allais-je vers la folie ou vers l'harmonie?' [Was I heading towards madness or harmony], the narrator asks. Imagination and creativity, so often exalted in Arnauld's texts, are also fraught with the fear of breakdown and rejection. Hearts are closed to her; the narrator even wonders what is left in life. A lack of belonging is expressed, too, in terms of the outsider, 'Je flâne d'une ville à l'autre, ou plutôt je cours en marge des villes sans m'arrêter nulle part. Et pourtant rien m'échappe'

[I wander from one town to another, or rather I do the rounds of the fringes of towns, stopping nowhere. Yet nothing escapes me]. This is a clear articulation of geographical and cultural displacement, of the itinerant outsider who does not belong anywhere.

An identity crisis is also eloquently evoked by metaphors of doubling that recall the twin spotlights that appear elsewhere. 'En me penchant sur la mer lucide je vis un autre moi-même s'avancer vers moi, les yeux démesurément ouverts, vraie créole marine' [Leaning on the lucid sea I saw another me approach, eyes incredibly wide, a true marine creole]. This separation of two selves speaks of an interrogation of her identity, perhaps an ideal self, here, who is not wandering on the land, troubled and insecure, but instead hails from the water. This self, emerging from the sea, reverberates with so many references to water and travel by boat that we have read, not least in 'Diorama' (Chapter 8). In this instance the word 'creole' makes particular allusion to the mixing of people or languages and may well relate to Arnauld's own situation as a Romanian Jew in 1930s' France, caught between — or, more positively, combining — histories, cultures, and languages.

The penultimate text, too, deserves to be considered here. 'Voyage autour de ma folie' [Journey through my madness] (*OC*, pp. 264–65) touches on travel, madness, and music. In spite of the first-person possessive in the title, the protagonist of the opening line is 'le Prince du Jazz'. He is joined by 'la Reine de la Marée', the two figures seemingly equating to 'les amis de ma vie intérieure' [friends from my interior life] (p. 265). Music, again, is the expression of creativity; water (the sea) its source. Both here assume personification in the form of royal figures, the stuff of fairy tales. They are like muses for the 'I' of the poem, or perhaps composite elements of Arnauld herself. A phrase from 'Je me suis serrée très fort contre la folie', just discussed, offers a refrain; the narrator's eyes are again 'démesurément ouverts' [incredibly wide], so much so that 'la folie elle-même ne peut plus supporter leur regard' [madness itself can no longer bear their gaze]. This ability to look and to perceive seems to be overwhelming, 'Mes yeux ne savent plus se fermer et le sourire se fait prière' [My eyes no longer know how to close and my smile offers a prayer] (p. 264). Vision and aurality go hand-in-hand once more and cannot be suppressed. The poem ends, 'Les fous ont perdus leur folie en route, et maintenant ce sont eux mes oiseaux sauvages' [The idiots have lost their madness en route, and now they are my wild birds] (p. 265).

In these instances notions of madness and creativity are linked. We inevitably think of the surrealist celebration of madness as a source of unfettered creativity, a means of accessing the unconscious, but Arnauld's writing suggests a more complex perception and even experience of mental illness or psychic disorder. As Chadwick has pointed out, the portrayal of madness in surrealist writing is strikingly gendered:

> Adopting madness as a creative pose for men and viewing it as a subject of scientific and poetic enquiry when it occurs in women [...] renders simulated madness a source of man's creativity, real madness a source of woman's. The man's is active, the woman's passive, powerless, and at the mercy of the unconscious.[15]

Unlike narratives that take women's madness as their object, such as, famously, Breton's *Nadja*, Arnauld's texts convey a first-person narrative of mental instability.[16] In their various instances they take in a complex range of representations of madness, from a perception of it as an accomplice to creativity, to visceral expressions of symptoms of fear and anxiety.

Arnauld cites Dante twice in this volume, each time taking a quotation from his *Divine Comedy*, once before each of the principle component elements. The first text, the 'Révélation du poème', also pays homage to him in its very first sentences. The protagonist arrives in Ravenna, 'la ville qui cache au monde le plus grand sanglot d'amour' [the town that conceals from the world the greatest sob of love] (*OC*, p. 227). As Martin-Schmets points out, this is the place of Dante's tomb. The lines that Arnauld includes before *La Nuit rêve tout haut* are taken from *Paradiso*, 'Thou art not on the earth as thou thinkest, but lightning flying from its own place never ran so fast as thou returnest to thine'. The verse before *Le Clavier secret* is an extract from *Inferno*, 'Through me the way into the woeful city | Through me the way to the eternal pain'.[17] These epigraphs set up for the reader the dramatic conflicts articulated in this volume, through transience and temporality, to pain and prophesy. Arnauld's citation of a poet from the past also speaks of her willingness to acknowledge precursors. It reminds us of her dismissal of Breton's selectiveness in 'Les Faux Managers' (Chapter 7). In *La Nuit rêve tout haut* she also refers twice to Petrarch and in forthcoming volumes, too, she will cite both Rimbaud and Shelley.

A short opinion piece by Arnauld is pertinent to several of the themes confronted in this chapter. Published in the magazine *Le Disque vert*, it is a brief celebration of the comte de Lautréamont.[18] Her very first point emphasises intertextuality. Stating that the author is drenched in English and French Romanticism, she underscores the idea that we are all intoxicated by those we love. 'Il aimait le Romantisme à travers un voile' [He loved Romanticism through a veil], she notes. This is an assertion that the modern writer can be inspired by their precursors even while seeing them, and writing, anew. A second point addresses madness, 'c'est la même folie que nous tous, poètes, portons en nous' [it is the same madness that all of us, poets, carry in us]. The alignment between creativity and madness is almost beyond doubt for Arnauld. She also encapsulates the tug between action and lyricism that runs through some of her texts, 'Lisez Lautréamont; il nous enseigne ceci: pour être efficacement révolutionnaire il ne faut pas dépouiller son cœur de ce qu'il a de plus humain' [Read Lautréamont; he teaches us this: to be an effective revolutionary one need not strip one's heart of what is most human]. Her approach is distinguished by empathy, both with precursors and peers.

In this chapter I have sought to emphasise the place of aurality and music in Arnauld's work. The term 'lyrisme', used in her 1924 letter to Tzara (cited in Chapter 5), seems carefully chosen. Most often personal and passionate, intense and emphatic, it encompasses grand themes of love, death, nature, time, destiny, and the sacred, often expressed in the first person singular. It exalts and insists on poetic expression. Importantly to this discussion, it seeks the rhythms and melodies of music. Although it dates back to the Middle Ages this is no straight atavistic turn. From Mallarmé to Kandinsky the interest in crossovers between literature, music, and also visual art are crucial emphases in the avant-garde and Modernism. As for the Surrealists, Coste, mentioned above, has written about the importance of music for Soupault, for example, in spite of Breton largely dismissing it for its bourgeois associations.[19] More recently, Dayan's comprehensive account of music in Dada paints a far more nuanced picture of its relevance to many of the avant-garde's key figures than had been understood before.[20] For Arnauld, it seems, sound was a longstanding preoccupation, as the advent of moving images and then sound opened up new possibilities for storytelling. It is surely no coincidence that this focus is crystallised in a period in which Dermée was establishing a career in radio. An expanding acquaintance with radio and film doubtless played a part in her conception of the poet in an age of modern technologies.[21]

This focus on sound led to further discussion of the situation of the (woman) poet, her fight against rejection and restriction, and her determination to be heard. We began with Fort's wish that she be recognised by her contemporaries and his belief in her legacy. Arnauld herself had expressed these same demands for her writing as early as 1924, in her letter to Tzara:

> Pourtant d'autres que vous ont étudié sans parti pris l'évolution lyrique des dernières années et ne tarderont pas à me donner ma place. Car on peut jongler avec les noms et les individus, selon l'opportunité, mais non avec les œuvres, qui ont du poids et ne se laissent pas manier comme des balles.[22]
>
> [Yet other people have studied the lyrical evolution of recent years, without bias, and will not hesitate to grant me my place. Because one can juggle with names and individuals, according to the occasion, but not with works, which are weighty and cannot be handled like balls.]

Flouquet echoed this in a 1932 interview with Arnauld, accusing their contemporaries of wilful neglect. Deriding the insincerity of these 'official' bosses of 'private schools' he surmised, 'J'imagine que, n'ayant pu l'enrégimenter, nos maîtres ont tout simplement tenté d'écarter un poète qui les précédait trop immédiatement' [I imagine that, unable to bring her into line, our masters simply tried to sideline a poet who preceded them too closely].[23] He points to her books as predating short-lived movements and outlasting the whims of politics. In his obituary of her, twenty years later, he repeats those accusations. Surrealism, he suggests, discarded her because she would not adhere to its principles. Some of the Dadaists, too (though notably not Tzara), slowly and obstinately sidelined and effaced her, he claims.[24]

Flouquet's observations about group politics, and their impact on the fate of Arnauld, were insightful. Despite both his championing of her and her own doggedness, her name and work would be sidelined from narratives for decades. Feminist scholarship, more latterly, has been instrumental in uncovering forgotten histories. Jeanine Moulin's inclusion of Arnauld in a 1963 anthology, for example, offered a rare, early interest in her, presenting her alongside two contemporaries, Adrienne Monnier (1892–1955) and Catherine Fauln (1911–1951). Moulin links them according to a growing insistence on formal experiment and resistance to explanation:

De toute manière, elles cessent de se cramponner aux normes de la description suivie et à la tradition des confessions rimées. Leur romantisme et leur narcissisme disparaissent. N'éprouvant plus au même degré le besoin de s'analyser, de défendre leurs droits, elle se sentent l'esprit libre pour se forger un langage et un jugement plus rigoureux.[25]

[In any case they stop confining themselves to the norms of description and rhyming confession. No longer feeling the same need to analyse themselves, or to defend their rights, they feel at liberty to forge a more rigorous language and verdict.]

This refusal to denote and explain, and instead to partake in what Moulin calls 'invention pure', is apparent in Arnauld's formulations. The next chapter will underscore another characteristic of her writing that has recurred since her early work, namely a recourse to the natural world. In particular I want to discuss her use of the natural environment as a means to express man's relationship to the psychological, social, and material world. This aspect was strikingly present in *La Nuit rêve tout haut*. While the structure of this study posits a principle focus for each chapter, it has become increasingly apparent that Arnauld's work is best read as a network of ideas and language, an openwork of reflections that offers more rewards the more the reader opens themself to it.

Notes to Chapter 9

1. Paul Fort, 'Une poétesse de la poésie nouvelle', *Mercure de France*, 50.291.980 (15 April 1939), 317–23 (p. 321) (*OC*, pp. 585–90 (p. 588)); consulted on microfiche in BnF. The conversation about lyricism was evidently a taxing one. It came up, too, in a review of *Point de mire* by Pascal Pia. He notes that he wants to use the word but is wary of it as a way of making difficult language more palatable and thinks Arnauld will not thank him for it. See Pascal Pia, 'Céline Arnauld: *Point de Mire*', *Le Disque vert*, 1.4 (August 1922) (not repr. in *OC*).
2. Fort, 'Une poétesse de la poésie nouvelle'.
3. Claude Coste, 'La Musique dans la vie et l'œuvre de Philippe Soupault', in *Présence de Philippe Soupault*, ed. by Myriam Boucharenc and Claude Leroy (Caen: Presses universitaires de Caen, 1999), pp. 275–92.
4. *Anthologie Céline Arnauld*, pp. 143–65. A short extract was also published in *Le Journal des poètes*, 4.3 (18 February 1934), 3.
5. The name might remind us of Arnauld's reference to 'La Tour de Nesle' in 'Ombrelle Dada' (see Chapter 5), at least in that they are homophonous.
6. Malcolm Bowie, 'The Modern Period: 1789–2000', in Sarah Kay, Terence Cave, and Malcolm Bowie, *A Short History of French Literature* (Oxford: Oxford University Press, 2003), pp. 193–314 (p. 235).
7. Peter Dayan, *The Music of Dada: A Lesson in Intermediality for our Times* (Abingdon & New York: Routledge, 2019).
8. See, for example, Apollinaire's 1917 essay 'L'Esprit nouveau et les poètes', in *Œuvres en prose complètes*, pp. 948–53. Poets are hailed here for their articulation of all that is true, as well as beautiful, in the physical world, from the natural to the new. Apollinaire describes their writing as surprising, prophetic, characterised by new combinations, heavy with multiple significations, and open to whatever literary form supports expression.
9. Arthur Rimbaud, letter to Paul Demeny at Douai, Charleville, 15 May 1871. See Arthur Rimbaud, *Lettres du voyant (13 et 15 mai 1871)*, ed. by Gérald Schaeffer (Geneva: Droz, 1975), pp. 133–44 (p. 137). Arnauld's articulations of 'projectivism', discussed in Chapter 7, again come to mind, including the notion of plumbing the inner self for its full range of emotions. For

more on the prophet-poet in the avant-garde see Russell, *Poets, Prophets and Revolutionaries*, and specifically on Rimbaud, 'The Poet as Seer: Rimbaud' (pp. 39–61).
10. Forcer, *Dada as Text, Thought and Theory*, p. 22.
11. Mansbach, 'Methodology and Meaning in the Modern Art of Eastern Europe'.
12. Sandqvist, *Dada East*, pp. 302–03. He cites Victor Karady, *Gewalterfahrung und Utopie: Juden in den europäischen Moderne* (Frankfurt am Main: Fischer Taschenbuch, 1999), pp. 146–71. See also Chapter 3 of *Dada East*, 'In Central and Eastern Europe', pp. 45–63, for some useful context on the complexity of economic, social, and cultural relationships between Central and Eastern Europe, especially Romania, and Western Europe.
13. This dialogue is one of several dramatic pieces that Arnauld published. Chapter 2 included an analysis of 'Jeu d'échecs', dealt with in relation to *Tournevire* as an example of the author's tendency towards work to be performed. In Chapter 8 I discussed the poetic narrative 'Diorama'. This preceded a 'passion en deux actes' bearing the title of the book, *L'Apaisement de l'éclipse* (1925). Set up by a passage 'Décors et Jeux de Scène', its list of characters includes seven women, five men, and three children. Arnauld's work on dramatic texts occurred and recurred from 1919 to 1933. These 'scripts' surely merit a fuller analysis. Suffice it to say that the spoken, the performed, the oral, were at the fore of her creative drive.
14. Kandinsky, 'Concerning the Spiritual in Art', p. 94.
15. Chadwick, *Women Artists and the Surrealist Movement*, p. 74.
16. Another notable narrative about mental illness written by a woman avant-gardist is Leonora Carrington's *En bas* [Down Below] (Paris: Fontaine, 1945). This explicitly autobiographical text relays the author's experiences in a Spanish asylum and provides a counterpoint to Breton.
17. Dante Alighieri, *The Divine Comedy of Dante Alighieri*, ed. and trans. by John D. Sinclair, 3 vols (Oxford: Oxford University Press, 1961), III (*Paradiso*), 23 (Canto I, 31), & I (*Inferno*), 47 (Canto III, 1–2).
18. Céline Arnauld, 'Le Cas Lautréamont', *Le Disque vert*, numéro spécial, 4.4 (January 1925), 98–99 (*OC*, p. 401). Arnauld also wrote a review of *Les Chants de Maldoror* and cross-references it in this article. See 'Les Chants de Maldoror', *L'Esprit nouveau*, 2 (November 1920), 208–10 (*OC*, pp. 405–08). This writer was heralded as an inspiration by other writers of the avant-garde including Breton and Tzara.
19. Coste, 'La Musique dans la vie et l'œuvre de Philippe Soupault'.
20. Dayan, *The Music of Dada*.
21. We know that Arnauld was heavily involved in helping Dermée with his work. Flouquet notes her help with preparation and editing, both technical and literary. This, together with domestic tasks, and later Dermée's ill health, left her less time for writing, he states ('La Mort de Céline Arnauld', *Le Journal des poètes*, 22.3 (15 March 1952), 4 (*OC*, p. 592).
22. Arnauld, letter to Tzara, 1924.
23. Pierre Louis Flouquet, in 'Céline Arnauld nous dit ... Mystère de l'image'.
24. Flouquet, 'La Mort de Céline Arnauld'.
25. Jeanine Moulin, 'Introduction', in *La Poésie féminine: époque moderne*, ed. by Jeanine Moulin (Paris: Seghers, 1963), p. 16. She includes a biography and three poems, 'Paupières' (*Poèmes à claires-voies*), 'Aubier' (*Guêpier de diamants*) and 'Le Bar des Algues' (*Le Clavier secret*), pp. 251–55. In her brief introduction she draws attention to the positive impact of the melting-pot of national and cultural backgrounds in this period, including the 'École de Paris'.

CHAPTER 10

Cycles of Time and Nature in *Heures intactes* (1936) and *Les Réseaux du réveil* (1937)

> Espérons que va sonner enfin cette *heure intacte* où Céline Arnauld sera glorifiée comme un vrai, un grand poète de France.[1]
>
> [Let us hope that the *unbroken hour* will finally chime when Céline Arnauld will be glorified as a true, a great poet of France.]

Heures intactes [Unbroken Hours] and *Les Réseaux du réveil* [Awakening Networks] appeared in quick succession, in 1936 and 1937 respectively, showing that Arnauld's creative production was far from defunct in the 1930s. The work was, however, more meditative and less quickfire than some of her contributions to journals in the 1920s. It has become apparent in previous chapters that the question of time is an important preoccupation in Arnauld's writing. The change from day to night and back to day was already touched on in Chapter 4 as part of an identification of mutability. Night as a time of isolation or reflection has been posited in narratives including *Tournevire* (Chapter 2), 'Diorama' (Chapter 8), and *La Nuit rêve tout haut* (Chapter 9). Sleepwalkers tread the line between states of sleeping and waking, dream and reality, respite and insight. Awakenings are rife, both actual, namely with the coming of dawn, and metaphorical, the arrival at understanding and expression. An awareness of the relative passing of time is strongly in evidence in many of Arnauld's texts.

Time was an important preoccupation of Modernism and the avant-garde. In some cases it is explored as a phenomenon that is experienced and perceived differently with modern technologies, for example in relation to modes of transport, including railways, aeroplanes, and submarines, as explored in Chapter 3. But the question of time is also relayed as integral to the natural world. In this chapter I want to focus on the evocation of cycles of time which, I propose, takes on a sustained importance in these two volumes, above all centred on interactions in nature, by and between plant, insect, animal, and human life. This thematic thread is used to discuss some common ground in two publications that are unalike in other ways. It is not meant as a device to conflate them; it is as much a means to delve into variations in form and tone that keep Arnauld's work moving, both in the sense of being dynamic and affective.

The very title of *Heures intactes* (OC, pp. 267–96) directs the reader's attention to the matter of time, while its structure demands a different kind of reading *in* time. The adjective 'intact' points to something unbroken, secure, whole, especially in the sense of a material object. Paired with time here, it suggests a lack of interruption, long segments of time to be either endured or enjoyed. Structurally the text differs from any other that Arnauld published, even though she still introduces it as 'poèmes'. It is made up of three parts, signalled by roman numerals. Unusually neither the sections nor the component poems are given titles, facilitating a more fluid reading of the text as continuous, potentially to be read in one go, as a single epic poem. There are, however, breaks between series of stanzas, and blank spaces. Sections of text could stand independently, to be read as poems, and indeed some fragments were reproduced both in journals and in Arnauld's 1936 anthology.[2] The tripartite structure is underscored by the fact that each begins with an epigraph. As discussed in the last chapter, Arnauld makes various explicit acknowledgements of her precursors and literary influences in her later works, in particular, either through direct quotations or by means of allusions within texts.

The first epigraph is a quotation from Rimbaud's 1873 *Une saison en enfer* [A Season in Hell], specifically from 'Matin' [Morning], the eighth of nine loose sections. It reads:

> Vous qui prétendez que des bêtes poussent des sanglots de chagrin, que des malades désespèrent, que des morts rêvent mal, tâchez de raconter ma chute et mon sommeil. Moi, je ne puis pas plus m'expliquer que le mendiant avec ses continuels *Pater* et *Ave Maria*. Je ne sais plus parler!
>
> [Those of you who believe that animals cry tears of sorrow, that the sick suffer, that the dead have nightmares, try to explain my fall, and my sleep. I can now no longer explain myself any better than a beggar mumbling his *Pater* and *Ave Maria*. I no longer know how to speak!][3]

Arnauld's reader, like Rimbaud's, is led to anticipate a dramatic battle of emotions but urged not to expect easy legibility. We recall the Baudelaire quotation that she chose as an introduction to 'Diorama' (Chapter 8), in which he asserted a refusal to answer to critics or to explain his writing. The quotation also expresses a terror of silence shared by Arnauld, as outlined in Chapter 9. The last line of Rimbaud's quotation tells us that the poet is exhausted to the point of being unable to express himself. He cannot talk or will not talk.

An interview with Arnauld provides us with a rare explicit comment on questions of explanation and articulation. In response to the question 'Un poème incohérent peut-il être beau?' [Can an incoherent poem be beautiful?], in a 1932 survey in *Le Journal des poètes*, she remains stubbornly lyrical as opposed to prosaic. She shifts the emphasis from poetry, or schools of poetry, to the poet, producing an elegy to their status as visionary, powerful, and divine, destined to be misunderstood. The similes she chooses align and fuse them with nature, such as, 'Il est le Nord terrible: neige et soleil; l'Orient de flamme: magie et songe; l'Occident sans âme: pluie et tempête' [He is the terrible North: snow and sun; the flaming West: magic and reflection; the soulless West: rain and storm].[4] We know of Arnauld's classification of her own poetry as ultra-modern. That affirmation ties in with Rimbaud's famously conflicted exhortation in *Une saison en enfer*, 'ce qu'il faut désormais, c'est être "absolument moderne"' ('One must be absolutely modern').[5]

The epigraph that introduces the second section is also a citation from Rimbaud, this time from his collection *Les Illuminations*, published in 1886. A quotation drawn from 'Conte', it reads: 'Peut on s'extasier dans la destruction, se rajeunir par la cruauté!' ('Can one rejoice in destruction, be rejuvenated by cruelty?').[6] The tone is set, here, for a metamorphosis through trial, for renewal out of devastation, and construction out of destruction. These are recurrent themes in exploring creative vitality, from the Romantics to the avant-garde. Half question, half exclamation, it is hopeful, at least, even as it evokes a painful journey. This second nod to Rimbaud cements an appreciation of him and encourages an intertextual reading. Connections between her work and that of Rimbaud were picked up by contemporary critics. In a 1936 review in *Mercure de France*, for example, the Belgian symbolist poet André Fontainas called her, 'une sœur d'art, de pensée, de sentiment, qu'il [Rimbaud] peut accueillir et reconnaître. Elle est un des poètes de ces temps' [a sister in art, thought and sentiment, whom he [Rimbaud] would welcome and recognise. She is one of the poets of our time].[7] In two of her own expositions of her writing Arnauld also acknowledges Rimbaud, the only writer aside from Dermée to whom she makes reference in any interviews. In 1950 she states, 'Je n'ai lu Rimbaud qu'après avoir publié *Point de mire* en 1921' [I read Rimbaud only after having published *Point de mire* in 1921]. In 1953 she reiterates the same point and date.[8] She is at pains, though, to clarify that the relationship to his work is not a straightforward case of influence and imitation. The connections are more complex.

It is evident, though, that *Heures intactes* takes inspiration from Rimbaud, above all his extended prose-poem, *Une saison en enfer*, both in form and theme. It pays homage in its reduced but signalled multipartite structure, its emotive rhetoric, and dramatic motifs. The battle through hell and hallucination, hope and damnation, that is enacted in Rimbaud's poem, is evident in Arnauld's poem. Other common ground is the attention to the seasons, the fantastic universe of childhood, and to the poet as visionary, previously identified in Chapter 9. Arnauld's poem begins by addressing a second person with the informal 'tu' issuing from the plural 'nous'. In the second part, and through the third, it switches to the first-person singular. This narrowing down to a first-person narrator leads the reader to an increasingly intense identification. Where Arnauld's poems are on occasion difficult to engage with, not least since they frequently eschew identifiable narrators, this work is lyrical and emotive. The text is punctuated by direct addresses, for example:'Ô sagesse' [Oh wisdom], 'Ô nuit' [Oh night], and 'Ô apaisement' [Oh appeasement] (*OC*, pp. 270, 272, 275), heightening its rhetorical effect.

The time-cycle of the day is dominant. The period between evening and dawn, as so often in Arnauld's writing, offers time for dreaming and thinking, to positive and negative effect. That tension is reflected in collisions that surprise and refuse closure, such as 'hanté par la clarté qui dévoile les âmes' [haunted by the clarity that unveils souls] (*OC*, p. 271). One is faced with one's own self, alone, in a time that offers extremes of experience, an emotional journey 'de merveille en merveille et de douleur en douleur' [from marvel to marvel, and from pain to pain] (p. 273). The thoughtfulness, reflection, and solitude it permits is both fruitful and afflictive. Dawn brings light and awakening but also its own agonies as reality and consciousness set in.

Weather is conjured up in all its beauty and drama. From snow to fog, mist, rain, wind, lightning, thunder, storms, and whirlwinds, to sun rays, light, heat, and flames, the world is in constant flux, alive with activity and seasonal change. The setting in *Heures intactes* is nature, with scarcely a reference to the urban experience so often associated with Modernism and the avant-garde. The fascination with trains and planes in earlier work, identified in Part I, is gone. This is a dynamic landscape of mountains, volcanos, glaciers, oceans, meteors, summits, rocks, fountains, geysers, and forests. It is one that seems unconfined by country or even continent; rather it is a transnational vision that takes in the full scope of the planet. The full majesty of nature maps on to the force of the narrator's emotions. She does not admire it from afar, as a spectacle, but is transformed by its action and violence. The marine environment is also present once again, the fluidity of water appealing to the poet. Here is an intelligent ecosystem, much of which is below the surface and cannot be seen; a world of connections and communications. Her will to grasp it intuitively, and to relate it dynamically, maps on to Bergson's theories of the apprehension of the material world as necessarily complex, mobile, and in flux.[9]

Another characteristic of this text is the recurrence of fire. Arnauld has employed metaphors of flames and burning before but here they are more dominant, recalling Rimbaud's journey to hell in *Une saison en enfer*. Given the epigraph that Arnauld chooses for part III of her extended poem, from Shelley's *Prometheus Unbound*, we might also think of Prometheus's gift of fire to humanity.[10] Fire in Arnauld's poem represents passion and light. We learn of 'Flammes du merveilleux' [Flames of the marvellous] (*OC*, p. 270) and 'l'incantation des flammes' [the incantation of flames] (p. 271). Eyes and hands burn with passion and iridescence. These contrast with evocations of cold, ice, and snow. Together they represent changes in mood and fortune, both seemingly necessary and required in a human life experienced to the full.

If Arnauld's preoccupations appear to border on the atavistic it is worth noting that the alignment of modernity with the city is only one aspect of the creative productions of the avant-garde. Because of Arnauld's rejection of Surrealism we are justifiably wary of drawing comparisons. But there are many examples of both visual art and poetry that take in tensions between natural and industrialised worlds. Just one example is Philippe Soupault's poem 'Est-ce le vent' [Is it the Wind].[11] With its far-ranging evocations of trees and forests, sand and sea, journeying and edges, night and day, remembering and forgetting, voice and song, we might be discussing typical elements in Arnauld's poetry. The natural world was also a source of the marvellous for the Surrealists, after all, including animal and insect worlds alongside the human.[12]

Much attention, too, has been paid to motifs of the natural world in work by women associated with Surrealism. While in large part scholarship has focused on the visual arts, Whitney Chadwick, Georgiana Colvile, and others have exposed how writers including Leonora Carrington and Gisèle Prassinos employed animals, insects, and plant life to evoke alternative and marvellous worlds, and to consider the confrontations or connections between the human and non-human.[13] We might also propose links to late nineteenth-century poets, those preceding and associated with French Symbolism. Baudelaire, Rimbaud, and Verlaine, for example, frequently drew on nature to make connections between outer, physical reality and inner, emotional states, all the time experimenting with form.

In Arnauld's poem, the human is intensely present, albeit dissipated and dispersed. We have seen how eyes and the mouth, representing vision and voice respectively, are prevalent in Arnauld's writing and they return here. Hands, too, are a strong bodily motif from the very first line, 'tes mains lourdes de délire et de lumiére' [your hands heavy with delight and light] (*OC*, p. 269). They are mostly powerful, especially those that are offered to the narrator: 'tes mains de flamme' [hands of flame] (p. 269); 'ses mains chargés de tremblantes merveilles' [hands laden with trembling marvels] (p. 273); 'Tes mains silencieuses flambent de bonté' [Your silent hands are aflame with goodness] (p. 293). Occasionally they falter, 'Tes mains qui s'enflammaient sur l'étendue du rêve | Sont-elles devenues des mains de fou?' [Your hands that were flaming with the extent of dreams | Have they become a fool's hands?] (p. 279). The narrator's hands, at times, represent uncertainty, 'J'ai les mains pâles et fiévreuses' [I have pale and feverish hands] (p. 289). One of the most poignant references is powerful in its repetition of the motif of hands:

> Écoute gémir me mains sous le poids de l'oubli
> [...]
> Mains sacrifiées mains crispées sur l'orage
> Mais aussi mains d'enfants tout imbibées de rêve! (*OC*, p. 296)

[Listen to my hands moan under the weight of forgetting | [...] | Hands sacrificed hands tensed on the storm | But also a child's hands imbibed with dreaming!]

Nostalgia for the past, a grasp of the realities of the present, and projection into the future — with the challenges this entails — are encompassed in these lines.

Shoulders, meanwhile, represents communion and comfort:

> J'ai des épaules de saule pleureur
> Des épaules d'enfant et des épaules grelottantes d'ivresse
> Mais des épaules de femme aussi! (*OC*, p. 289)

[I have weeping willow shoulders | The shoulders of a child and shoulders shivering with drunkenness | But a woman's shoulders too.]

The body struggles to carry the narrator's emotional burden. At times she is more capable than others, this sequence suggests, but she is candid about the trials she faces, exalting childhood for its raw state. Fragments of the body variously symbolise a gamut of emotions. They are connected only loosely to a whole. The narrator's identity is dispersed and elusive.

A rare summary of Arnauld's writing life, published in an anthology of women's writing, picks up on the rapport between the human and non-human in her *œuvre*. Its editor, Moulin, writes, 'Sa tête frôle les nuages, sa poitrine reçoit tous les arbres avec leurs cris d'oiseaux, ses bras enveloppent les cimes. Confondue avec l'univers, elle murmure des paroles d'une enivrant ambiguïté' [Her head brushes the clouds, her chest welcomes all the trees with their birdcall, her arms wrap around their tops. Merged with the universe, she murmurs words marked by an intoxicating ambiguity]. This poetic elegy echoes a bodily dissipation that nevertheless suggests a generative communion with the sights and sounds of nature. Moulin likewise identifies an in-betweenness, 'sa silhouette flotte entre deux eaux, entre le réel et l'irréel, entre ce qu'on est convenu d'appeler le bon sens at la folie' [her silhouette floats between two waters, between the real and unreal, between what we are used to calling common sense and madness].[14] Her review draws out key currents in Arnauld's work, from the evocation of the fragmented, vaporous physical body, to the indeterminate distinction between robust or insecure mental health. Both are vividly mapped on to the landscape.

Though body parts have been included in Arnauld's earlier writings they become more prevalent in her later volumes, the human assuming more physicality. Fears, anxieties, and hopes are projected onto it. It is a nexus of interactions with other individual humans and society. The human and her relationship with her surroundings, too, are examined, often aligned or conflated. As the psychologist Marc Wittmann observes, 'The brain does not simply represent the world in a disembodied way as an intellectual construct, but rather the organism interacts with the whole with the environment. In this notion, a mind separate from the body [...] does not exist, but rather our mind is body-bound. We think, feel, and act with our body in the world. All experience is embedded in this body-related being-in-the-world'.[15]

The industrial mechanisation that threatened and excited writers and artists of Modernism and the avant-garde in the 1910s and 1920s sometimes resulted in a rejection of representations of the body. Formally, a turn against figuration is tied to what Sally O'Reilly calls 'the cool detachment of modernism'.[16] Yet the body was still an important question for the avant-garde, even as new formal strategies were developed. It was dissected and reconfigured, for example, in literary and visual forms, from dadaist mechanomorphic diagrams to surrealist *corps exquis* [exquisite corpses].[17] In the 1930s, in changing cultural, political, and personal circumstances, Arnauld seems to bring the body back to view in her writing. It is still, notably, a 'body-in-pieces', to use Nochlin's term. Instead of coherent descriptions of external appearances, elements of the body suggest 'the sense of social, psychological, even metaphysical fragmentation that so seems to mark modern experience — a loss of wholeness, a shattering of connection, a destruction or disintegration of permanent value'.[18] Arnauld's searching eyes and seeking hands are verbally-rendered equivalents to the painted and sketched representations that Nochlin underscores. The impression of a dissolute, partial, vulnerable body comes across strongly in *Heures intactes*, the 'intact' almost a plea for solidity or wholeness. Her recourse to a more meaningful natural belonging is also illuminated by Nochlin's outlining of a will to overcome the 'disintegrative effects' so acutely felt in the urban environment by the seemingly opposite call for a higher unity or totalisation.[19]

Memory is also a theme. References to childhood recur, fêted by Surrealism as a prelogical state of experience. Childhood is arguably an even more acute source of nostalgia for Arnauld as an émigré, with her past and present at odds. There are plentiful articulations of remembering: 'Je tourne sans cesse les pages de ma vie' [Ceaselessly I turn the pages of my life], declares the narrator self-consciously (OC, p. 272). The possibility of a linear narrative, a coherent story of selfhood, is challenged by forgetting, which is frequently called up. The narrator grapples with organising a continuum of time:

> Regardons le passé comme une floraison ingénue de rêves
> L'avenir comme une nature morte
> Tandis que le présent est l'éruption du volcan (OC, p. 270)
>
> [Let us view the past as an ingenuous flourishing of dreams | The future as a still life | Whilst the present is the eruption of the volcano]

The innocent self of the past is already eroding, while the uncertain present, for Arnauld's narrator, is described as volatile, like a violent explosion. The future, meantime, is scarcely imaginable, a static still life.

Since Arnauld uses the example of the still life, we might refer to reflections on painting that work across art forms, and that bridge or blur conceptual boundaries between the nineteenth and twentieth centuries. In his 1863 essay 'Le Peintre de la vie moderne' Baudelaire writes, 'La modernité, c'est le transitoire, le fugitif, le contingent, la moitié de l'art, dont l'autre moitié est l'éternel et l'immutable' ('By "modernity" I mean the ephemeral, the contingent, the half of art whose other half is the eternal and the immutable').[20] These tensions between the transitory and the eternal are apparent in Arnauld's poetry. It is taut, looking back and looking ahead, but above all intensely informed by enquiry in the present. Composed of vivid imagery and motifs, to which our attention is drawn, her works nevertheless leave much unsaid and uncertain, like gaps on a canvas. Russell's characterisation of Apollinaire's work applies to Arnauld too:

> He views the past with both nostalgia and a recognition that it must depart, and the future with both resignation and hope. Both are exhilarating and frightening. For each threatens to deny that part of himself which feels its allegiance to the opposing sense of time.[21]

A fear of dissolution of the self over time is keenly expressed by Arnauld in *Heures intactes*. The most poignant point in this text is the first lines of the second section, 'Je connais toutes les misères | Et tous les chemins qui mènent au suicide' [I know all the miseries | and all the paths that lead to suicide] (OC, p. 276). With the benefit of hindsight, namely our knowledge of Arnauld's death by suicide in 1952, this statement strikes us as painfully self-aware and even prophetic. It is an epic expression of emotion that has as much in common with Romantic or Dantean verse as with avant-garde or modernist poetry, and which assumes an intense personal dimension. All have in common a profound exploration and experience of the conflicts of doubt and the definite, the fugitive and the permanent. Body, self, space, and time are shown to be inextricable in intensely-felt human experience. The 'heures intactes' signalled by the title can pass slowly — in solitude, self-doubt, or depression — or quickly, in creative flow and vitality. A heightened awareness of the passing of time is inherent in the project of facing and embracing the sensations of the moment.

The relationship between the nocturnal and diurnal is neatly encompassed by the successive titles *Heures intactes* and *Les Réseaux du réveil*. Where the former can be read as denoting night and solitude, the latter proposes awakening. Appearing in print one year after *Heures intactes*, *Les Réseaux du réveil* returns to the format of a collection of named poems (*OC*, pp. 299–323). These twelve poems share ground thematically with *Heures intactes*, including emphases on time and place, and the human individual enmeshed in the context of the dramatic natural world. The titles alone offer a flavour of these themes. Some combine the natural environment with reflection, such as 'Vallée des songes' [Valley of Dreams] and 'Buisson de rêves' [Stream of Dreams]. Others point to time, joining moments with moods, from 'Festival de minuit' [Midnight Festival] to 'L'Aube jeune et alerte' [The Young Alert Dawn]. The moon, waves, a storm, and spring feature in other titles. Cycles of time and weather are again at the forefront as the object of contemplation and as metaphorical markers of emotional experience.

The volume begins with an intriguing one-line imperative, 'Faisons éclater nos secrets comme des pivoines!' [Let us burst open our secrets like peonies!] (p. 301). The contrast between previous direct addresses, in which *tu* or *vous* have been employed, above all in the Dada period, and this more communal exhortation is striking; this is a shared imperative. The vibrancy and vitality of the exploding peony is a powerful introductory snapshot. In the twelve poems that follow, hope and love are foregrounded in beautifully-crafted celebrations of the natural world.

While the exploding peony does not make another appearance its burst of energy is felt in many references to flora in this collection. The rose, for example, is selected by Arnauld as a signifier laden with connotations. Normally symbolic of love, it is used to various effects in these poems. Typically, she is not satisfied with cliché but instead wants to dissect and deploy this object differently. It features in all but two of the poems in this volume, that is in ten texts. The daisy also appears in abundance. We might read this use of flora as an acceptance of transience. The short but vivid lives of blossoms are preferable to dullness and stagnation. They exist in the present. In a recent book on Dada and time, Maria Stavrinaki has argued for the 'presentism' of Dada. She proposes that it is characterised by a refusal of fossilised past or utopian future in favour of a concentration on the ambiguities of the present moment. Her claims for a 'vertiginous mix of death drive and *élan vital*' can aptly be applied to Arnauld's grapplings with time.[22]

The final three poems in this volume are presented here for their conspicuous optimism. 'Et revoici la joie!' [And Here again is Joy!] (*OC*, pp. 318–19) follows its exclamatory title with a similarly emphatic and effective single word 'Vagues!' [Waves!]. Human and nature are inextricable:

> Prophètes et poètes sur le bord d'un rayon assis
> Parlent à l'amitié neigeuse des vagues
> Ils écoutent la fuite des souvenirs et des songes
> Et se grisent de lueurs d'infini (*OC*, p. 318)

[Prophets and poets seated on the edge of a ray | Speak to the snowy friendship of the waves | They listen to the drift of memories and musings | And get drunk on infinite glimmers]

This four-line stanza is a wonderful depiction of the poet as visionary, inspired and intoxicated by the edges and expanse of the natural environment. We have already discussed ideas of the poet as prophet, ahead of their time, prevalent in so many manifestations of the avant-garde. Russell has pointed to variations in belief in the future according to contexts of time and place. A discussion of Apollinaire and Futurism, for example, identifies a pre-war optimism, in the early years of the avant-garde, in the possibilities of art and role of the artist. The timespan of Arnauld's work sees her engage in very different periods of belief and despair but her attachment to the poet-as-prophet, ahead of their time, is a constant. Russell's drawing-out of tensions in Apollinaire's work between the personal and the collective, and the need for constant innovation balanced with acknowledgement of the past, resonates, too, with some of the ambiguities in Arnauld's work.[23]

'Un ciel de joie épanoui après l'orage' [A Joyous Sky blooming after the Storm] (*OC*, pp. 320–21) denotes the drama of a tempestuous sky and sea, occasionally collapsed into each other. It is saturated with the notion of change, of the hope that succeeds despair. Russell's observations of Apollinaire's poems as 'marked by alternating passages of exuberance and quietude, idealistic expansiveness and melancholy retreat' apply here too.[24] The human first-person narrator intervenes, again, in fragments: a heart (burned by the sand), hands (vibrating, placed on the sea), head (rolling with the waves), and lips (pale, dreams deposited on them by the wind). Both poems call up marine and celestial landscapes to map sentiment and passion. The narrator-poet is in sync with her environment. Indeed, in one rare articulation of her writing Arnauld likewise makes use of nature. She compares expression unhindered by formal rules to both the splendour of an aurora borealis and the myriad productive branches of a tree.[25]

The final poem in this volume leaves the reader on a similarly high note of optimism and productivity. 'Plus haut que l'amour' [Higher than Love] (*OC*, pp. 322–23) picks up in its title the 'haut' of *La Nuit rêve tout haut*. This height can signify both sound, defiantly emitted, and altitude, a reaching-up to summits or the sky. In the first five-line stanza alone the heart is mentioned three times. But it is also creativity, the ability to articulate and write, that are the pinnacle for Arnauld, sought after and sketched out so lyrically throughout her work. The declarative 'Ô cœurs si lourds de peine!' [Oh hearts so heavy with pain] is followed immediately by 'Ô têtes où naissent des mondes!' [Oh heads in which worlds are born!], this sixth line indented for emphasis. These worlds — and words — are born of struggle, she recognises, 'Mais le cœur en peine est l'axe du poème!' [But the heart in pain is the axis of the poem] (p. 322). This line, standing alone, is indeed at the core of the poem and her production. Designations of Apollinaire's oscillations between the 'visionary and melancholic' and 'personal expansion and contraction' are likewise pertinent to Arnauld.[26]

The poem's refrains are emphatic and build momentum, above all in the second stanza:

> Plus haut que l'amour il y a les nuages
> Plus haut que la gloire se place la vie
> Plus haut que les yeux il y a le ciel (OC, p. 322)

> [Higher than love there are the clouds | Higher than glory stands life | Higher than eyes there is the sky]

The rhetorical effect of repetition is exultant, optimistic, and infectious. It recurs in the seventh stanza, too. A miracle occurs:

> Tremblante d'avoir mis la merveille
> Plus haut que l'amour
> Plus haut que la fuite des visages (OC, p. 322)

> [Trembling at having captured the marvellous | Higher than love | Higher than the swift passing of faces]

Communion with society, connoted here by fleeting faces, is taxing and transitory, only momentarily enjoyed, as the narrator seeks an elevated consciousness.

Far from being isolated examples these texts form part of a network of associations that began in *Poèmes à claires-voies* and persists as far as *Les Réseaux du réveil*. From openworks to networks, Arnauld's reiterations are both intentional and abundant. Indeed the term 'claires-voies' reappears in two instances in this collection, in both cases applied to hearts ('cœurs à claires-voies', in 'Oreiller de lune' and 'Festival de minuit', OC, pp. 308, 312). The heart is porous, vulnerable, and open in these applications. In *Heures intactes*, too, the qualifier is applied to rain, 'les claires-voies de la pluie' (OC, p. 281), drawing attention succinctly to the transparency and insolidity of a rain shower, through which objects can be only semi-glimpsed. Its application to forgetting, 'les claires-voies de l'oubli' (p. 294), again blurs the material and the immaterial. Memory loss is not total, it implies; remembering can slip through and surprise us. The term *réseaux*, meantime, is polysemic. The notion of networks extends from the natural world to the man-made. It can apply to rays of light, crystalline structures, or rivers; to the criss-crossing lines of textile or architectural patterns; to communications, electricity, or transport systems.

The harmony expressed in this volume is far removed from the defensive-aggressive rhetoric of the writing discussed in the context of the Dada era, with its provocative stance, and the articulation of confusion and conflict in some texts from the mid-1920s. Where other humans and social interactions have given rise to conflict, the landscape imagined prior to, or beyond the built, social, and cultural environment seems to offer a means of articulation, of intense and painful seeking, and the greatest potential for solace. It is worth returning to a quotation from 'Diorama', cited in Chapter 7, 'Les mains des poètes et des artistes seront aussi nouvelles et fragiles que cette fleur qui est le réveil-matin de l'aurore' [The hands of poets and artists will be as new and as fragile as the flower that is daybreak's alarm-call] (*OC*, p. 180). Imagery discussed in this chapter comes together in this vision of the poet, from hands to flora to natural awakenings. This was Arnauld's conception of projectivism.

Arnauld specifies a place, Monaco, and a date, summer 1936, for this dazzlingly optimistic volume. It was also the year in which an anthology of her work was produced. The collection bears witness to confidence and joy, to progress and creativity, to the arrival in a clearing after a fight through the thicket. A harmony and peace are exuded, succeeding the pain evoked so desolately elsewhere, not least in the previous volume *Heures intactes*, and bearing witness to the optimistic idea that mental struggle and suffering can be generative. The awakenings of *Les Réseaux du réveil* bring a welcome consciousness and capacity for presence in time and in the environment. In the next chapter, however, we will see another extreme change of tone that should scarcely surprise us, given the trajectory of political events in Europe. A first, very different, text from 1939 will bear witness not only to Arnauld's individual, psychological battles, but also to the drastic political context of an approaching war.

Notes to Chapter 10

1. Fort, 'Une poétesse de la poésie nouvelle', in *OC*, p. 590.
2. In one case three extracts appear in a different order than in *Heures intactes*. See Céline Arnauld, 'Poèmes', *Souvenir de la réception de Madame Céline Arnauld et Monsieur Paul Dermée aux amis de 1914, Les Actes poétiques*, 8 (15 December 1937), [n.p.]. This reinforces a notion of contingency in narrative structure.
3. Arthur Rimbaud, *Une saison en enfer*, in *Œuvres*, ed. by Suzanne Bernard (Paris: Garnier, [1960]), p. 239 (Martin-Schmets did the work of tracing the source of this quotation and others; *OC*, p. 269); *Rimbaud Complete*, trans. and ed. by Wyatt Mason (New York: Modern Library, 2003), p. 218.
4. Céline Arnauld, 'Notre enquête hebdomadaire: un poème incohérent peut-il être beau?', *Le Journal des poètes*, 2.7 (9 January 1932), 1 (*OC*, p. 441). The other respondents were Gustave Khan, André Marcou, and Ribemont-Dessaignes.
5. Rimbaud, *Une saison en enfer*, p. 207; *Rimbaud Complete*, p. 220.
6. Arthur Rimbaud, *Les Illuminations*, in *Œuvres*, ed. by Bernard, pp. 245–309 (p. 259); *Rimbaud Complete*, p. 227.
7. André Fontainas, 'Revue de la quinzaine: les poèmes', *Mercure de France*, 271.919 (1 October 1936), 112–13 (*OC*, pp. 540–41 (p. 541)).
8. Céline Arnauld, in 'Poésie et réalité: interview du poète Céline Arnauld', interview with P. L. Flouquet, *Le Journal des poètes*, 1 (January 1950), 3 (*OC*, p. 446), and 'Comment je suis venue à la poésie', in *Anthologie des écrivains du Vè*, ed. by Gérard de Lacaze-Duthiers (Paris: Pierre Clairac, 1953), pp. 38–39 (*OC*, p. 456). Rimbaud was of course also acknowledged as a precursor by Arnauld's close peers, including Tzara and Breton.
9. Bergson, *L'Évolution créatrice*.
10. The quotation is the final nine lines of Shelley's 1820 four-act play *Prometheus Unbound* in French translation.
11. Philippe Soupault, 'Est-ce le vent', *La Révolution surréaliste*, 7 (15 June 1926), 15.
12. For a discussion of this poem see Coste, 'La Musique dans la vie et l'œuvre de Philippe Soupault', pp. 275–92.
13. See, for example, Whitney Chadwick, *Women Artists and the Surrealist Movement*, pp. 141–80; Georgiana M. M. Colvile, 'Beauty and/Is the Beast: Animal Symbology in the Work of Leonora

Carrington, Remedios Varo and Leonor Fini', in *Surrealism and Women*, ed. by Caws, Kuenzli and Raaberg, pp. 159–81; Kirsten Strom, *The Animal Surreal: The Role of Darwin, Animals, and Evolution in Surrealism* (New York: Routledge, 2017), pp. 73–84. These texts confront discourses around woman and nature, as either an imposed cliché or potentially as a source of power.
14. *La Poésie féminine*, ed. by Moulin, p. 251.
15. Marc Wittmann, *Altered States of Consciousness: Experiences out of Time and Self*, trans. by Philippa Hurd (Cambridge, MA: MIT Press, 2018), p. 82.
16. Sally O'Reilly, *The Body in Contemporary Art* (London: Thames & Hudson, 2009), p. 13.
17. See Elza Adamowicz's important work in this area: *Dada Bodies: Between Battleground and Fairground* (Manchester: Manchester University Press, 2019); *Surrealist Collage in Text and Image: Dissecting the Exquisite Corpse* (Cambridge & New York: Cambridge University Press, 2005). I also conclude that representations of the body and embodied experience were a critical issue for women in *Dada's Women*, pp. 195–205.
18. Nochlin, *The Body in Pieces*, pp. 23–24.
19. Ibid., p. 53.
20. Baudelaire, 'Le Peintre de la vie moderne', p. 69; *The Painter of Modern Life and Other Essays*, pp. 4–5.
21. Russell, *Poets, Prophets and Revolutionaries*, p. 78.
22. Maria Stavrinaki, *Dada Presentism: An Essay on Art and History*, trans. by Daniela Ginsburg (Stanford, CA: Stanford University Press, 2016), p. 22.
23. Russell makes close analyses of exemplary poems such as 'Toujours' [Always], pertinent to time and forgetting, and 'Les Collines' [The Hills], with its depictions of the poet placed above his fellow men, his identity torn between past and future (*Poets, Prophets and Revolutionaries*, pp. 62–95). He also draws on explicit articulations of key themes in the essay 'L'Esprit nouveau et les poètes', noted as a reference point in Chapters 3 and 8 of this book.
24. Russell, *Poets, Prophets and Revolutionaries*, p. 66.
25. Arnauld, in 'Céline Arnauld nous dit … Mystère de l'image', p. 1.
26. Russell, *Poets, Prophets and Revolutionaries*, p. 66.

CHAPTER 11

❖

War, Exile, and Precarious Peace: *La Nuit pleure tout haut* (1939) and *Rien qu'une étoile, suivi de Plains-chants sauvages* (1948)

While there are only two years between the second volume discussed in the previous chapter and the first publication to be presented here, there is nevertheless a huge leap to negotiate in terms of historical events as we enter the context of war. With Fascism already on the rise in the mid-1930s it is safe to assume that Arnauld and Dermée were aware of the mounting peril to their work and lives and that they would have been following closely events in France and in Europe. In October 1936, for example, they were both signatories of the 'Manifeste de l'Association des écrivains pour la défense de la culture' [Manifesto of the Association of Writers in Defence of Culture], in support of anti-Fascist action in Spain. In a 1932 interview with Flouquet, Arnauld had underscored the urgency of political engagement more generally:

> Aujourd'hui, où les lamentations de la misère humaine traversent les murs les plus épais, le poème est de moins en moins un éclat de rire, et de plus en plus, si beaux que soient les mots qu'il fait scintiller — un cri d'indignation, et un chant de révolte.[1]
>
> [Today, as the lamentations of human misery pierce the thickest walls, the poem is less and less a burst of laughter and — however beautiful the words that enliven it — more and more a cry of indignation, and a song of revolt.]

Poetry as revolt might remind us of Dada but times had changed. Lamentation and indignation would become evident in her work of the late 1930s in a newly-imploding Europe. Arnauld's writing of this period offers rich clues to an environment of escalating tensions.

The title of her 1939 publication *La Nuit pleure tout haut* [The Night Weeps Aloud], in its reworking of the name of her 1934 collection *La Nuit rêve tout haut*, encapsulates the transformation she had anticipated in the 1932 interview just cited. The subject of the sentence remains the same but the change in verb points compellingly and worryingly to the changes wrought in five years. The dreaming of the personified night has given way to weeping; optimism has ceded to foreboding. What was glorious and celebratory ('tout haut'), when applied to a dream state, becomes negatively declarative and unrestrained when applied to the shedding of tears. The title signals an outpouring, a warning, something inflicted rather than chosen, a reaction to the present or immediate past rather than an expression with creative potential and hope for the future. As noted in Chapter 10, nocturnal time is marked by intensity, for Arnauld. It is a time to interrogate both the unconscious and reality, in all their manifestations.

La Nuit pleure tout haut is designated by the author as a single poem, the only instance in which she published a book-length poem signalled as such. Printed across twenty-two pages it is notable for its layout. Rather than continuous text, it restarts at different points on the page, with white space between sections. This attention to the page reminds us of the typographical experiments of the avant-garde and its precursors, above all Mallarmé.[2] Each page is a short musing, a new thought, the blank spaces suggesting hesitancy and reflection. Arnauld had experimented with typographical layout in some of her earlier publications. Her willingness to do so again suggests a return to a more radical way of writing that responds to the climate and underscores the urgency of her project. The power of the blank spaces to militate against complacency or passivity in the reader is reinforced by the varying styles, presentation, and lengths of each. From short bursts of continuous prose centred and justified on a page, to short passages separated by blank lines and set with hanging indents, to sections set out in stanzas, there are any number of variations. The effect on the reader is to make room for thought, to instil pauses in reading, and to renew the impact of each, fresh intervention. Questions and exclamations are frequent. Some sections are placed in quotation marks to heighten the effect of direct, passionate delivery. Others draw on repetition and renewal — the same phrase underscored, or an expression slightly altered, varied, returning in a different form.

Thematically the poem oscillates between expressions of love and solitude, vigour and death, night and day, light and dark, hope and foreboding. Night may bring terrors but it also facilitates dreams. Daytime can be a terrifying place too. Love invokes fear of the opposite, solitude, even as it comforts. The first-person narration makes the poem feel deeply personal and authentic. It is powerfully emotive, encouraging a connection between the reader and narrator that has been more challenging to establish in other work that rather instils a critical distance and requires decoding. The notion of a life's journey, so central in 'Diorama', is reprised here in a poem that can feasibly be read as autobiographical. There is a semi-narrative from childhood to the present, a necessary journeying evoked by boat. One stanza can be interpreted as a love poem to Dermée. These biographical readings are more viable here than in any of Arnauld's work so far.

Emotions are laid bare, more so than in previous work that signifies rather through suggestion. A declaration at the foot of the third page summarises a struggle that was discussed in the previous chapter, 'Depuis mon enfance j'ai avancé dans la vie solitaire, gorgée de songes, d'illusions, d'amour! Quelquefois la folie me guette! Une folie où le merveilleux est roi' [Since childhood I have edged forwards in a solitary life, filled with musings, with illusions, with love! Sometimes madness stalks me! A madness in which the marvellous is king] (*OC*, p. 329). A blank expanse on the page before this text underscores both reflection and solitude. The term 'le merveilleux', meanwhile, has strong associations with Surrealism, of course. Identified and promoted by Breton, in his 1924 'Manifeste du surréalisme', and further theorised by Pierre Mabille in 1940, this expansive concept exalts the discovery of the extraordinary in day-to-day experience.[3]

If dreams provide access to the marvellous, so too does childhood, another state beloved of Surrealism for its access to the unconscious. In Arnauld's text there are references to the child launched into the world, its mother and father lost. 'L'enfance' [childhood] is personified, given a voice. It appears like a spectre, a version of the narrator haunting her:

> Tu as grandi en marge de la vie, entourée de livres et d'étoiles. Mais à quoi rêvais-tu donc? Ah! Oui, le coffre aux trésors, les livres oubliés par un certain aïeul, un prophète sans doute! Tu as brisé mes poupées? On va briser l'idole que tu es, on va t'égorger, colombe! (*OC*, p. 337)

> [You grew up on the margins of life, surrounded by books and by stars. But what did you dream about? Ah! yes, a treasure trove, books left behind by a certain forbear, likely a prophet. You've broken my dolls? The idol that you are will be broken, your throat will be slit, dove!]

The marginalised child-dreamer-writer is here evoked. But her hopes are dashed — her dolls broken, the dove's throat slit. The precarity of hanging on to a creative life is palpable. Another two pages on and adolescence reprises the warning that life 'égorgera la colombe!' [will slit the dove's throat!] (*OC*, p. 339).

The motif of the dove is central to this poem. Birds are usually invoked by Arnauld to represent freedom, both of movement (flight, ascension) and of expression (song, voice). That association persists in *La Nuit pleure tout haut*, but what the birds represent is severely threatened as well as feted. The dove carries huge symbolic weight. On the very first page a gruesome possibility is introduced, 'Dans mes mains s'agite une colombe; si la vie me quitte, on lui tord le cou' [In my hands a dove stirs; if I die, they will strangle it] (*OC*, p. 327). The bird's fate is intimately bound up with that of the narrator. The death of one will mean the death of the other. The death of the individual, of the author, is the death knell of peace. The dove, and thus the writer, her freedom and expression, are under threat.

The relationship between the bird and the narrator is established more explicitly in this poem than in other instances of Arnauld's work that work on looser allusive connections. On the ninth page the analogy is clear, 'Et pourquoi ne serais-je pas une colombe, puisque je suis l'amour, donc le cœur du poëme, puisque je suis la douleur, puisque je suis la splendeur?' [And why should I not be a dove, since I am love, thus the heart of the poem, since I am pain, since I am splendour?] (*OC*, p. 335). Though framed as an enquiry, this is an assertion of the writer's all-encompassing drive to express the most pertinent aspects of living and feeling. A doom-laden and prescient warning is issued, 'priez, jetez vos livres, on égorge la colombe, on taille dans la douleur, on va briser l'idole' [pray, throw away your books, they are slitting the dove's throat, they are carving out pain, they will break the idol] (p. 333). The context is both personal and political.

The violence of slicing and cutting and hacking here shares some tendencies with the rhetoric of Arnauld's and the Paris Dadaists' earlier metaphors of attack on the status quo. But where those texts of the 1920s sought to revolutionise culture via provocation, the violence here far exceeds the irony and playful bravado of Dada. The situation in the 1930s was altogether more urgent and demanded a less equivocal response. Youth is given a voice in two passages punctuated with speech marks; it levels accusations of complacency and issues warnings to a generation on the brink of another war. The stakes are high. This poem, written in February 1939, can quite aptly be read as a premonition of the war that would be declared in September. That reading, and the power of the poem, are supported paradoxically by its apparent destruction at the hands of the National Socialists. A note in a rare bibliographical listing of Arnauld's works reads, 'détruit par les Allemands' [destroyed by the Germans].[4]

Flames and burning, prevalent and powerful in *Heures intactes*, now prophesy visions of destruction that would turn out to be frighteningly accurate. The very first line, 'Rose brûlée par des sables!' [Rose burned by the sands!] (*OC*, p. 327) is succeeded by references to burning evil, burning eyes, and burning arms. Hands become febrile. A thermometer in flames appears, its temperature rising, as well as a bouquet of flames. A boat crossing a burning river explicitly references Dante's journey to hell ('Dans la barque du Dante j'ai traversé un fleuve en flammes') (p. 335). The environment is no longer one of possibility, alterity, or escape for the author, but a frightening backdrop of destruction. Each vision builds dramatically and inexorably towards apocalypse.

But *La Nuit pleure tout haut* is arguably also a poem about poetry, about the hope offered by writing and the imaginary world, and the danger of abandoning that vocation. There are numerous meta-textual references to the poem, the poet, and poetry. Books and song merge and overlap as expressive utterances from the bird or human. The imaginary world offers salvation. But an encroaching reality is inescapable, 'Pour obtenir la grâce divine, tu t'es réfugiée dans un monde imaginaire. Prends garde, la vie se vengera d'avoir été négligée, elle brisera tes rêves' [In order to obtain divine grace, you sought refuge in an imaginary world. Watch out, life will avenge itself for having been neglected, it will shatter your dreams] (*OC*, p. 339). The 'prends garde' reminds us of the warning at the end of Arnauld's 1920 poem 'Avertisseur', 'Prenez garde aux tombes ouvertes' [Watch out for open graves] (*OC*, p. 81). The perils of the interwar period are laid bare, with these lines culminating in the slitting of the dove's throat. The child's (and here adolescent's) love of the imaginary, beloved too of the Surrealists, is not enough to ward off the reality of another war.

Stars perform different functions. Martin-Schmets has singled out one occurrence for comment, 'Je porte mon étoile comme une croix de douleur' [I wear my star like a cross of pain] (*OC*, p. 332). In a footnote he ponders the possibility that the author might be referring to the yellow star imposed by the Nazis, but concludes that this line precedes that development, albeit only by a matter of months in the case of Poland, and longer in France. Arnauld's star has been an ever-changing companion in her work. Here it can be read as a sign for elevated creativity but it is far from stable. 'Une étoile bleue, une étoile de douleur, une étoile d'oubli, une étoile de mort est suspendue au plafond, vacille, soutient la vie, s'éteint à l'aube' [A blue star, a star of pain, a star of forgetting, a star of death is suspended from the ceiling, it sways, sustains life, is extinguished at dawn] (p. 333). This inspiration requires nurturing and cannot be taken for granted.

'Douleur' recurs, placed in opposition to 'rêve' and 'songe'. The final line is a single word, 'sanglot' [sob] (*OC*, p. 348). It is a powerful conclusion to an affective poem, rendered more moving by our knowledge of political events to come. Written in February of the year of the outbreak of war, and published on the last day of June, the poem stands as a courageous, powerful testament of an individual life about to be thrown into insecurity and a horrifying prophecy of Europe's descent into war. A heartfelt, moving, foreboding piece of work, it is also, arguably, a premonition, riddled with stark warnings about persecution and censorship. It can be considered a judgement on the failure of government and society to deal with the rise of Fascism, and the insufficiency of writing to counter it.

We only have scant details about what Arnauld and Dermée did during the war years. Their nephew, Pierre Janssen, related that they escaped the occupied zone for Toulouse, staying there from 1941 until the liberation of France in 1945, but he knew few details.[5] It was almost a decade after *La Nuit pleure tout haut*, published on the cusp of war, that Arnauld brought to print another collection. *Rien qu'une étoile, suivi de Plains-chants sauvages* [Nothing but a Star, followed by Wild Plain-Songs]. Printed in November 1948, it is our only index of her wartime production and experiences. It would also be her last book.

The size and format of this text distinguishes it immediately from the rest of Arnauld's single-authored books. Measuring 19 x 28 cm it makes an immediate impact. Its material format is more suited to a journal or periodical than a volume of poetry and, I propose, is strongly reminiscent of a songbook. On the cover the author's name is printed in the top right-hand corner. The first element of the title, 'Rien qu'une étoile', stretches across the foot of the page. Both are in upper case. The huge space in between is left blank. This is a work that invites contemplation even at first glance.

The first page (*OC*, p. 351) presents the reader with some stark signposting. It points emphatically to the war years:

> DANS LE GOUFFRE NOIR DU CIEL DE GUERRE NOUS SUIVIONS DÉSESPÉRÉMENT
> UNE ÉTOILE QUI BRILLAIT D'UN ÉCLAT DANTESQUE!
> NUIT APRÈS NUIT DE CETTE ÉTOILE NAQUIT LA CONSTELLATION ESPOIR.
>
> [IN THE BLACK ABYSS OF THE SKY OF WAR WE DESPERATELY FOLLOWED A STAR
> THAT SHONE WITH A DANTESQUE BRIGHTNESS!
> NIGHT AFTER NIGHT FROM THIS STAR WAS BORN THE CONSTELLATION HOPE.]

I have respected Arnauld's use of the upper-case, its typography leaving little doubt as to the context and tone of this volume. The next page offers a clear indication of the period in which these texts were written, namely 1940 to August 1944. In this dark period of war Arnauld's night-time terrors had taken on greater resonance and consequence. Hope, nevertheless, persisted, the star taking on that symbolic value. It may or may not be coincidence that the title picks up a phrase that appears in a poem by Breton. The last line of Breton's 'Du rêve' reads 'Une étoile rien qu'une étoile perdue dans la fourrure de la nuit' [A star nothing but a star lost in the fur of the night].[6] It seems unlikely that Arnauld would knowingly pay homage to Breton, even though his poem was published earlier, in 1945. More likely she is drawing on her own work with its preponderance of stars as motif. More relevant is her acknowledgement of Dante, building on references in *La Nuit rêve tout haut*.

The first poem, 'Rien qu'une étoile' (*OC*, p. 353) shares its name with the volume. It is succeeded by eleven more poems that together set out the precariousness and provisional nature of wartime circumstances. The introductory poem may well be read as autobiographical, with its allusions to flight and fragility. 'Nous avons pris le large' [We set forth] the first stanza states, in an uncommonly prosaic line that is, however, ensconced in more poetic renderings of displacement. The narrator feels herself dissipating:

> Absente à demi-ivre
> Ô cœur miroir des colombes
> Ni reine ni comblée mais rien qu'une étoile...

[Half-drunk absent | Oh heart mirror of doves | Neither queen nor complete instead nothing but a star...]

Symbolic icons from Arnauld's repertoire, including the dove and star most recently discussed in relation to *La Nuit pleure tout haut*, and the mirror, from as early as *Tournevire*, are reprised and are here menaced; the flame trembles, the sun is walled up, the whirlwind of a cygnet shut away. The terms 'immolant' and 'murés' surely point to the fate, metaphorical and literal, of those fleeing occupation, forced to hide.

In two poems, 'Notre-Dame de Paris' (*OC*, p. 354) and 'Cathédrale des poètes' [Cathedral of Poets] (*OC*, p. 355), Arnauld writes longingly of the capital city. Where dreamlike natural landscapes had predominated in recent volumes, here, forced into exile from Paris, she expresses her longing for that home. There are rare specificities. In 'Notre-Dame de Paris' she points to her hinterland as being between the Seine and the Garonne. In 'Cathédrale des poètes', too, she expresses her betwixtness, 'Loin de Paris vagabondante' [Far from Paris, a vagabond], she is caught between two locations, 'Je suis ici et là-bas' [I am here and over there.] The liminal spaces we have observed in many of her other texts, highlighted in Chapter 4 as a focal point, are geographically real and concrete in this volume.

The final stanza of 'Notre-Dame de Paris' paints a vivid picture of wartime Paris:

> Voici Paris pleurant tout haggard
> Esmérelda délire au vent
> Au vent d'autan plein d'imprévu criblé de cris
> La pluie atrocement tombe — ailes brisées des colombes
> Sur la Parvis de Notre-Dame de Paris

[Here is Paris crying, distraught | Esmerelda delirious in the wind | The southerly wind heavy with the unforeseen, bristling with cries | The rain falls horribly — the broken wings of doves | On the square of Notre-Dame de Paris]

The cultural heart of Paris is in mourning and mourned, as she asserts in the second poem, 'Cathédrale des poètes', 'Et c'est toujours Paris qui me hante' [And it is always Paris that haunts me]. Rarely is this poet so frank in her depictions. In the first poem, for example, she designates unequivocally 'la détresse de l'exil' [the distress of exile] and in the second poem she describes herself as 'captive'. The huge symbolical and actual value of the capital city for Arnauld is nowhere more keenly felt than when she is removed from it.[7]

A reading of the poems in sequence is instructive. 'Les merveilleuses nuits de Paris' [the marvellous nights of Paris], in the fourth poem 'Fraîcheur' [Freshness] (*OC*, p. 356), offers a modified echo of 'les merveilleuses aubes' [the marvellous dawns] in the previous poem, 'Cathédrale des poètes' (*OC*, p. 355). Roses, a sustaining thread through this set of poems, signify both the blooming of nature and the window of Notre-Dame. Death, however, looms large in this dangerous context, nowhere more so than in the poems 'Puisqu'il faut que je meure' [Since I Must Die] (*OC*, pp. 361–62) and 'Les Corbeaux bleus de la mort' [The Blue Ravens of Death] (*OC*, p. 363).

Another noteworthy text in this journey of jeopardy is 'L'Appel' [The Call] (*OC*, p. 357). This relatively short and accessible poem is a powerful plea for liberty, as in the second of its three stanzas:

> Liberté liberté
> Toujours le même appel
> Dans les minuits du monde

[Freedom freedom | Always the same appeal | In the midnights of the world]

It is clearly also a demand for political freedom. Arnauld's poetry has frequently called up the night and dreamt of deliverance but this is a potent instance of the word 'liberté'. The poem would be published in *Le Journal des poètes* in February 1946. Displaying the characteristics of action and rhetoric associated with Dada-era manifestos, it is nevertheless far removed from that period. The urgency for this poet in exile is apparent.

Plains-chants sauvages, the second element of this publication, was written between 1945 and 1947. The indications of writing-time in this volume map out for us two very different historical contexts. Twenty-four texts provide indices of a period of prolific post-war writing for Arnauld. The term 'plains-chants' translates into English as 'plainchants' or 'plainsongs', referring to a Gregorian chant, or any monophonic medieval liturgical music without strict meter, traditionally sung without accompaniment. Arnauld's reference may have been to Catholicism, the institutional connotations rendered freer by the addition of the adjective. It suggests musical voices prior to or outside convention or logic. The word 'sauvages' calls up something wild or unconstrained, primordial or primitive. The many references to the Church, occurring also in *Rien qu'une étoile*, are interesting and even perplexing. As with her stance towards a second language, perhaps Arnauld's approach to a religion that was not her first permits her a critical distance.

There are both laments and love songs in this collection, written in a postwar peace that nevertheless remained precarious for Arnauld. Cycles of time build on *Les Réseaux du réveil*. In 'Ma peine s'éveille' [My Pain Awakens], for example, the first verse begins with 'ma peine s'éveille avec le jour', the second with 'ma peine s'éveille avec la nuit' (*OC*, p. 371). This focus on awakening follows a poem 'Pour éveiller l'aurore' [To Awaken the Dawn] (*OC*, p. 370). Language is self-referential, with frequent references to poetry. In 'Des étoiles de fine taille' [Finely-crafted Stars] the title is echoed by 'Des poèmes de fine taille' [finely-crafted poems] (*OC*, p. 368). In the first poem, 'Plains-chants sauvages' we read 'le cœur en peine est l'axe du poème' (*OC*, p. 367), a repetition of the same line from the poem 'Plus haut que l'amour' in *Les Réseaux du réveil*. The effect is a self-reflective ode to the poems themselves. Intertextual references reinforce a sense of self-consciousness. The expression 'claires-voies' occurs again in the poem 'Plains-chants sauvages' (p. 368), and 'rêver tout haut' makes a reappearance in 'Ma peine s'éveille' (p. 371). Favoured vocabulary threads through these poems, from flora to avian life, time-cycles to skyscapes, hearts to hands. As we near the end of this body of work the impression of a fabric of openwork is reinforced. Once difficult to comprehend, Arnauld's vocabulary now guides us, in a sense familiar and graspable.

The final text in this collection, 'Clairières' [Clearings] (*OC*, p. 390), consists of a first-person narrative set out in three short paragraphs. Printed in upper-case, it reminds us of the short introductory passage to *Rien qu'une étoile*, the two texts offering bookends to these final volumes from the 1940s. The very first line sets an optimistic tone, 'Maintenant les clairières de toutes les nuits du monde s'ouvrent devant moi' [Now the clearings of all the nights in the world open up before me]. As with the *clair* of 'claires-voies', the word 'clairières' encapsulates a promise of clarity and relief. Daybreak will always come, the narrator declares, a chink of light will appear to illuminate even those years in which she was enveloped. She describes herself as having been wrapped in sails, battered by the cruel winds of the past, a phrase 'comme pour la tombe' [as if for the tomb] suggesting shrouding. The second paragraph picks up the forward trajectory of the first line:

> JE SUIS L'AMIE DES OISEAUX MIGRATEURS QUI VOLENT VERS LA FINALITÉ DES RÊVES. ILS DÉCOUVRIRONT UNE ROSE POUR ÉPOUSER LE CHANT DANS LA SPLENDEUR D'UN BAISER.
>
> [I AM THE FRIEND OF MIGRATORY BIRDS THAT FLY TOWARDS THE FINALITY OF DREAMS. THEY WILL DISCOVER A ROSE TO JOIN THEIR SONG IN THE SPLENDOUR OF A KISS.]

The qualifier 'migratory', here, offers a clear nod to the author as émigré, her flight and dreams rewarded by love and creativity. The third part, finally, is struck through with an awareness of mortality. I am the friend of those departed, the narrative voice declares, the departed who will never return, the departed who will have neither rest nor sleep. The final sentence concludes this refrain, 'L'amie des grands navires, ces oiseaux fabuleux qui se couchent pour mourir au cœur des tempêtes' [The friends of the great ships, these fabulous birds that lay down to die in the heart of storms]. This final sentence contains within it several of Arnauld's emphases, from boats, to birds, to belonging in the environment in all its drama and changeability. It privileges hope and communion, even as it accepts the inevitability of death.

The short passage, in its entirety, succeeds in conveying a tripartite experience of struggle, creativity, and death. Its relative brevity, upper-case typography, layout in blocks, and status as the last text in what would be the author's final single-authored volume, tempt us to adopt it retrospectively as an epitaph of her life. 'All that is solid melts into air,' wrote Karl Marx in the *Communist Manifesto* one hundred years earlier (1848), pointing to the dynamic but destructive nature of capitalist society. Arnauld's life was shot through with precarity — psychologically, professionally, and materially — from the relative instability of Romania's history that constituted her cultural background, to her life in France. Marx's phrase is taken up fruitfully by Marshall Berman to expound the formal reflections and expressions in visual arts and writing of the modernist period. He points to vaporousness and fluidity, to Baudelaire's fragile 'floating existences'.[8] That phrase applies to Arnauld's dreamlike fragmented-constructed visions, to uncertainty but also mobility, to despair then dynamism, to the glimpses, the gaps, the chinks of light that pierce dark periods and difficulties. These creative renewals are the openings that permit the writer to continue.

In a review of Lautréamont's *Les Chants de Maldoror*, Arnauld draws attention to twin poles of suffocating emotion and *joie de vivre* and wonders how to express this oscillation. She writes:

> N'est-ce pas d'avoir devant soi un grand espace, d'embrasser à la fois tout l'univers, l'immensité des eaux et des champs, de parcourir les vieilles rues de Paris, d'errer au bord de la Seine sans pensée ni désir, d'arrêter pour quelques temps cette horloge infatigable qu'est le rêve?[9]

> [Is it not to have before oneself a great space, to embrace at once the whole universe, the immensity of the waters and fields, to walk through the old streets of Paris, to wander on the banks of the Seine with neither thought nor desire, to stop for a while the indefatigable clock that is dreaming?]

While she was referring to Lautréamont and to his character Maldoror, she simultaneously betrays here her own preoccupations.

Arnauld's sense of precarity has permeated her writing and the little we know of her life. It has also plagued her legacy. In his early article on this forgotten poet Martin-Schmets posed the following question ironically, in reference to Dada poetry, 'Une femme, toute de raison, de délicatesse, de raffinement dans cette galère?' [A woman, reasonable, delicate, and refined, in this crazy mess?].[10] He likewise articulated the question of neglect as a feminist issue, 'Les poétesses étant plus rare que les poètes (si j'en crois les statistiques des anthologies même les plus récentes), il s'en suit que je connais encore moins de poétesses dadaïstes' [Female poets being rarer than male poets, (if I am to believe in the statistics of even the most recent anthologies), it follows that I know even fewer female Dada poets].[11] Martin-Schmets's style is somewhat disarming. He uses the diminutive 'poétesse', includes the qualifier 'épouse Paul Dermée' in the title of the article, and his starting-point is Dermée, but his point is a feminist one. He makes bold claims about the relationship between the two poets, alleging that Dermée used Arnauld's name, when it suited, to advance his own ambitions. She was, he proposes, 'plus connue, plus appréciée [better-known, better-liked]; thus Dermée sends her forward 'à l'assaut' [on the assault] while he stays 'à l'arrière' [at the back].[12] The language is appropriate to the avant-garde, reminding us of the term's origins in war, and its adoption in the nineteenth century by Henri de Saint-Simon to designate radicalism in the arts.[13] In the formulation above, a woman leads the vanguard.

Arnauld's own comments on her situation are scarce. A notable exception is her contribution to a 1931 anthology, edited by the poet and art critic Élie Moroy, which gathered testimonies from women writers.[14] Arnauld's short text, which I encountered relatively late in my research, is a gift both for its explicit autobiographical statements and reflections on her writing that support some of my readings. Respondents were asked to comment on three areas. On the first, the characteristics of her work, she sets up a metaphor of an unnamed town in which she has been enclosed since childhood. Made up of sun-rays and a transparent wall that cannot be crossed, it reflects her inner life and quest for expansion. The setting-out of this place is typical of her propensity to describe thinking in terms of reflections of light and surfaces in the exterior world. The city as an alluring yet at times imprisoning home is also familiar to us from her writings. She is candid, here, about her priorities — to refuse reason in favour of her unconscious mind. 'Révoltée, j'ai trouvé mon refuge dans cet asile qui comme l'océan passif peut connaître des tempêtes. J'ai voué une lutte sans merci à la réalité' [Rebelling, I found refuge in this asylum which, like the passive ocean, can yet experience storms. I waged a merciless war against reality]. She writes of her rejection of aesthetics and logic, the priority of her own inner universe, and of the madness that lies in wait for her. Her celebration of the unconscious and inner mind reminds us here, more than anywhere, of what she has in common with the precepts of Surrealism, even if not with its protagonists.

The more unusual element in this text is her assertiveness as a writer. The second of the three sections reads:

> Mais quand tous les poètes, et ceux qui ont une âme de poète, auront compris et senti la profondeur de mes chants, mon rôle dans la littérature féminine, et dans toute la littérature — car je ne fais pas de différence entre celle des femmes et celle des hommes — sera également unique, et mon œuvre remplira de poésie et de lyrisme tous les cœurs. Tel est mon rêve.[15]

> [But when all poets, and those who have a poet's soul, have understood and felt the depth of my songs, my role in women's literature, and in literature as a whole — since I do not make any distinction between that of women and that of men — will be likewise unique, and my work will fill hearts with poetry and lyricism. Such is my dream.]

The 'likewise' follows from a reference made to Nietzsche's Superman. It is an assertion of a combination of strangeness and humanity, of her voice as being distinct from the crowd, and of her uniqueness. Her self-confidence and ambition are striking in this passage. In response to a question about the place of her work in a history of women's writing she calls for its acknowledgment in writing as a whole.

The third and final part of this piece of writing addresses the question of women's writing in contemporary literature. Of the contemporary woman Arnauld writes, 'elle est la camarade et l'égale des hommes' [she is the comrade and the equal of men], and 'elle est bohème, vagabonde et errante' [she is bohemian, vagabond, and errant]. This woman no longer waits for men to fall admiringly at her feet, she claims; she is out in cafés rather than at home in the artificiality of the salon; she will one day be a *flâneur*, her liberty permitting her to stand alongside Shakespeare, Byron, Shelley, and Rimbaud. In a direct and prosaic pronouncement Arnauld predicts that, following progress in teaching, the sciences, the revolutionary movement, and all intellectual activities, women will take their place in literature. 'Le rôle de la littérature féminine sera considérable' [the role of women's literature will be considerable], she announces. It is difficult to over-state the thrill of coming across this manifesto for women writers by an individual who consistently fought to express herself and her independence but who rarely made such explicit pronouncements.

Jennifer E. Milligan has drawn attention to a 'forgotten generation' of women writers in France between the wars, to the difficult context in which they worked, and to their 'outstanding, innovative and prolific' contributions. She asserts:

> Through no fault of their own they have been partly eclipsed by the reception accorded to their Anglo-American modernist counterparts, and more importantly they have been marginalised by the way in which they have been represented by the literary establishment.[16]

Arnauld surely counts among this forgotten generation. Sixty-five years earlier, Moroy, the editor of the anthology of women's testimonies to which Arnauld contributed, had insisted on 'un mouvement conscient que nul historien n'oserait méconnâitre' [a conscious movement that no historian would dare to disregard].[17] Arnauld's struggle to make her voice read and heard is palpable in her writing. Attention to her work, long overdue, does justice to her persistence. The two volumes discussed in this chapter were scarcely reviewed in their time and have since fallen into obscurity.[18] They deserve to be read as powerful, evocative renditions of one Jewish woman's foreboding ahead of the 1939–1945 war and a subsequent attempt to regain optimism.

Notes to Chapter 11

1. Arnauld, in 'Céline Arnauld nous dit ... Mystère de l'image'. This is in response to the question whether the poet should be absent from the world. Her reference to the poet as 'un appareil enregisteur extrêmement sensible', following an emphatic 'No!', recalls Breton's concept of a recording device (see Chapter 7). In a 1950 interview she reiterates her absolute belief in the *poète engagé*; 'Poésie et réalité: interview du poète Céline Arnauld', *Le Journal des poètes*, 1 (January 1950), 3 (*OC*, p. 445).

2. For a recent analysis of the blank or white space in literature and visual arts see Eric Robertson, '"Le Blanc Souci de notre toile": Writing White in Modern French Poetry and Art', *French Studies*, 71 (2017), 319–32
3. Breton, *Manifestes du surréalisme*; Pierre Mabille, *Le Merveilleux* (Paris: Les Éditeurs des quatre vents, 1946). For discussions of *le merveilleux* as a literary genre see Tzvetan Todorov, *Introduction à la littérature fantastique* (Paris: Éditions du Seuil, 1970).
4. *Bibliographie de la littérature française 1940–49*, ed. by S. Dreher and M. Rolli (Lille: Librairie Giard; Geneva: Librairie E. Droz, 1958). Martin-Schmets also claims this, on the grounds that she had a Jewish name and would have featured on the Otto lists of banned works that began 23 September 1940 (*OC*, pp. 557–59). It is also noted in an untitled review of *Rien qu'une étoile* by Aimé Patri, 'La Poésie, *Paru*, 52 (July 1949), 32–33 (*OC*, pp. 567–68).
5. Pierre Janssen: 'Pendant la guerre [...] parce qu'elle était juive [...] ils se sont réfugiés à Toulouse pour ne pas être dans la zone occupée. Ils y sont restés 1941 jusqu'à 1945. Je ne sais pas sous quel papier elle a vécu pendant la guerre' [During the war [...] because she was Jewish [...] they took refuge in Toulouse to be out of the occupied zone. I don't know what papers they used during the war], interview with Hemus, 12 November 2007. It is worth noting also that Dermée was a Freemason and therefore vulnerable to persecution. Freemasons were perceived by Hitler as pro-Jewish and anti-German. Many were interned in concentration camps, and lost their lives, as political prisoners.
6. André Breton, 'Du rêve', in *Signe ascendant: suivi de Fata Morgana, Les États généraux, Des épingles tremblantes, Xénophiles, Ode à Charles Fournier, Constellations, Le La* (Paris: Gallimard, 1968), p. 74. The poem was written in October 1943, in New York.
7. For an exposition of the significance of Paris in the Romanian imagination see Spiridon, '"Bucharest-on-the-Seine"'. As briefly noted in Chapter 8, Spiridon emphasises its importance as *lieu de mémoire*, a place somewhere between history and nostalgia, for all kinds of writers and circumstances, including those exiled and displaced. Certainly the identification with Paris as adopted and familiar home, rather than any affinity with France as a whole, is apparent in these texts.
8. Marshall Berman, *All That is Solid Melts into Air: The Experience of Modernity* (New York: Simon & Schuster, 1982), pp. 21 & 144, n. 15.
9. Arnauld, 'Les Chants de Maldoror'.
10. Martin-Schmets, 'Céline Arnauld, épouse Paul Dermée, poète dadaïste', p. 172.
11. Ibid. p. 171.
12. Ibid., p. 176.
13. See Sascha Bru, *The European Avant-Gardes, 1905–1935: A Portable Guide* (Edinburgh: Edinburgh University Press, 2018), for a recent and readable account of the broader avant-garde, including p. 216 for notes on the origins of the term.
14. Céline Arnauld, 'Autour d'une ville ...', in *La Littérature féminine définie par les femmes écrivains: enquête sur les lettres de ce temps*, ed. by Élie Moroy (Geneva: M. Burgi, 1931), pp. 4–5 (not in *OC*).
15. Ibid., pp. 4–5.
16. Jennifer E. Milligan, *The Forgotten Generation: French Women Writers of the Inter-war Period* (Oxford & New York: Berg, 1996), p. 209.
17. Élie Moroy, 'Prélude', in *La Littérature féminine*, ed. by Moroy, [n.p.].
18. Some texts were published in *Le Journal des poètes* in 1946 and 1948. In contrast with the pre-war proliferation of magazines in which Arnauld featured, this magazine became her most constant outlet in the 1930s and 1940s and printed her anthology. She was part of the editorial committee from 1932.

CONCLUSION

A Triple Margin: Gender, Nationality, and Ultra-Modernity

Avant dada, pendant le règne de dada, et après dada, il y a quelque chose qui est plus que tout, qui est l'essence même de notre existence: la poésie.[1]

[Before Dada, during the reign of Dada, and after Dada, there is something that means more than anything, that is the very essence of existence: poetry.]

When Dermée died, having long been ill with cancer, two days after Christmas on 27 December 1951, at the age of just thirty-eight, Arnauld was left isolated. Dermée's nephew, Pierre Janssen, recalled visiting her in the flat she had shared with her husband at 16 rue Cassini, near the observatory in the fourteenth arrondissement in Paris, for just over thirteen years, since October 1928. He noted how she felt she had been deserted by her literary friends and colleagues. She began selling off the books and paintings given to them over the years by their peers, to generate income to keep afloat, 'comme elle n'avait pas les moyens' [since she didn't have the means].[2] On 21 February 1952, a little under two months after her husband's death, she rang her doctor to signal her intention to take her own life. By the time he arrived, after calling the emergency services, Arnauld was dead, having turned on the gas in her flat. According to Janssen, she had left an envelope with the exact amount of money required to arrange her funeral. She had not wanted to be a burden, he claimed, and had prepared carefully.[3]

It is a terrible end to a questioning life. Janssen was firm in the belief that his aunt's decision was driven not only by grief at the loss of her spouse but also by financial despair. Here was a woman who had sought to live by her writing but who could not make a sufficient living, finally, especially alone. A newspaper report on 25 February 1952 of Arnauld's death is set out under three headlines, their different font types and diminishing sizes shouting out degrees of sensation:

> Une femme de lettres se suicide à la téléphone
> en décrivant son agonie à son médecin
> Elle s'est asphyxiée au gaz parce qu'elle ne pouvait survivre à son mari.[4]
>
> [A woman of letters commits suicide over the telephone | relaying her last moments to her doctor | She gassed herself because she could not go on living without her husband.]

The article refers to her as 'Caroline Janssen', one more in a line of names that string together a fractured identity: Carolina, Caroline, Céline; Goldstein, Janssen, Arnauld. Further into the article her pen name and some of her achievements are mentioned, including publications, but Arnauld's life and work subsequently fell into neglect and it would be more than five decades before some of us would be on her trail. It is only now that Céline Arnauld / Carolina Goldstein is assuming some kind of definition in accounts of the avant-garde.

Dada's Women was a first attempt to demonstrate the existence of women who had hitherto been side-lined in narratives and histories of Dada. In the chapter on Arnauld in that book I drew out some parallels between her work and that of her male colleagues, aiming to show unequivocally her participation in the Parisian group. Already under discussion was the inevitable dilemma of how to make her work 'fit' at the same time as showing its characteristics and contribution, of how to include her but not let her be absorbed, of how to underscore her individuality without isolating her from her contemporaries. That initial study paved the way for a measure of confidence not only to consider her texts in relation to Dada but to respect them as a standalone body of work. Arnauld was prolific at an explosive point of avant-garde literary activity in Paris, teetering on the cusp of Dada and Surrealism. But she wrote before 1920 and she would write after it. The epigraph to this chapter is an articulation of this longer view by Arnauld herself. In fact it refers to Tzara. An extract from a review of his 1924 *Sept manifestes Dada*, it hails him as a poet above all else.[5] It can be applied equally to her, and neatly summarises the approach taken in this book.

In terms of formal innovation, the current study has sought to bring to light the writer's experiments with language and with genres. From poems to manifestos, dialogues to narratives, prose-poems to novels, her texts are often difficult to categorise. Performance and theatricality, orality and aurality are important markers. The reader asks themselves whether works are poetic, theatrical, or filmic. Their attention is drawn to the page, the structure, the conventions or anti-conventions of literary forms and genres. Too often lazily dismissed as nihilist, avant-garde writing is seen, instead, to be creative, constructive, and innovative. Arnauld's love of language, spoken and written, is palpable.

As Tzara famously stated, 'La pensée se fait dans la bouche' [Thought is made in your mouth].[6] Immediacy, spontaneity, and materiality are at the fore in unfettered sounds and images. The medium is verbal but, as with music, which is so frequently called up in Arnauld's work, rhythm and tone, alliteration and assonance, are paramount in producing feeling and imagery. Logic and linearity, sense and semantics, take a back seat. The narrator is often unspecified, ambiguous, nebulous. The point of view is in some cases akin to a camera lens, scoping across a scene, taking in facets and fragments, avoiding intervention between the reader and the image, and evincing omniscient conclusions. This is the poet as projector and the reader as spectator, piecing together half-glimpsed but commanding scenes that spark revelations.

Arnauld's interventions in the Dada era were implicitly experimental and sometimes explicitly radical. In a handful of texts she proclaimed, promoted, and perpetuated Dada by name. She partook in the aggressive rhetoric of renewal, and vehemently rejected critics of the new. In prose pieces akin to manifestos she launched attacks on outdated aesthetic conventions, the Arts with a capital A, and conformism. Other texts are less directly confrontational but challenge the reader with their refusal to be read passively. Arnauld was not simply a follower. *Projecteur*, notably, should be recognised as a rich, untapped seam in a network of ephemeral publications that form the legacy of the avant-garde. Through it we can draw attention to Arnauld as a pioneering poet, manifesto writer, networker, promoter, and editor; as an innovative woman Dadaist in an otherwise staunchly male landscape.

That magazine, in addition, demonstrates that she was not uncritical of the groups with which she was associated, and not short of her own ideas and ambition. She was presciently conscious of the historicising of Dada and the danger of being selective in the recounting of events and people, and resisted being annexed to one or other movement for posterity. Some of her work anticipates the automatic writing techniques developed by Breton and Soupault, and the preponderance of dreams, the marvellous, and liminal states is crucial to her writing. A line from 'Diorama' comes to mind, 'Le rêve c'est la vraie réalité du poète. L'autre réalité, n'est qu'une chaise pour se reposer' [Dreaming is the poet's true reality. The other reality is nothing but a chair on which to rest] (*OC*, p. 185). It is a statement to rival, or indeed align with, any surrealist pronouncement. But she was quick to condemn Breton for his management methods, for his rigid definitions and excommunications, which she perceived as limiting to writers. And she hoped to find new directions for her writing that took on the challenges of modernity and emerging technologies, networks, and communications. Out of this came her notion of projectivism, a testament to her commitment to the modernist project of making new, and to her own vision. She was awake to creative technologies, above all film, that were changing perception and expression. Her journal exemplifies an investigation of the slippages between film and writing.

Arnauld's poetry plays with the ambiguities and inconsistencies of language, and with the indecipherability of the linguistic sign. She challenges the reader's expectations of textual stability and meaning, pulling the rug from under their feet. The reader's understanding is thwarted, their desire to read clear meaning in the text upset, as the poet taunts that desire — sometimes even explicitly — to decipher and to make sense of non-sense. Reading the avant-garde text becomes an uncanny, unsettling experience, and Arnauld understands all too well the impetus to overcome this and settle on more familiar patterns of meaning. Hence her challenge to the reader in the poem 'Énigme-personnages', 'Tu ne trouveras jamais la clé' [You will never find the key'] (*OC*, p. 400). The possibility for passive absorption is replaced by a demand to decode the text. And sometimes the overwhelming compulsion to make full, rational sense of the text must be abandoned to the pleasure of the language. New strategies and, in a sense, capitulation are required. There is a danger that the experience is so de-stabilising that the reader steps back from the text, stops short of engaging with it, and ultimately finds it too esoteric. If successful, however, the reader will question the process of communication, the use and mis-use of language as a sign system, and even their own perceptions of reality. The materiality of language, its deconstruction and reconstruction, is at the heart of her work. It is manipulated and renewed to arrive at different states of consciousness. In some cases it is explicitly underscored, where she makes reference to 'parole', to voices, to mouths, and hands that produce words in speech and in written acts, and to the poet as prophet. In its refusal of the plain and transparent, in favour of metaphor and allusion, her writing owes much to Symbolism.

It seems fitting to cite Tzara again, 'À priori, c'est-à-dire les yeux fermés, Dada place avant l'action et au-dessus de tout: *Le Doute*. DADA doute de tout' ('A priori, in other words with its eyes closed, Dada places before action and above all: *Doubt*. DADA doubts everything').[7] Dada is not absolute allegiance to a doctrine. In her incessant questioning both of action and lyricism, and in her admittance of gaps, Arnauld is Dada in spirit and philosophy. Like many of her peers, she questions the role of the poet in modernity, from activist revolutionary on the one hand, that is avant-garde, to independent, free, and purely visionary on the other, refusing to explain or account for her work. She writes, 'Malgré tous les manifestes, malgré toutes les guerres civiles, il faut rester poète et plus encore: poète pur' [Aside from all the manifestos, aside from all the civil wars, one has to remain a poet and, more than that, a pure poet].[8] Her body of writing is a quest, sometimes painful, sometimes passionate, to locate a new role for the word and for the wordsmith in modernity. Her texts are frequently self-reflective; they are poetry about poetry.

Thematically, this study has underscored Arnauld's interest in fantasy, fairy tale, and folklore, in the crossovers between a landscape of the past, modernity, and the otherworldly, establishing enquiries not only connected to gender but to nationality. Oral storytelling and song are elements in prose work as early as 1919's *Tournevire*, her openness to people and texts arguably connected to a hybridity of cultural and national experiences that destabilise and disrupt categories. French literature is inevitably a nexus of culture for her. She acknowledges her near-precursors and peers, in references and homages to Baudelaire and Rimbaud and, most compellingly, Apollinaire. She also ranges beyond that, historically and geographically, from Shakespeare to Shelley, and Dante to Nietzsche. Her approach is characterised less by absolutism and purity and more by synthetism and intertextuality. She reacts forcefully against exclusion, both in her writing and her dealings with others. Though estranged from Surrealism, she shares some common ground with it. The unconscious, childhood, dreams and apparitions, madness, and linguistic liberation are at the fore, elements that were explored programmatically by her peers in that group.

Arnauld is far from reactionary. As well as exploring experiences of modernity, including new forms of transport, with their accelerated speed in experience and perception, she was an early adopter of film as an art form, making use of its vocabulary in her writing, and exploring formal conventions in the context of image-making's effect on creativity. In many ways her work anticipates techniques of film-making, above all her intense interest in the effects of light and the roving eye. Other characteristics of her work that may once have been dismissed as romantic and atavistic can be considered differently in the age of the Anthropocene.

Her sustained evocations of the natural environment, including marine-, celestial-, and landscapes, her interests in the ecologies of the insect and avian worlds as alternative universes, gain new currency in a twenty-first century facing up to the damage wrought by humans.

The incredible richness of her creative output in the 1930s has been especially surprising and rewarding. I was wary of tackling the work she produced after the period of the avant-garde, fearing that it might have lost its experimental force. Instead I found it to be moving, expressive, and generous. It built on words, expressions, and themes from earlier work, rendered more comprehensible in an increasingly urgent political context by systems of repetition, variance, and intertextuality. The search for voice, words, and language is legible in some of these texts. In some of these later works a human narrator comes back into view, but she is still fragmented, in pieces, to be constructed by the reader.

Where a rejection of the past tends to characterise the stated aims of the avant-garde, here we see the acknowledgement of multiple poetic inspirations and influences. And yet the work still refuses easy closure and insists on linguistic invention over realism and narrative ease. This period does not represent a return to the past, then. Instead it demonstrates the co-existence of thematic concerns in nineteenth- and twentieth-century writing that denies clean breaks between poets and militates against the tendency to categorise writing too distinctly and too neatly. The avant-garde desire to break with the past could never be complete after all.

Finally, Arnauld's writing in the lead-up to the 1939–1945 war and during those years reveals yet another set of techniques and concerns. *La Nuit pleure tout haut*, written in 1939, was prescient in its engagement with the rise of Fascism. Its lyrical lament to the threat to peace, symbolised by the dove under violent attack, is visceral and powerful. The poems written between 1940 and 1944, moreover, are invaluable for their expression of concealment and precariousness in dangerous times. They eloquently and movingly convey the fear and desolation of the war years and offer an ode to the city of Paris from which Arnauld was exiled. They alone justify the task of restoring this poet, whose writing life spans such dramatic political and cultural change. The neglect of her work has been a loss not only to narratives of Dada, it transpires, but for interwar and wartime writing in France.

Arnauld's comments on gender are scarce and she did not write explicitly about nationality or religion, but thematic subtexts and linguistic allusions persist. Questions around identity, language, and selfhood permeate her writing. Names, places, and times are often shifting and ambiguous, nebulous and uncertain, resulting in a sort of transnational resistance. Her status as a non-native speaker of French appeared to permit a generative consciousness and questioning, an oscillation between admiration and play, encouraged by the experiments of the avant-garde. Free imagination and language revolution offered a malleable home, in which tradition, knowledge, and fluency were posited as less vital. A closed system of culture might prove to be more porous. The structures and hierarchies of language were deliberately opened to attack and reconfiguration by the projects of the avant-garde.

But the very real frustrations that Arnauld experienced in her life are evident in glimpsed moments — in her letter to Tzara, her disgust with Breton, her end to life. Ambition and assertion are trailed by fears of rejection and isolation. She was insistent and consistent in her wish to be viewed independently from any group or crowd, casting herself as the vagabond and never a member of the troupe. In a 1950 interview she was still adamant, 'Je suis fière de mon indépendance dans le mouvement moderne. Je ne reconnais l'influence d'aucune de mes compagnons de route, même ceux que j'admire le plus' [I'm proud of my independence in the modern movement. I don't acknowledge the influence of any of my peers, even those I admire the most].[9]

Confrontation played out in sync with Dada tendencies, at one point, as irony and satire, directed at an imagined enemy. But it featured critically, too, in relation to a sense of non-belonging. As war approached, playfulness was superseded by a bitter reality. Sandqvist has written of the Romanian writer in western Europe as 'doubly-bound'. Sjöberg has examined the 'double outsiderdom' of the Jewish-Romanian writer abroad, as being too radical for the conservative Jewish community and too Jewish to be part of the mainstream population. Suleiman points to the woman avant-gardist as 'doubly-marginal'. All note that the avant-garde in itself implies marginality or liminality. These conundrums are further complicated in Arnauld's case. She can be said to be triply intolerable, by being avant-garde, by being Jewish-Romanian, and by being a woman.

Women were overlooked in accounts of the avant-garde for far too long, as were questions of gender, nationality, and diversity. Avant-garde groups did not exist in a cultural vacuum, they did not operate outside all convention, and they were not homogeneous. Even as their proclamations were vociferous, they were as susceptible to prejudice, power struggle, and egotism as any other movement. It is through recognising diversity and variety that the more nuanced facets of avant-garde groups can be fully appreciated, as well as their impact on movements and figures that came after them. Classifications — of the avant-garde and of Modernism — have been tested by greater resistance to temporal linearity, cultural containment, and selectivity.

The problem of the death of the avant-garde has been a topic of heated debate in literary and art-historical discourse. How can a movement sustain its radicalism without being absorbed into mainstream culture? Isn't its demise inevitable from the start? Avant-garde artists around the hubs of Dada and Surrealism were generally conscious of this issue. In its early days in Zurich, Dada sought to resist the commodification of culture through artistic practices that operated on principles of ephemerality. Pragmatically the magazines and small presses associated with Dada and Surrealism proposed accessibility for unconventional writers. The bastions of culture were derided, and alternative avenues sought for artistic expression that bypassed the status quo and the stultifying demands of the academy. Even then, writers and painters fell prey to the temptations of status and power, from the desire to communicate their ideas to a wider audience, to the writing of self-aggrandising directorships and autobiographies. Dogma, hierarchy, exclusion, and closing ranks were anathema to Arnauld, as a foreigner, a Jew, and a woman.

The question is not only a general theoretical polemic, but an individual crisis. What happens to the burning young man who rebelled against the strictures of society, as he ages? Can he do without the finance of the publishers, art galleries, and collectors forever? How to lead the life of an angry rebel as the decades pass and new artists and writers increasingly perceive you as the old guard? In spite of the fact that this vocabulary veers towards the masculine, that is towards the 'angry young man,' the problem for the 'angry young woman' is arguably yet more severe. She had fewer models of rebellion to begin with and fewer female peers in the avant-garde. Having rejected, often, the conventional expectations of marriage, housekeeping, childbearing, motherhood, and decorum, she is at the edges of social acceptability, neither quite at home in the male group, nor in female society according to the norms of the times. What happens to the avant-garde woman writer, then, when *her* fires die down?

Here we might reiterate the affirmative aspect of lost voices by turning to the critic Paul Mann, and this time to a theoretical death. In his discussion of the idea that the avant-garde was doomed to failure he states, 'in the end one will also find that something is always missing from discourse, always omitted, denied, concealed, lost, skipped over, ignored. Perhaps only in this residuum is the death of the avant-garde belied'.[10] Forgotten voices like Arnauld's, in their return, are a crucial force in reminding us of the value, vitality, and diversity of the avant-garde. A theory of the avant-garde that takes account of its margins is a way forward. A reclamation of its heterogeneous and amorphous nature, carried out by scholarship, does justice to its more utopian aims.

The front cover of this book shows two very different images of Arnauld. The first is a portrait by Henri Laurens that was included in *Tournevire*. It is a valuable index of the writer in her cultural milieu and a thoroughly modern representation. Evincing mimesis and figuration it speaks of the author's place in the avant-garde. Without revealing much of the individual it pays homage to this mysterious writer who left traces in words.[11] The second is a photographic portrait given to me by her heirs, the Janssens. Seemingly taken by Philippe Halsman, the photographer based in Montparnasse in the 1930s renowned for his portraits of writers and actors, it too is of its time. But it permits a more conventional, human aspect to this figure who has been largely obliterated from literary histories. It ties into a story of a life lived precariously, by a woman who wore bright nail varnish, loved to socialise with her peers at the writers' haunt La Coupole and who was affectionately described as 'coquette' by her nephew and his wife. Less anecdotally, the emotive and occasionally confessional works of her later writing life afford us glimpses of a life. Taken together (and I do not mean to create a polemic) they combine to represent the action and lyricism for which the author hoped to be remembered.[12] The opposing forces she articulated ('les deux phares') may have challenged her but she continued to seek out the spaces in-between, the inexpressible. This was the work not of a couple of years around 1920 but a lifetime's writing vocation.

I return to the first review I cited in this book, this time quoting a longer section, 'On ne peut classer dans aucune école cette jeune poétesse: elle est en dehors de tout mouvement. Elle constitue à elle seule une école et un mouvement' [One cannot classify this young woman poet in any school: she is beyond any movement. She constitutes a school and a movement of her very own].[13] The three parts of this book have coalesced into three broad areas: Modernism, avant-garde, and ultra-modern, but the boundaries are porous. Arnauld was a modernist poet, she was a Dada poet, she was a projectivist poet, she was an ultra-modern poet. With its frets, gaps, and endless readability, her work — having endured against the odds — is ultra-modern openwork.

Notes to the Conclusion

1. Céline Arnauld, 'Les Livres — lettres' [review of *Sept manifestes Dada* by Tristan Tzara], *L'Esprit nouveau*, 28 (January 1925), 2338–41 (p. 2338) (*OC*, pp. 437–38).
2. Pierre Janssen, interview with Hemus, 12 November 2007. As he listed the artists they had known ('Marinetti, Picabia, Éluard, Apollinaire') I was heartbroken at the dispersal of these materials, which he had witnessed as crammed from floor to ceiling in their apartment. Even after Arnauld's death he recalled, 'J'étais tellement sousmergé de livres' [I was so submerged in books]. He was, of course, a young man, called to deal with his aunt's death, and compelled to deal with their accumulated materials. His fondness for his aunt was apparent in my interview with him. His wife Josette, too, was kind about the woman she called 'tante Carola' in her correspondence with me.
3. The funeral took place on 27 February 1952. Josette Janssen kindly wrote to me (23 June 2006) with the receipt for funeral services as confirmation. Although her death was covered in the newspapers, the BnF had no date of death until I informed them of it. Arnauld's marginalisation continued long beyond that final period in Paris.
4. A photocopy was given to me by Josette Janssen but without the title of the newspaper in which it appeared. Pierre Janssen recalls that two Paris-based Romanian cousins attended the funeral.
5. The timing of this review, published in January 1925, is notable. Appearing just a few months after Arnauld's letter to Tzara of October 1924, first cited in Chapter 5, it shows generosity in its appraisal of Tzara and of Dada. She characterizes the latter as 'une époque ardente [...] qui a passionné le monde entier' [a fervent period that [...] impassioned the whole world]. Arnauld, 'Les Livres — lettres', p. 2339 (*OC*, p. 438).
6. Tristan Tzara, 'Dada manifeste sur l'amour faible et l'amour amer' (in *Lampisteries*, p. 12; *Seven Dada Manifestos and Lampisteries*, p. 35).
7. Cited by Béhar, in Tzara, *Dada est tatou*, p. 227; *Seven Dada Manifestos and Lampisteries*, p. 38.
8. Arnauld, 'Les Livres — lettres', p. 2339 (*OC*, p. 438).
9. Arnauld, in 'Poésie et réalité'.
10. Mann, *The Theory Death of the Avant-Garde*, p. 7.
11. According to Lista, Laurens also made a polychrome stone bust of her but I have not been able to locate this (see *Dada libertin & libertaire*).
12. The other images reproduced in this book militate against a simple binary and propose kaleidoscopic representations and relationships. Two sketches, by the French artist Louis Favre, at the start of Part III, and the Polish-Jewish Cubist Alice Halicka, at the start of Part I, offer their versions of likenesses. A note by Artaud on Halicka's portrait as 'une classification de son âme' [a classification of her soul] is at odds with my findings that pinning down Arnauld's identity is taxing. See Artaud, 'Livres reçues: *Point de mire*'.
13. Lacaze-Duthiers, 'Céline Arnauld'.

BIBLIOGRAPHY

The primary bibliography below gives an overview of Arnauld's publications and lists selected reviews of her work. The *Œuvres complètes* brings almost all of these texts, and more, together.

Works by Céline Arnauld

Books

Lanterne magique, poèmes (1914) [no copies survive]
Tournevire, roman poétique (Paris: Éditions de L'Esprit nouveau, 1919)
Poèmes à claires-voies (Paris: Éditions de l'Esprit nouveau, 1920)
Point de mire, poèmes (Paris: Jacques Povolozky & Cie, Collections Z, 1921)
Guêpier de diamants, poèmes (Antwerp: Éditions Ça ira, 1923)
L'Apaisement de l'éclipse, passion en deux actes; précédé de 'Diorama', confession lyrique (Paris: Écrivains réunis, 1925)
La Nuit rêve tout haut et Le Clavier secret (Paris: Collection des D. I. de L'Esprit nouveau, 1934)
Heures intactes, poèmes (Brussels: Éditions du 'Journal des poètes', 1936)
Anthologie Céline Arnauld: morceaux choisis de 1919 à 1935 (Brussels: Cahiers du Journal des poètes, 1936)
Les Réseaux du réveil (Paris: G. L. M., 1937)
La Nuit pleure tout haut, poème (Paris: Librairie Paul Magné, 1939)
Rien qu'une étoile, suivi de Plains-chants sauvages, poèmes (Paris: Montbrun, 1948)
ARNAULD, CÉLINE, and PAUL DERMÉE, *Œuvres complètes. Tome 1 — Céline Arnauld*, ed. by Victor Martin-Schmets (Paris: Classiques Garnier, 2013)

Edited Journal

Projecteur (21 May 1920)

Contributions to Journals (listed chronologically)

'Phrase', 'Réponse', 'Avertisseur', and 'Réponses', *Z*, (March 1920), 3, 5–6
'Énigme-personnages', *Dadaphone*, 7 (March 1920), [n.p.]
'Sous-marin', *391*, 12 (by 27 March 1920), [n.p.]
'Dangereux', *Cannibale*, 1 (25 April 1920), [n.p.]
'Entre voleurs', *Proverbe*, 4 (April 1920), [n.p.]
'Ombrelle Dada', *Littérature*, 13 (May 1920), 19
'Prospectus Projecteur', 'Luna Park', and 'Les Ronge-Bois', *Projecteur* (21 May 1920), [n.p.]
'Mes trois péchés Dada', *Cannibale*, 2 (25 May 1920), [n.p.]
'Le Cirque, art nouveau', *L'Esprit nouveau*, 1 (15 October 1920), 97–98

'Périscope', *391*, 14 (November 1920), [n.p.]
'Les Chants de Maldoror' [review of Lautréamont], *L'Esprit nouveau*, 2 (November 1920), 208–10
'Les Livres' [reviews of *Pensées sans langage* by Francis Picabia, *La Défense de Tartuffe* by Max Jacob, and *La Femme assise* by Guillaume Apollinaire], *L'Esprit nouveau*, 3 (15 December 1920), 359–63
'Les Livres' [reviews of *Vers de circonstance* by Stéphane Mallarmé and *Le Pan-pan au cul du nu nègre* by Clément Pansaers], *L'Esprit nouveau*, 4 (January 1921), 471–73
'Chevaux de frise', *Bleu*, 3 (January 1921), [n.p.]
'Rabindranath Tagore' [review of *Le Jardinier d'amour*], *L'Esprit nouveau*, 5 (February 1921), 559–62
'Pilori', *Creación*, 1 (Madrid: April 1921), 18
'Envoi du Japon', 'Extrait de Saturne', *Le Pilhaou-Thibaou*, (July 1921), [n.p.]
'Jeux d'anneaux', *Action*, 2.9 (October 1921), 19–20
'Surnom', *Ça ira*, 16 (November 1921), 101
'Le Cinéma: Le Signe de Zorro', *Action*, 10 (November 1921), [n.p.]
'Le Cinéma: Le Gosse', and 'Ouvrages reçus', *Action*, hors série (December 1921), [n.p.]
'Fête', *Action*, 3.12 (March-April 1922), 41
'Souffrances d'émail', *Zenit*, 24 (May 1923), [n.p.]
'La Lyre des toits', *Les Images de Paris*, 4.40 (April 1923), [n.p.]
'Les Cordes du rail', *Contimporanul*, 2.41 (May 1923), 1
'Cavatine de marées', *Het Overzicht*, 16 (May-June 1923), 65
'Livres nouveaux' [review of *L'Homme de la pampa* by Jules Supervielle, *En péniche* by Philippe Thual, and *Les Étrangères* by André Harlaire], *L'Esprit nouveau*, 20 (January 1924), [n.p.]
'Le Zèbre handicapé' [review], *Interventions*, 2 (January 1924), 2
'Livres nouveaux' [reviews of *L'Équipage* by Joseph Kessel, *Ledentu le phare* by Iliazd, and *Mektoub* by Syo], *L'Esprit nouveau*, 21 (March 1924), [n.p.]
'Lettres' [reviews of *Rahab* by Waldo Franck, *Fable des origines* by Henri Michaux, and *Le Paradis à l'ombre des épées* by Henry de Montherlant], and 'Livres nouveaux — lettres [review of *Cygne* by Rabindranath Tagore], *L'Esprit nouveau*, 23 (May 1924), [n.p.]
'Livres nouveaux — lettres' [review of *Un vagabond joue en sourdine* by Knut Hamsun, *Colin-Maillard* by Louis Hémon, and *Élégies bruxelloises* by Léon Kochnitzky], *L'Esprit nouveau*, 24 (June 1924), [n.p.]
'Livres nouveaux — lettres' [review of *Essais amoureux d'un homme ingénu* by Pio Baroja, *Voyage dans l'Inde* by Waldemar Bonsels, and *Enchantements* by Hélène Lémery], *L'Esprit nouveau*, 25 (July 1924), [n.p.]
'Le Banquet' [*Apollinaire* issue], *L'Esprit nouveau*, 26 (October 1924), [n.p.]
'Les Faux Managers', *Le Mouvement accéléré* (November 1924), [n.p.]
'Les Livres — lettres' [review of *Sept manifestes Dada* by Tristan Tzara, *Les Reines de la main gauche* by Pierre Naville, *Les Voyageuses de l'Île fermée* by Henry Petiot, and *Poèmes 1920–23* by Paul-Gustave van Hecke], *L'Esprit nouveau*, 28 (January 1925), 2338–41
'Le Cas Lautréamont', special issue of *Le Disque vert*, 4.4 (January 1925), 98–99
'Avion', 'Les Tournois du Vent', and 'Charlot prince des rêveurs', *Documents internationaux de l'Esprit nouveau*, 1 (Spring 1927), [n.p.]
'Le Bocage des cygnes', *Integral*, 13–14 (1927), [n.p.]
'Cortège marin', *Muba*, 1 (1928), [n.p.]
'Aux portes de l'océan', *La Revue mosane*, 1 (January 1929), 10
'Voyage autour de ma folie', *La Revue mosane*, 6 (June 1929), 8
'Le Bar des algues' [with Polish translation], *L'Art contemporain*, 1 (April 1929), 36–37

'Je me suis serrée très fort contre la folie', *Le Journal des poètes*, 1.3 (18 April 1931), 1
'Notre enquête hebdomadaire: un poème incohérent peut-il être beau?', *Le Journal des poètes*, 2.7 (9 January 1932), 1
'Le Rideau se lève', *Le Journal des poètes*, 2.9 (23 January 1932), 3
'Céline Arnauld nous dit ... Mystère de l'image', interview with P. L. Flouquet, *Le Journal des poètes*, 2.21 (30 April 1932), 1
'Griffes de lumière', *Le Phare de Neuilly*, 1 (1933), 34–35
'La Nuit rêve tout haut' [extract], *Le Journal des poètes*, 4.3 (18 February 1934), 3
'A travers la tempête, le vent hagard' [untitled poem], *Le Dernier Carré: cahiers mensuels de la poésie*, 4 (May 1935), [n.p.]
'Poèmes', *Souvenir de la réception de Madame Céline Arnauld et Monsieur Paul Dermée aux amis de 1914, Les Actes poétiques*, 8 (15 December 1937), [n.p.]
'L'Appel' and 'Nocturne', *Le Journal des poètes* (February 1946), 12
'Plaints-chants sauvages', 'L'Ondine', and 'Pour éveiller l'aurore', *Le Journal des poètes*, 7 (September 1948), 1
'Poésie et réalité: interview du poète Céline Arnauld', interview with P. L. Flouquet, *Le Journal des poètes*, 1 (January 1950), 3

Contributions in anthologies

'Le Banquet', in Guillaume Apollinaire and others, *Apollinaire* (Paris: Éditions de l'Esprit nouveau, [1919–1924]), [n.p.]
'Levée d'écrou', in *Le Cahier des muses: textes autographes de Juliette Adam, Céline Arnauld et autres*, ed. by Charles d'Éternod and Élie Moroy (Geneva: Eggimann, 1922), p. 8
'Autour d'une ville ...', in *La Littérature féminine définie par les femmes écrivains: enquête sur les lettres de ce temps*, ed. by Élie Moroy (Geneva: M. Burgi, 1931), pp. 4–5
'Comment je suis venue à la poésie', in *Anthologie des écrivains du Vè: Paris et le quartier Latin, souvenirs et impressions*, ed. by Gérard de Lacaze-Duthiers (Paris: Pierre Clairac, 1953), pp. 38–39

Selected Reviews of Arnauld's Work

[Anon.], 'Céline Arnauld: opinions de la critique' [pamphlet of collected reviews] (Antwerp: Éditions Ça ira, [*c.* 1923?])
—— *La Critique et Céline Arnauld* [pamphlet of collected reviews] (Paris: [*c.* 1925?])
ARTAUD, ANTONIN, 'Livres reçues: *Point de mire*', *Action*, 12 (Paris: March-April 1922), [n.p.]; repr. in *Œuvres Complètes*, 26 vols (Paris: Gallimard, 1956–1994), II, 227–28
BOUCHARY, JEAN, '*Point de mire*', *La Vie des lettres et des arts*, n.s. 11 (August 1922), 345
BOUSQUET, JOE, 'Les Livres de poésie', *Courrier des poètes*, 1, *Les Cahiers du Journal des poètes*, 14 (20 June 1936), 50–53
DANTINE, ÉMILE, 'L'Œuvre admirable de Céline Arnauld', *La Revue mosane*, 6 (June 1929), 3–7
DUNAN, RENÉE, 'Encycliques: *Poèmes à claires-voies*', *Action*, 3 (April 1920), 62
FLOUQUET, PIERRE-LOUIS, 'La Mort de Céline Arnauld', *Le Journal des poètes*, 22.3 (15 March 1952), 4
FONTAINAS, ANDRÉ, 'Revue de la quinzaine: les poèmes', *Mercure de France*, 47.271.919 (1 October 1936), 112–13
FORT, PAUL, 'Une poétesse de la poésie nouvelle', *Mercure de France*, 50.291.980 (15 April 1939), 317–23
HERTZ, HENRI, 'Panorama des livres' [includes a paragraph on *Heures intactes*], *Europe*, 42.156 (15 September 1936), 540–41

LACAZE-DUTHIERS, GÉRARD DE, 'Céline Arnauld', *Interventions*, 1 (December 1923), 2
—— 'A travers Paris', *L'Œuf dur*, 9 (April 1922), 16
MARTIN DU GARD, MAURICE, 'Les Livres' [brief note on *Point de mire*], *L'Œuf dur*, 8 (March 1922), 16
PATRI, AIMÉ, 'La Poésie' [review of *Rien qu'une étoile*], *Paru*, 52 (July 1949) 32–33
PIA, PASCAL, 'Céline Arnauld: *Point de mire*', *Le Disque vert*, 1.4 (August 1922)
RICHARD, ÉLIE, 'Le Jardin des supplices' [review of *Point de mire*], *Les Images de Paris*, 34 (September-October 1922), [n.p.]
—— 'Le Jardin des supplices' [review of *Guêpier de diamants*], *Les Images de Paris*, 48 (December 1923), [n.p.]
SAISSET, FRÉDÉRIC, 'Les Livres; Les Poèmes', *La Nervie* (September-October 1923), 225

Other Primary and Secondary Sources

ADAMOWICZ, ELZA, *Dada Bodies: Between Battleground and Fairground* (Manchester: Manchester University Press, 2019)
—— *Surrealist Collage in Text and Image: Dissecting the Exquisite Corpse* (Cambridge & New York: Cambridge University Press, 2005)
ADES, DAWN, ed., *The Dada Reader* (London: Tate Publishing, 2006)
ALLMER, PATRICIA, *Angels of Anarchy: Women Artists and Surrealism* (Munich: Prestel, 2009)
—— 'Feminist Interventions: Revising the Canon', in *A Companion to Dada and Surrealism*, ed. by David Hopkins (Chichester: Wiley-Blackwell, 2016), pp. 366–81
ALLMER, PATRICIA, ed., *Intersections: Women Artists / Surrealism / Modernism* (Manchester: Manchester University Press, 2016)
APOLLINAIRE, GUILLAUME, *Calligrammes: Poems of Peace and War (1913–1916)*, trans. by Iain Lockerbie (Berkeley & Los Angeles: University of California Press, 1980)
—— 'L'Esprit nouveau et les poètes', in *Œuvres en prose complètes*, Bibliothèque de la Pléiade (Paris: Gallimard, 1991), pp. 948–53
BARNET, MARIE-CLAIRE, 'To Lise Deharme's Lighthouse: *Le Phare de Neuilly*, a Forgotten Surrealist Review', *French Studies*, 57.3 (2003), 323–34
BARON, JACQUES, *L'An du surréalisme, suivi de L'An dernier* (Paris: Denoël, 1969)
BASS, JACQUELYNNE, *Marcel Duchamp and the Art of Life* (Cambridge, MA: MIT Press, 2019)
BAUDELAIRE, CHARLES, *Œuvres complètes*, ed. by Claude Pichois, 2 vols, Bibliothèque de la Pléiade (Paris: Gallimard, 1975–1976)
—— *The Flowers of Evil*, ed. by Marthiel and Jackson Mathews (New York: New Directions, 1989)
—— 'Le Peintre de la vie moderne', in *Œuvres complètes*, 7 vols (Paris: Calmann Lévy, 1885–1903), III, 68–73
—— 'The Painter of Modern Life', in *The Painter of Modern Life and Other Essays*, trans. and ed. by Jonathan Mayne (London: Phaidon, 1964), pp. 1–40
BECKETT, SAMUEL, *En attendant Godot* (Paris: Bertrand-Lacoste, 1993)
—— *Waiting for Godot* (London: Faber & Faber, 2015)
BÉGHIN, LAURENT, and HUBERT ROLAND, 'La Première Série du *Journal des poètes* (1931–1935) de Pierre-Louis Flouquet et son réseau de médiateurs', *Textyles*, 52 (2018), 93–110
BENJAMIN, WALTER, *Illuminations*, trans. by Harry Zorn (London: Pimlico, 1999)
BERGSON, HENRI, *L'Évolution créatrice* (Paris: Alcan, 1917)
BERMAN, MARSHALL, *All That is Solid Melts into Air: The Experience of Modernity* (New York: Simon & Schuster, 1982)
BOHN, WILLARD, *Marvelous Encounters: Surrealist Responses to Film, Art, Poetry and, Architecture* (Lewisburg, PA: Bucknell University Press, 2005)

Bohn, Willard, ed., *The Dada Market: An Anthology of Poetry* (Carbondale & Edwardsville: Southern Illinois University Press, 1993)
Bowd, Gavin, ed., *France-Romania: Twentieth-Century Cultural Exchanges*, special issue of *Forum for Modern Language Studies*, 36.2 (2000)
Bowie, Malcolm, 'The Modern Period: 1789–2000', in Sarah Kay, Terence Cave, and Malcolm Bowie, *A Short History of French Literature* (Oxford: Oxford University Press, 2003), pp. 193–314
Breton, André, *Manifestes du surréalisme* (Paris: Gallimard, 2014)
—— *Manifestoes of Surrealism*, trans. by Richard Seaver and Helen R. Lane (Ann Arbor: University of Michigan Press, 1972)
—— *Nadja* (Paris: Gallimard, 2000)
—— *Œuvres complètes*, ed. by Marguerite Bonnet, 4 vols, Bibliothèque de la Pléiade (Paris: Gallimard, 1988–2008)
—— *Signe ascendant: suivi de Fata Morgana, Les États généraux, Des épingles tremblantes, Xénophiles, Ode à Charles Fournier, Constellations, Le La* (Paris: Gallimard, 1968)
—— *What is Surrealism? Selected Writings*, trans. by Franklin Rosemont (New York: Pathfinder, 1978)
Bru, Sascha, *The European Avant-Gardes, 1905–1935: A Portable Guide* (Edinburgh: Edinburgh University Press, 2018)
Buffet-Picabia, Gabrielle, 'Gambit de la Reine', *Dada*, 4–5 (February 1919), 19
Burmeister, Ralf, Michaela Oberhofer, and Esther Tisa Francini, eds, *Dada Africa: Dialogue with the Other* (Zurich: Scheidegger & Spiess, 2016)
Carrington, Leonora, *The Debutante and Other Stories* (London: Silver Press, 2017)
——, *En bas* (Paris: Fontaine, 1945)
Caws, Mary Ann, *The Poetry of Dada and Surrealism* (Princeton, NJ: Princeton University Press, 1970)
Caws, Mary Ann, Rudolf E. Kuenzli, and Gwen Raaberg, eds, *Surrealism and Women* (Cambridge, MA, & London: MIT Press, 1991)
Chadwick, Whitney, *The Militant Muse: Love, War and the Women of Surrealism* (London: Thames & Hudson, 2017)
—— *Mirror Images: Women, Surrealism and Self-representation* (Cambridge, MA: MIT Press, 1998)
—— *Women Artists and the Surrealist Movement* [1985] (London: Thames & Hudson, 1991)
Cixous, Hélène, *Le Rire de la Méduse et autres ironies* (Paris: Éditions Galilée, 2010)
—— 'The Laugh of the Medusa', trans. by Keith Cohen and Paula Cohen, *Signs*, 1.4 (Summer, 1976), 875–93
Colliani, Tania, 'Les Avant-gardes et la narration: pour une poétique anti-prosaïque', *Cahiers de Narratologie*, 24 (2013), 1–13
Colvile, Georgiana M. M., 'Beauty and/Is the Beast: Animal Symbology in the Work of Leonora Carrington, Remedios Varo and Leonor Fini', in *Surrealism and Women*, ed. by Mary Ann Caws, Rudolf E. Kuenzli, and Gwen Raaberg (Cambridge, MA, & London: MIT Press, 1991), pp. 159–81
Coste, Claude, 'La Musique dans la vie et l'œuvre de Philippe Soupault', in *Présence de Philippe Soupault*, ed. by Myriam Boucharenc and Claude Leroy (Caen: Presses universitaires de Caen, 1999), pp. 275–92
Dante Alighieri, *The Divine Comedy of Dante Alighieri*, ed. and trans. by John D. Sinclair, 3 vols (Oxford: Oxford University Press, 1961)
Dayan, Peter, *The Music of Dada: A Lesson in Intermediality for our Times* (Abingdon & New York: Routledge, 2019)
Dell, Simon, 'After Apollinaire: *SIC* (1916–19); *Nord-Sud* (1917–18); and *L'Esprit nouveau*

(1920–5)', in *The Oxford Critical and Cultural History of Modernist Magazines*, ed. by Peter Brooker and others, 3 vols in 4 (Oxford: Oxford University Press, 2013), III, 143–59

DERMÉE, PAUL, 'Guillaume Apollinaire', *L'Esprit nouveau*, 26 (June–July 1924), [n.p.]

DERMÉE, PAUL, and MICHEL SEUPHOR, eds, *Documents internationaux de l'esprit nouveau*, repr. with a preface by Hubert Juin (Paris: J. M. Laplace, 1997)

DREHER, S., and M. ROLLI, eds, *Bibliographie de la littérature française 1940–49* (Lille: Librairie Giard; Geneva: Librairie E. Droz, 1958)

DRIJKONINGEN, FERNAND, 'Un tableau-manifeste de Picabia: le double monde', in *Marcel Duchamp*, ed. by Klaus Beekman and Antje von Graevenitz (Amsterdam: Rodopi, 1989), pp. 97–112

ECO, UMBERTO, *The Open Work*, trans. by Anna Cancogni (Cambridge, MA: Harvard University Press, 1989)

ESHLEMAN, CLAYTON, *The Gospel of Céline Arnauld* (Berkeley, CA: Tuumba Press, 1977)

FORCER, STEPHEN, *Dada as Text, Thought and Theory* (Oxford: Legenda, 2015)

——*Modernist Song: The Poetry of Tristan Tzara* (Oxford: Legenda, 2006)

FORSTER, E. M., *Aspects of the Novel* (Harmondsworth: Penguin, 1966)

FREYTAG-LORINGHOVEN, ELSA VON, *Body Sweats: The Uncensored Writings of Elsa von Freytag-Loringhoven*, ed. by Irene Gammel and Suzanne Zelazo (Cambridge, MA: MIT Press, 2011)

GAMMEL, IRENE, *Baroness Elsa: Gender, Dada and Modernity — A Cultural Biography* (Cambridge, MA: MIT, 2002)

GANCEVICI, OLGA, 'Littérature féminine des avant-gardes roumaines', in *Les Oubliés des Avant-Garde*, ed. by Barbara Meazzi and Jean-Paul Madou (Chambéry: Université de Savoie, 2006), pp. 183–96

GELBER, MARK H., and SAMI SJÖBERG, eds, *Jewish Aspects in Avant-Garde: Between Rebellion and Revelation* (Berlin: De Gruyter, 2017)

GOLL, IVAN, 'Manifeste du surréalisme', in *Surréalisme*, 1 (October 1924), [n.p.]

HAYDEN, SARAH, 'Céline Arnauld: Six Poems Translated by Sarah Hayden', *Translation Ireland*, 20.1 (2017), 139–51

HEMUS, RUTH, 'Céline Arnauld: Dada Présidente?', in *The French Avant-Garde*, ed. by Stephen Forcer and Emma Wagstaff (Nottingham: Nottingham French Studies, 2012), pp. 67–77

——'Céline Arnauld's *Poèmes à Claires-Voies* (Openwork Poems)', in *Lost in Transmission: Preservation, Radicalism, and the Institutionalisation of the Avant-Garde(s)*, ed. by Rebecca Ferreboeuf, Fiona Noble, and Tara Plunkett (Basingstoke: Palgrave Macmillan, 2016), pp. 71–85

——'Dada's Film Poet: Céline Arnauld', in *Modernism's Intermedialities: From Futurism to Fluxus*, ed. by Rhys Davies and Chris Townsend (Newcastle upon Tyne: Cambridge Scholars Publishing, 2014), pp. 66–80

——'Dada's Paris Season', in *The Oxford Critical and Cultural History of Modernist Magazines*, ed. by Peter Brooker and others, 3 vols in 4 (Oxford: Oxford University Press, 2013), III, 180–202

——*Dada's Women* (London & New Haven, CT: Yale University Press, 2009)

——'The Manifesto of Céline Arnauld', in *Dada and Beyond*, ed. by Elza Adamowicz, Eric Robertson, and Andrew Rothwell (Amsterdam & New York: Rodopi, 2011), pp. 121–31

HENTEA, MARIUS, *TaTa Dada: The Real Life and Celestial Adventures of Tristan Tzara* (Cambridge, MA, & London: MIT Press, 2014)

HOPKINS, DAVID, *Dada and Surrealism: A Very Short Introduction* (Oxford: Oxford University Press, 2004)

——*Marcel Duchamp and Max Ernst: The Bride Shared* (Oxford: Clarendon Press, 1998)

HUGNET, GEORGES, *L'Aventure Dada (1916–1922)* (Vichy: Seghers, 1971)

JONES, AMELIA, *Irrational Modernism: A Neurasthenic History of New York Dada* (Cambridge, MA, & London: MIT Press, 2004)
JÜRGS, BRITTA, *Etwas Wasser in der Seife: Portraits dadaistischer Künstlerinnen und Schriftstellerinnen* (Berlin: Aviva, 1999)
KAMENISH, PAULA K., *Mamas of Dada: Women of the European Avant-Garde* (Columbia: University of South Carolina Press, 2015)
KANDINSKY, WASSILY, 'Concerning the Spiritual in Art', in *Art in Theory 1900–1990: An Anthology of Changing Ideas*, ed. by Charles Harrison and Paul Wood (Oxford & Cambridge, MA: Blackwell, 2001), pp. 87–94
KARADY, VICTOR, *Gewalterfahrung und Utopie: Juden in den europäischen Moderne* (Frankfurt am Main: Fischer Taschenbuch, 1999)
KUNSTHAUS ZURICH, ed., *Dadaglobe Reconstructed* (Zurich: Scheidegger & Spiess, 2016)
LEBEL, JACQUES, *Marcel Duchamp*, trans. by George Heard Hamilton (New York: Grove Press, 1959)
LISTA, GIOVANNI, *Dada libertin & libertaire* (Paris: l'Insolite, 2005)
MAHON, ALYCE, ed., *Dorothea Tanning* (London: Tate Modern, 2019)
MABILLE, PIERRE, *Le Merveilleux* (Paris: Les Éditeurs des quatre vents, 1946)
MALLARMÉ, STÉPHANE, *Œuvres complètes*, ed. by Bertrand Marchal, 2 vols, Bibliothèque de la Pléiade (Paris: Gallimard, 1998–2003)
MANN, PAUL, *The Theory Death of the Avant-Garde* (Bloomington & Indianapolis: Indiana University Press, 1991)
MANSBACH, S. A., ed., *Graphic Modernism: From the Baltic to the Balkans, 1910–1935* (New York: New York Public Library, 2007)
—— 'Methodology and Meaning in the Modern Art of Eastern Europe', in *Between Worlds: A Sourcebook of Central European Avant-Gardes, 1910–1930*, ed. by Timothy O. Benson and Éva Forgács for the Los Angeles County Museum of Art (Cambridge, MA, & London: MIT Press, 2002), pp. 290–303
MAREK, JANE E., *Women Editing Modernism: 'Little' Magazines and Literary History* (Lexington: University Press of Kentucky, 1995)
MARINETTI, F. T., 'Destruction of Syntax — Imagination without Strings — Words-in-Freedom 1913', in *Futurist Manifestos*, ed. by Umbro Apollonio (New York: The Viking Press, 1973), pp. 95–107
MARTIN-SCHMETS, VICTOR, 'Bibliographie analytique des revues littéraires belges: *La Revue mosane*', in *Le Livre et l'estampe: revue semestrielle de la Société Royale des Bibliophiles et Iconophiles de Belgique* (Brussels, 1994), p. 104
—— 'Céline Arnauld, épouse Paul Dermée, poète dadaïste', in *Les Oubliés des Avant-Garde*, ed. by Barbara Meazzi and Jean-Paul Madou (Chambéry: Université de Savoie, 2006), pp. 171–82
MELZER, ANNABEL, *Dada and Surrealist Performance* (Baltimore, MD, & London: The John Hopkins University Press, 1994)
MIÈGE, GUY, *A New Dictionary: French and English, with Another English and French*, (London: printed for Thomas Basset, 1679)
MILLIGAN, JENNIFER E., *The Forgotten Generation: French Women Writers of the Inter-war Period* (Oxford & New York: Berg, 1996)
MOORHEAD, JOANNA, *The Surreal Life of Leonora Carrington* (London: Virago, 2017)
MOROY, ÉLIE, ed., *La Littérature féminine définie par les femmes écrivains: enquête sur les lettres de ce temps* (Geneva: M. Burgi, 1931)
MOULIN, JEANNE, ed., *La Poésie féminine: époque moderne* (Paris: Seghers, 1963)
NIETZSCHE, FRIEDRICH, *Ainsi parlait Zarathoustra*, trans. by Henri Albert (Paris: Mercure de France, 1924)

——— *Thus Spoke Zarathustra: A Book for Anyone and Nobody*, trans. by Graham Parkes (Oxford: Oxford University Press, 2005)

NOCHLIN, LINDA, *The Body in Pieces: The Fragment as a Metaphor of Modernity* (London: Thames & Hudson, 2001)

O'REILLY, SALLY, *The Body in Contemporary Art* (London: Thames & Hudson, 2009)

PIERRE, JOSÉ, *Tracts surréalistes et déclarations collectives* (Paris: Le Terrain vague, 1980)

POP, ION, ed., *La Réhabilitation d'un rêve: une anthologie de l'avant-garde roumaine* (Paris: Maurice Nadeau, 2006)

POUPARD-LIEUSSOU, YVES, and MICHEL SANOUILLET, eds, *Documents Dada* (Paris: Weber, 1974)

PROUST, MARCEL, *A la recherche du temps perdu*, ed. by Jean-Yves Tadié, 4 vols (Paris: Gallimard, 1987–1989)

——— *In Search of Lost Time*. Vol. 1, *The Way by Swann's*, trans. by Lydia Davis (London: Penguin, 2002)

——— *Remembrance of Things Past*. Vol. 3, *The Guermantes Way*, trans. by C. K. Scott-Moncrieff (London: Chatto & Windus, 1927)

QUINNEY, ANNE, ed., *Paris-Bucharest, Bucharest-Paris: Francophone Writers from Romania* (Amsterdam & New York: Rodopi, 2012)

RASULA, JED, and TIM CONLEY, eds, *Burning City: Poems of Metropolitan Modernity* (Notre Dame, IN: Action Books, 2012)

REVERDY, PIERRE, *Œuvres complètes. Nord-Sud, Self-Defence et autres écrits sur l'art et la poésie (1917–1926)* (Paris: Flammarion, 1975)

REY, XAVIER, 'Céline Arnauld: *Projecteur*', in *Dada*, exhibition catalogue, 5 October 2005–9 January 2006 (Paris: Éditions Centre Pompidou, 2005), p. 88

RIBEMONT-DESSAIGNES, GEORGES, 'Cafard', *Cannibale*, 1 (April 1920), [n.p.]

RIMBAUD, ARTHUR, *Lettres du voyant (13 et 15 mai 1871)*, ed. by Gérald Schaeffer (Geneva: Droz, 1975)

——— *Œuvres*, ed. by Suzanne Bernard (Paris: Garnier, [1960])

——— *Rimbaud Complete*, trans. and ed. by Wyatt Mason (New York: Modern Library, 2003)

ROBERTSON, ERIC, *Arp: Painter, Poet, Sculptor* (New Haven, CT, & London: Yale University Press, 2007)

——— '"Le Blanc Souci de notre toile": Writing White in Modern French Poetry and Art', *French Studies*, 71 (2017), 319–32

RUSSELL, CHARLES, *Poets, Prophets and Revolutionaries: The Literary Avant-garde from Rimbaud through Postmodernism* (New York & Oxford: Oxford University Press, 1985)

ROSEMONT, FRANKLIN, *What is Surrealism? Selected Writings* (New York: Pathfinder, 1978)

ROSEMONT, PENELOPE, *Surrealist Women: An International Anthology* (London: Athlone Press, 1998)

SANDQVIST, TOM, *Dada East: The Romanians of Cabaret Voltaire* (Cambridge, MA: MIT Press, 2006)

SANOUILLET, MICHEL, *Dada à Paris* (Paris: Flammarion, 2005)

——— *Dada in Paris*, revised and expanded by Anne Sanouillet, trans. by Sharmila Ganguly (Cambridge, MA: MIT Press, 2009)

——— *Francis Picabia et 391: revue publiée de 1917 à 1924 par Francis Picabia*, 2 vols (Nice: Centre du XXè siècle; Paris: Eric Losfeld, 1960–1966)

SANOUILLET, MICHEL, and DOMINIQUE BAUDOUIN, eds, *Dada: réimpression intégrale et dossier critique de la revue publiée de 1917 à 1922 par Tristan Tzara*, 2 vols (Nice: Centre du XXe siècle, 1976–1983)

SAUSSURE, FERDINAND DE, *Cours de linguistique générale* [1916] (Paris: Payot, 1972)

SAWELSON-GORSE, NADIA, *Women in Dada: Essays on Sex, Gender and Identity* (Cambridge, MA: MIT Press, 2001)

SEUPHOR, MICHEL, and OTHERS, *Une vie à angle droit* (Paris: Éditions de la Différence, 1988)
SJÖBERG, SAMI, 'Any Other Transnationalism: Romanian Jewish Emigrants in Francophone Avant-Garde Literature', *French Studies*, 73.1 (2019), 33–49
SOUPAULT, PHILIPPE, 'Est-ce le vent', *La Révolution surréaliste*, 7 (15 June 1926), 15
SPIRIDON, MONICA, ' "Bucharest-on-the-Seine": The Anatomy of a National Obsession', in *Paris-Bucharest, Bucharest-Paris: Francophone Writers from Romania*, ed. by Anne Quinney (Amsterdam & New York: Rodopi, 2012), pp. 23–35
SPITERI, RAYMOND, 'What Can the Surrealists Do?', in *The Oxford Critical and Cultural History of Modernist Magazines*, ed. by Peter Brooker and others, 3 vols in 4 (Oxford: Oxford University Press, 2013), III, 219–43
SPIVAK, GAYATRI CHAKRAVORTY, *A Critique of Postcolonial Reason: Toward a History of the Vanishing Present* (Cambridge, MA: Harvard University Press, 1999)
STAVRINAKI, MARIA, *Dada Presentism: An Essay on Art and History*, trans. by Daniela Ginsburg (Stanford, CA: Stanford University Press, 2016)
STOPPARD, TOM, *Travesties* (London & Boston, MA: Faber & Faber, 1975)
STROM, KIRSTEN, *The Animal Surreal: The Role of Darwin, Animals, and Evolution in Surrealism* (New York: Routledge, 2017)
SULEIMAN, SUSAN RUBIN, *Subversive Intent: Gender, Politics and the Avant-Garde* (Cambridge, MA, & London: Harvard University Press, 1990)
—— 'Writing Past the Wall', in *'Coming to Writing' and Other Essays by Hélène Cixous*, ed. by Deborah Jenson (Cambridge, MA: Harvard University Press, 1991), pp. v–xii
TODOROV, TZVETAN, *Introduction à la littérature fantastique* (Paris: Seuil, 1970)
TYSLIAVA, JUOZAS, 'Marche contre la terre', *Muba*, 1 (1928), 3
TZARA, TRISTAN, *Dada est tatou: tout est dada*, ed. by Henri Béhar (Paris: Flammarion, 1996)
—— *Lampisteries: sept manifestes Dada* (Paris: Pauvert, 2001)
—— *Seven Dada Manifestos and Lampisteries*, trans. by Barbara Wright (London: Calder, 1992)
VICOVANU, ROXANA, 'L'Esprit nouveau et les avant-gardes', in *Les Oubliés des Avant-Garde*, ed. by Barbara Meazzi and Jean-Paul Madou (Chambéry: Université de Savoie, 2006), pp. 103–22
WITTMANN, MARC, *Altered States of Consciousness: Experiences out of Time and Self*, trans. by Philippa Hurd (Cambridge, MA: MIT Press, 2018)
YAARI, MONIQUE, and TIMOTHY SHIPE, eds, *From Dada to Infra/Noir: Dada, Surrealism and Romania*, special issue of *Dada/Surrealism*, 20.1 (2015)

Web-based resources

Association pour l'étude du surréalisme <http://melusine-surrealisme.fr> [accessed 10 April 2020]
Digital Dada Library at the International Dada Archive, University of Iowa Libraries <http://sdrc.lib.uiowa.edu/dada/index.html> [accessed 1 March 2020]
Monoskop: Wiki for avant-garde and modernist magazines, including numerous reprints <https://monoskop.org/Avant-garde_and_modernist_magazines> [accessed 1 March 2020]

INDEX

Adamowicz, Elza 138 n. 17
Allmer, Patricia 3, 7 n. 10
Apollinaire, Guillaume 5, 35–36, 44, 56, 119, 120, 133, 135–36, 154
  'La Colombe poignardée et le jet d'eau' 38
  'Cortège' 51
  'L'Esprit nouveau et les poètes' 45 n. 4, 125 n. 8, 138 n. 23
  'Lundi rue Christine' 40
  'Paysage' 105
Aragon, Louis 30, 61, 68, 74, 76
  'Café crème' 80
Arensberg, W. C. 68
Arnauld, Céline:
  as Carolina Goldstein 4, 14–17, 152
  correspondence written by 61, 87, 123–24, 156
  life:
    birth 14
    death 6, 133, 151–52
    marriage 14
  journals (published):
    Projecteur 5, 74–83, 101, 153
  journals (planned but not published):
    Ipéca / I.P.K. 75–76
    M'Amenez'y 35, 75–76
  poems and prose:
    'A tâtons' 44
    'L'Apaisement de l'éclipse' 104
    'Apothéose' 51–52
    'L'Appel' 145
    'L'Aube jeune et alerte' 134
    'Avertissement aux lecteurs' 3, 7, 88–90, 101, 108, 116
    'Avertisseur' 36, 39–41, 53, 67, 81, 142
    'Avion' 94
    'Le Banquet' 36
    'Le Bocage des cygnes' 92
    'Buisson de rêves' 134
    'Cathédrale des poètes' 144–45
    'Cavatine de marées' 102, 103
    'Cavatine de velours' 103
    'Les Chants de Maldoror' 92, 147
    'Charlot, prince des rêveurs' 93–94
    'Chevaux de frise' 102
    'Un ciel de joie épanoui après l'orage' 135
    'Cinéma' 33 n. 12
    'Le Cinéma: *Le Gosse*' 78, 92–93

    'Le Cinéma: *Le Signe de Zorro*' 92
    'Le Cirque, art nouveau' 92
    'Claires-voies' 37–39, 41, 43, 44
    'Les Claires-voies du sommeil' 103
    'Clairières' 146–47
    'Les Corbeaux bleus de la mort' 145
    'Les Cordes du rail' 91, 102
    'Dangereux' 70–72
    'Dans l'abîme' 57 n. 2
    'Des étoiles de fine taille' 146
    'Dévidoir des songes' 104–05
    'Dialogue lyrique du guêpier' 108
    'Diorama' 3, 5–6, 16, 18, 24, 87–88, 102, 108–13, 117, 118, 122, 127, 128, 136, 140, 153
    'Énigme-personnages' 65–67, 153
    'Entre voleurs' 36, 45 n. 7
    'Envoi du Japon' 62
    'Et revoici la joie!' 134–35
    'Extrait de Saturne' 62–64
    'Farandole' 33 n. 12
    'Les Faux Managers' 83, 85–87, 101, 123
    'Festival de minuit' 134, 136
    'Fête' 48, 57 n. 2
    'Fraîcheur' 145
    'Guêpier de diamants' 107–09
    'Je me suis serrée très fort contre la folie' 121–22
    'Jeu d'échecs' 30–32, 48, 63, 126 n. 13
    'Jeux d'anneaux' 48, 49–51, 54
    'Levée d'écrou' 58 n. 13
    'Luna Park' 28, 80–81, 82
    'La Lyre des toits' 102
    'Ma peine s'éveille' 146
    'Mes trois péchés Dada' 67–68
    'Le Musicien des marées' 103
    'Notre-Dame de Paris' 144–45
    'Ombrelle Dada' 47, 68–70, 76, 82
    'Oreiller de lune' 136
    'Périscope' 48, 54, 55–56, 62
    'Plains-chants sauvages' 146
    'Plus haut que l'amour' 135–36, 146
    'Point de mire' 52, 53–54, 78
    'Porte-peine' 52–53, 54
    'Pour éveiller l'aurore' 146
    'Prospectus Projecteur' 77–78, 81, 82, 91, 116
    'Puisqu'il faut que je meure' 145
    'Réponses' 65
    'Rien qu'une étoile' 144

'Les Ronge-Bois' 80, 81, 82
'Somnambule' 51
'Souffrances d'émail' 91, 102, 105–07
'Sous-marin' 36, 41–43
'Surnom' 48, 54
'Surtout ne regarde pas' 44, 57 n. 2
'Symphonie' 44, 57 n. 2
'Tempête' 57 n. 2
'Terrasse des songes' 103
'Les Tournois du vent' 94
'Travaux songeux' 103
'Vallée des songes' 134
'Le Velours de l'espace' 103
'Voyage autour de ma folie' 122
projectivisme 5, 19, 82, 87–90, 91, 92, 109, 110, 137, 153, 158
relationship with Dada 1, 4, 5, 7, 14, 17, 35–36, 57, 61–62, 64–72, 74–83, 85, 88–89, 90–91, 112–13, 124, 147–48, 152–56, 158
relationship with Surrealism 5, 55–57, 62, 83, 85–91, 94, 112, 124, 130–31, 133, 141, 148, 154
single-authored books (planned but not published):
  La Lune dans le puits 30
  Le Musicien des marées 30
  Serpentine 30
single-authored books (published):
  Anthologie Céline Arnauld 26, 30, 96, 102, 108, 115, 117, 121, 128, 137
  L'Apaisement de l'éclipse, 3, 5, 30, 56, 83, 92, 108, 113, 126 n. 13
  Guêpier de diamants 5, 17, 30, 102–09, 110, 113
  Heures Intactes 6, 127–34, 136, 137, 142
  La Lanterne magique 4, 5, 11, 16, 17–19, 77, 109, 110
  La Nuit pleure tout haut 6, 139–43, 144, 155
  La Nuit rêve tout haut et Le Clavier secret 6, 94, 113, 115–25, 127, 135, 139, 144
  Poèmes à claires-voies 5, 17, 30, 35–45, 56, 75, 105, 110, 113, 136
  Point de mire 5, 17, 30, 44, 47–57, 110, 113, 125 n. 1, 129
  Les Réseaux du réveil 6, 44, 127, 134–37, 146
  Rien qu'une étoile, suivi de Plains-chants sauvages 6, 143–47
  Tournevire 5, 17, 19–20, 22–32, 42, 44, 45 n. 3, 63, 108, 110, 111, 113, 118, 127, 144, 154, 157
Arp, Jean 14, 68
  'la couille d'hirondelle' 55
Artaud, Antonin 47–48, 56, 103, 158 n. 12
automatic writing 23, 29, 55–56, 86, 90, 153
avant-garde 55–56, 61–64, 85–95, 112, 127, 129, 130, 132, 135, 140, 148, 152–55, 158
  and central and Eastern Europe 12–17, 30, 91–92, 101–02, 121
  death of 156–57
  and music 115–16, 119, 124

and women 1–4, 17, 64, 83 n. 4, 101, 120, 148–49, 156

Baron, Jacques 31
Baudelaire, Charles 41, 102, 109–10, 114 n. 10, 128, 131, 133, 147, 154
Beckett, Samuel, En attendant Godot 31
Benjamin, Walter 22, 93
Bergson, Henri 90, 130
Berman, Marshall 147
Boesch, Ina 2
Bohn, Willard 31, 45 n. 7, 39, 76, 84 n. 20
Bouchary, Jean 54
Bowie, Malcolm 119
Brauner, Victor 13
Breton, André 5, 55, 61, 68, 74, 75, 80, 82, 83, 85–87, 90, 95, 101, 123, 124, 153, 156
  'Du rêve' 144
  'Manifeste du surréalisme' 29, 90, 141
  Nadja 29–30, 41, 123
  'Parfums d'Orsay' 80
Buffet-Picabia, Gabrielle 34 n. 28, 114 n. 13
  'Le Gambit de la Reine' 32

Cahun, Claude 3
Carrington, Leonora 3, 131
  En Bas 126 n. 16
  The Hearing Trumpet 3
Caws, Mary Ann 3, 114 n. 14, 137 n. 13
Chadwick, Whitney 3, 122, 131
Chaplin, Charlie 78, 92–94
chess 30–32, 93
childhood 11, 18, 32, 110, 118, 129, 131, 140–41, 148, 154
Citroen, Paul, Metropolis 41
Cixous, Hélène 111–12
Clair, René, Entr'acte 93
Cocteau, Jean 35, 64
collage 5, 35–38, 41, 44, 79, 80, 106
Colliani, Tania 29
Colvile, Georgiana 131
Constructivism 1
Coste, Claude 115–16, 124
Crevel, René 85
Cubism 35, 37, 44, 64–65, 91

Dada:
  exhibitions (recent) 2–3, 6, 11–12
  and music 124
  and women 1–4, 6, 11, 14, 32, 61–62, 64, 74, 101, 147–48, 152
  in Berlin 13, 41
  in Paris 1, 13–14, 30, 61–62, 65, 74, 76–77, 85–86
  in Zurich 11–13, 55, 71, 156
Daguerre, Louis 109
Dante Alighieri 123, 133, 142, 143–44, 154
  Divine Comedy 123

Dayan, Peter 119, 124
Degas, Edgar 55
Deharme, Lise 83 n. 4, 84 n. 13 & 25
Delaunay, Robert 41
Delaunay, Sonia 41
Dermée, Paul 4, 26, 30, 36, 41, 57, 64, 65, 68, 70, 72, 78, 82, 83, 85–86, 91, 92, 94–96, 113, 124, 129, 139, 140, 143, 148
  as Camille Gérard Zéphirin Janssen 14
  correspondence written by 75–76
  death 151
  'Philosophie de l'histoire' 80
  'Signalement' 79–80
  'L'Un pour l'autre' 78–79
Divoire, Fernand 23
Doucet, Jacques 76
Ducasse, Isidore (Le comte de Lautréamont) 69, 123
  Les Chants de Maldoror 92, 147
Duchamp, Marcel 2, 32, 93
  Fountain 2
  as Rrose Sélavy 15
Duchamp, Suzanne 1
Dunan, Renée 35, 37, 44, 75, 78
  'Dadaphysis' 79
  'Hyper Dada' 81–82
  'Les Méditations du saladier' 79

Eco, Umberto, The Open Work 37
écriture féminine 111–12
Éluard, Paul 11, 36, 68, 75, 76
  as Paul Draule 15, 79
  'Julot' 78
Ernst, Max 3
Eshleman, Clayton 15
Expressionism 39, 91, 104

Fairbanks, Douglas, The Mark of Zorro, 92
fairy tales 5, 24–25, 27, 29–30, 32, 104, 107, 122, 154
Fascism 139, 143, 155
Fauln, Catherine 124
Favre, Louis 92, 100, 158 n. 12
Festival Dada, Salle Gaveau 30, 82
First World War 13, 38, 40, 49, 51, 54
flâneur 41, 102, 149
Flouquet, Pierre-Louis 96, 97 n. 31, 124, 139
Fontainas, André 129
Forcer, Stephen 4, 28, 32, 81, 101, 107, 109, 120
Forster, E. M., Aspects of the Novel 23, 25, 28–29
Fort, Paul 115, 124
Freud, Sigmund 55, 88
Freytag-Loringhoven, Elsa von 2
  God 2
Futurism 1, 13, 47, 91, 135

Gammel, Irene 2
Gancevici, Olga 20 n. 7

Gleizes, Albert 85
Goll, Ivan 85
  'Manifeste du surréalisme' 44, 56, 82–83
Grosz, George, Leben und treiben in Universal-City, 12 Uhr 5 Mittags 41

Halicka, Alice 10, 158 n. 12
Halsman, Philippe 157
Hayden, Sarah 57 n. 2, 84 n. 20
Heartfield, John:
  as John Herzfelde 14
  Leben und treiben in Universal-City, 12 Uhr 5 Mittags 41
Hennings, Emmy 1
Herman, Max 92
Hilsum, René 76
Höch, Hannah 1, 2
Hoerle, Angelika 2–3
Hugnet, Georges 69, 71
Hugo, Victor 27
Huidobro, Vincente 85, 96 n. 16

Janco, Georges 12, 13
Janco, Jules 12, 13
Janco, Marcel 12, 13, 91
Janssen, Josette 21 n. 17, 158 n. 2, 3 & 4
Janssen, Pierre 15, 16, 143, 151, 157
Jones, Amelia 2
journals and pamphlets:
  Action 35, 48, 82
  Bleu 102
  Bulletin Dada 61
  Ça ira 48, 91, 102
  Cannibale 61, 64, 67, 70, 76
  Le Cœur à barbe 61
  Contimporanul 91, 102
  Creación 91
  Dada 71, 74
  Dada soulève tout 64
  Dadaphone 65, 75
  Dd O^4 H^2 74
  Le Disque vert 91, 123
  Documents internationaux de l'Esprit nouveau 93, 94–95, 97 n. 29
  L'Esprit nouveau 36, 82, 92, 96 n. 19
  Het Overzicht 91, 102
  Les Images de Paris 54, 102
  Integral 92
  Le Journal des poètes 95–96, 128, 145, 150 n. 18
  Littérature 61, 68–69, 75–76, 82
  Mercure de France 129
  Le Mouvement accéléré 83, 85–86
  Muba 91
  Le Pilhaou-Thibaou 61, 62, 85
  La Pomme de pins 64, 85
  Plus de cubisme 65

Projecteur, see Arnauld, Céline, journals (published)
Proverbe 11, 36, 64, 75, 76
Z 36, 39, 41, 64–65, 70, 72, 75, 76
Zenit 91, 102
391: 23, 36, 41, 48, 55, 61, 62, 75
Joyce, James 13
Juin, Hubert 85, 90, 95
Jürgs, Britta 2

Kahlo, Frida 3
Kamenish, Paula K. 2, 45 n. 7, 67, 73 n. 14, 80, 84 n. 8 & 20
Kandinsky, Wassily 124
    'Concerning the Spiritual in Art' 87, 121
Kupka, François (aka František or Frank) 85

Lacaze-Duthiers, Gérard de 107
Laurens, Henri 22, 157
Lautréamont, comte de, *see* Isidore Ducasse
Le Corbusier, aka Charles-Édouard Jeanneret 92, 94
Lenin, Vladimir 13
lyricism 54, 61–62, 69, 71–72, 87, 92, 108, 115, 123–24, 148, 154, 157

Mabille, Pierre 141
Mallarmé, Stéphane 119, 124, 140
'Manifeste de l'Association des écrivains pour la défense de la culture' 139
Man Ray 12, 93
Mann, Paul 157
Mansbach, Steven 30, 121
Marinetti, F. T. 23, 41, 55
Martin-Schmets, Victor 4, 66, 116, 117, 123, 142, 147–48
Marx, Karl, *Communist Manifesto* 147
Meliès, Georges:
    L'Éclipse du soleil en pleine lune 28
    La Lanterne magique 19–20
Melzer, Annabel 32
le merveilleux 86, 141
Mićić, Ljubomir 91
Miller, Lee 3
Milligan, Jennifer E. 149
Modernism 13, 16, 23, 41, 53, 56–57, 102, 105, 112, 124, 127, 130, 132–33, 147, 153, 156, 158
Mondrian, Piet 91
Monnier, Adrienne 124
Moroy, Élie 148–49
Moulin, Jeanine 124–25, 132

Nietzsche, Friedrich 103, 109, 154
Nochlin, Linda 55, 56, 112, 132–33

Olson, Charles 96 n. 10
Oppenheim, Meret 3
O'Reilly, Sally 132

Ozenfant, Amedée 92, 94

Pansaers, Clément 102
Petrarch, Francesco 133
Picabia, Francis 2, 23, 36, 48–49, 55, 61, 62, 64–65, 67, 68, 70, 74, 75, 76, 85
    'Cabinet du Docteur Aïsen' 64
    Le Double Monde 75
    'Handicap' 79
    L'Œil cacodylate 61
    'Le Rat circulaire' 75
    Relâche 93
Pierre, José 95
Prassinos, Gisèle 131
Proust, Marcel, *Du côté de chez Swann* 18–19, 70, 77, 89

Quinney, Anne 13–14, 17

Rafalowski, Aleksander 91
Reverdy, Pierre 33 n. 10, 65
Ribemont-Dessaignes, Georges 30, 64, 68, 74, 85
    'Cafard' 64
    'Pneumatique' 80
    'ZA' 76
Richard, Élie 54
Rimbaud, Arthur 120, 123, 131, 149, 154
    'Le Bateau ivre' 106, 110
    Les Illuminations 129
    Une saison en enfer 6, 128–29, 130
Robertson, Eric 58 n. 12, 150 n. 2
Romanticism 52, 105, 123, 129, 133, 154
Russell, Charles 57 n. 5, 125–26 n. 9, 133, 135
Russolo, Luigi 91

Saint-Simon, Henri de 87, 148
Saisset, Frédéric 103
Salon des Indépendants 68, 76
Sandqvist, Tom 12–13, 16, 121, 156
Satie, Eric 85, 93
Saussure, Ferdinand de 89
Sawelson-Gorse, Nadia 2
Schneider, Nadine 2
Second World War 4, 6, 113, 137, 139, 142–45, 149, 150 n. 5, 155
Segal, Arthur 12, 13
Serner, Walter 68
Seuphor, Michel 91, 94–95
Shakespeare, William 27, 149, 154
    The Tempest 36
Shelley, Percy Bysshe 123, 149, 154
    Prometheus Unbound 130
Shipe, Timothy 20 n. 8
Sjöberg, Sami 16, 51, 102, 114 n. 7 & 12, 156
Soupault, Philippe 30, 55, 61, 68, 75, 76, 124, 153
    'Est-ce le vent' 130
    'Salutations distinguées' 79

Spiridon, Monica 102, 150 n. 7
Spivak, Gayatri Chakravorty 15
Stavrinaki, Maria 134
Stazewski, Henryk 91
Sudhalter, Adrian 12
Suleiman, Susan Rubin 17, 156
Surrealism 1, 5, 6, 13, 16, 17, 44, 55, 56–57, 61, 62, 68, 86, 88–91, 94, 112, 124, 133, 141, 148, 152, 154, 156
    and film 82–83
    and the novel 22, 23, 29, 30
    and women 3, 122–23, 130–31
Symbolism 13, 89, 106, 119, 120, 131, 154

Taeuber, Sophie 1, 2
Tanning, Dorothea 3, 34 n. 29
Tatlin, Vladimir, *Monument to the Third International* 77
Townsend, Chris 93
transport 40–44, 53–54, 56, 66–67, 71, 111, 113, 127, 136, 154
Tysliava, Juozas 91

Tzara, Tristan 4, 12, 13, 23, 30, 31, 57, 61, 64, 65, 68, 69, 74, 75, 76, 79, 85, 87, 123, 124, 156
    'Le Cierge et la vierge' 79
    'Dada manifeste sur l'amour faible et l'amour amer' 94, 152, 154
    'Dada Manifesto' 71
    'Mouvement Dada' letterhead 74–75
    as Samuel Rosenstock 14, 15
    Sept manifestes Dada 152

ultra-modern 7, 20, 30, 88, 90, 93, 129, 158

Vantongerloo, Georges 91
Varo, Remedios 3
Voronca, Ilarie 13, 91

war, *see* First World War or Second World War
Wittmann, Marc 132

Yaari, Monique 20 n. 8

www.ingramcontent.com/pod-product-compliance
Lightning Source LLC
LaVergne TN
LVHW061252060426
835507LV00017B/2031